EUROPEAN INTEGRATION IN BRITISH POLITICS 1950-1963:
A STUDY OF ISSUE CHANGE

"But it seems that the Government had a true account of it (plague in Holland), and several councils were held about ways to prevent it coming over; but all was kept quiet and very private. Hence it was that this rumour died off again, and people began to forget it".

Daniel Defoe. <u>A Journal of the Plague Year.</u>

90 0690806 8

European Integration in British Politics 1950-1963: A Study of Issue Change

JEREMY MOON
Department of Politics
University of Western Australia

Gower

Published by
Gower Publishing Company Limited,
Gower House,
Croft Road,
Aldershot,
Hampshire GU11 3HR,
England

and

Gower Publishing Company,
Old Post Road,
Brookfield,
Vermont 05036,
U.S.A.

Reprinted 1987

British Library Cataloguing in Publication Data

Moon, Jeremy
  European integration in British politics 1950-1963: a
  study of issue change.
  1. Great Britain---Politics and government---1945-1964
  2. Great Britain---Foreign relations---Europe
  3. Europe---Foreign relations---Great Britain
  I. Title
  320.941   DA589.7

Library of Congress Cataloging-in-Publication Data

Moon, Jeremy, 1955-
  European integration in British politics, 1950-1963.

  A revision of the author's thesis (Ph.D.--University of
Exeter)
  Bibliography: p.
  Includes index.
  1. European Economic Community--Great Britain--Public
opinion. 2. Public opinion--Great Britain. 3. Great
Britain--Politics and government--1945-1964. I. Title.
HC241.25.G7M63 1985   337.1'42   85-12721

ISBN 0-566-00786-X

Printed in Great Britain by
Athanaeum Press Limited, Newcastle upon Tyne

Contents

FIGURES

TABLES

Preface

This study is a revised version of my PhD thesis completed in the Politics Department, University of Exeter. I am grateful for all the encouragement and assistance I received there, particularly from my supervisor, Dr. David Steel. The revision of the thesis was conducted in the Department of Politics, University of Strathclyde, where I also received considerable help and support. Special thanks are due to Margaret Totterdell and Grace Hunter who typed the manuscript with patience and enthusiasm beyond the call of duty.

Jeremy Moon
Glasgow
March 1985.

Introduction

This book is primarily concerned with issues in politics; how and why they change over time, and the implications such changes may have for an understanding of the policy-making process. The central variable which will be posited and elaborated upon to illustrate such changes is 'issue anatomy' - the manner in which issues are depicted and perceived. Students of politics have had an intuitive recognition that the presentation of political issues is a crucial feature of the policy process. This was also recognised by a rather frustrated practitioner who stated that

'The simple fact is that arithmetic and accountancy bear little or no resemblance to economics in general, and the 'art' of presenting huge public expenditure figures in particular. In the preparation of a public expenditure White Paper, a whole variety of 'assumptions' have to be made (economic jargon for 'guessing') about such matters as earnings, prices, shortfall, along with a host of other 'estimates'. Any one of these variables could ensure that the picture painted was such as to require action of the kind which officials believed to be right, and, as they were genuinely convinced, in the national interest. The trouble was that a slightly different 'assumption' or 'guesstimate' could give a rather different picture, to the tune of say £1 billion less on the estimated borrowing requirement - and therefore considerably reduce the case for an equivalent public expenditure cut.' (Barnett, 1982, p.22).

The present study will attempt to advance our understanding of issue change with reference to a study of the European question in British politics 1950 to 1963. More specifically, by means of a content analysis of Parliamentary debate on the question of British membership of the ECSC and the EEC during these years, it will seek to identify, explain, and 'assess the policy implications of changes in the anatomy of the issue over four sub periods of this thirteen year period.

This study is born out of some dissatisfaction with previous approaches to the study of issues: insufficient attention seems to have been given to the fact that issues are neither static nor monolithic. In other words, issues change over time, both in terms of their salience within the political system, and in terms of the broad arguments associated with them. In order to highlight these essential characteristics of political issues, this analysis first gives prime attention to the nature of the European question itself, and in the light of the findings, it will turn to examination of competing views of the groups and organisations involved with the issue. However, to approach every policy-making study solely from a group perspective may be myopic. Traditional interest group studies are limited first by the exclusion of non group factors. Attitudes towards issues within the political system may not be explained solely in group terms, and the relationships between widely held political perceptions and policy outcomes should be an important line of enquiry. Secondly, straightforward interest group studies are not normally fruitful when an issue was at a low ebb, and groups fairly inactive! However, analysis of just such a situation may provide important illumination of the policy-making process. A study which concentrates on the issue enables analysis of such junctures, in addition to occasions when a question enjoys high political salience and all manner of political organisations and groups are active.

As will be outlined in Chapter 1 students of politics have made reference to changes which issues undergo. The debate between pluralist and elite theorists about the nature of political influence has been characterised by differing perceptions of what constitute political issues and differing explanations of their particular status within the political system. Work in this debate has provided insights into a wide range of political issues, from the highly public issue, characterised by a high level of group participation, on the one hand, to the non issue, characterised by an absence of public cognisance and group involvement, on the other. Building on these concepts, other studies have been conducted which have given more attention to the issues themselves and, although shortcomings of these will be discussed, they are used to provide a framework in the construction of the concept of issue anatomy.

The aim of the study is to develop the notion of issue salience and to propose that of issue anatomy in order to depict issue change and to consider the relevance of this to policy-making. The term issue salience refers to the stature which an issue achieves at any one time. Although, as will be outlined, I prefer not to use the term 'agenda status', issue salience is related to the idea which has been developed that issues rise and fall on the political agenda. A measure of issue salience will be provided, and this examined with reference to other relevant indicators.

By the anatomy of a political issue, I am referring to the dominant characteristics attributed to that issue, or to put it another way, which features of the question are to the fore in any one period. Again, a means of measurement will be posited, and the anatomy derived for the issue in any one period will be contrasted with competing views of the issue occurring within the political system.

As the purpose of the study is to illustrate issue change, it was clearly necessary to select an issue which was judged in advance to be capable of illustrating this reasonably well: there are no pretensions of random selection here! It could be argued anyway that no single issue is necessarily representative of other issues within a political system, though the representativeness of that chosen will be discussed in the concluding chapter.

This book is concerned with tracing the advent and change in nature of the European question in British politics, and commences shortly after the Second World War when certain European countries were preparing to organise themselves into an economic bloc, which emerged as the ECSC. It culminates in early 1963 when, although General de Gaulle vetoed British membership of the EEC, the issue had emerged as one central to British politics, where it has remained. Consequently, much of the book is devoted to periods when it appeared that membership of a European community was almost as far from British minds as membership of COMECON! The

3

purpose is neither to decry nor justify Britain's disregard for membership. Rather, it is believed that the study of the limited status of a political issue is as valid as the more familiar study of the peaks of political activity. Further, the European issue from 1961 to 1963 must be viewed in the context of earlier British attitudes. A study of the emergence of a political question should involve careful scrutiny of the circumstances from which the issue emanated.

The criticism may be put forward that it is impossible to study what is not there. In one sense this is of course true. However, two retorts can be made. First, in the case of the European question, at least since the inception of the Schuman Plan discussions, if not before, there was always 'something there'. Britain could never be totally unaware of what has happening in Europe, nor that some, if not all of the six original members, desired British participation in the process of integration. The British Governments of the period received invitations to participate in the process of integration, as well as information on the progress achieved, and as will be seen in later chapters, such communications were occasionally made more widely available (e.g. in White Papers and Parliamentary debate). Thus the limited responses to European initiatives constitute 'something there' for analysis, if not always very much. Secondly, when one policy alternative appears to attract little support, it is always instructive to examine which alternatives receive predominant consideration in that period, and to attempt to explain such priorities.

The question arises as to the basis on which the relationship of Britain to these two particular European organisations (ECSC and EEC) and not any other ones is described as a single issue. The factors which unify the ECSC and the EEC are first, that the latter evolved out of the former, and secondly, that they both embodied attempts at economic integration with some surrender of national sovereignty (the extent of this has been subject to fluctuation) and a pooling of economic resources. This distinguishes them from other organisations (e.g. OECD, EFTA) which attempted to secure economic cooperation, but possessed none of the unifying institutions of the ECSC and EEC, nor entailed the surrender of some economic autonomy. Whilst of course the precise terms on which Britain could have joined the Six fluctuated, the nature of the organisations remained essentially the same, only varying significantly in the scope of their activities.

4

The first chapter will introduce the two main components of
issue change which will be utilised in the case study,
explaining their theoretical context and their relevance to
our understanding of the policy making process.   Following
a brief historical account of the European question in
British politics 1951-63 in chapter three, the method by
which these concepts will be utilised is unfolded in the
fourth chapter.   A content analysis of debate on the
European issue in the House of Commons will be outlined,
indicating how the salience and anatomy of the issue can be
quantified for four individual spans of time within the
overall period chosen, in order to highlight changes within
the issue from one of these sub-periods to another.   These
sub-periods are identified as P1, P2, P3 and P4, and are
defined by relevant historical watersheds.   P1 begins with
the announcement of the Schuman Plan (which paved the way
for the creation of the ECSC) in 1950.   P2 begins with the
advent of a new British Conservative Government in 1952.
P3 begins with the Messina Conference in 1955 (which
heralded the formation of the EEC in 1957).   P4 begins in
January 1961, from which time most historians of the issue
have perceived an overt shift in establishment attitudes
towards British membership of the EEC.   P4 ends when the
first British application for EEC membership was vetoed by
the French President, General de Gaulle, in January 1963.

The results of the content analysis conducted will then be
outlined, and presented in such a way as to illustrate any
broad differences between the issue in the periods P1 to P4,
and also to provide more detailed characterisation of the
issue's anatomy in each of these periods.

The following four chapters are addressed to the issue
within these shorter periods, and will attempt to account
for the respective salience and anatomy which prevailed, and
any changes which took place from the previous period.
Each of these chapters will discuss the views of the issue
and the contribution to its debate of a variety of groups in
the British political system, alongside those of the
Government, political parties, the civil service and the
press.   This exercise is a product of the view that an
issue does not exist in a vacuum, but rather is the result
of wider political phenomena.   It may be the result of the
operation of a dominant, unquestioned political ideology (as
might be argued by elite theorists) or the upshot of a
variety of competing political viewpoints (as might be
argued by pluralist writers).   In any event, the second and
related object of these chapters is to consider the
implications of the findings of each period for an

understanding of the policy-making process at work, and of the resultant policies. The concluding chapter will draw together these findings and evaluate the usefulness of the concepts of salience and anatomy for an understanding of the European question in the years covered, and will assess their wider applicability.

These is no doubt that the tracing of causality in the market of perceptions and ideas is an extremely complex task. Wyn Grant has warned that

> 'The measurement of interest group effectiveness poses a number of grave and probably insurmountable problems.' (1978, p.13).

This has a double application in the case of the present study: first in Grant's original context of relating group strategy to policy outcome, and secondly in that of accounting for such intervening variables as the perceptions of the salience and anatomy of an issue. Grant added however that 'nevertheless the issue is of such importance and general interest that it cannot be ignored.' (1978, p.13). This rider is considered as significant as the warning. Positivism in the relationship between overall findings for salience and anatomy, and the views and influence of particular groups and interests is not claimed. However, it is considered that due note should be taken of these two concepts, and that they are susceptible to influence. Salience and anatomy do not exist independent of the contemporary dynamics of the political system and the political actors therein, yet they may also have a reinforcing effect upon evaluations of political issues and thus be relevant to an understanding of political outcomes.

1 Issue change

The study of political issues has important links with the debate over political influence and power which has been waged, at times vehemently, over the last quarter of a century. This debate has been concerned not only with the nature and exercise of these concepts, but also with the value of the study of political issues in throwing light upon notions of influence and power. It is unfortunate that the terms political power and political influence have been used interchangeably and without precision : a habit which undermines their usefulness. Also, the terms have become value-laden: intuitively the term political influence has become associated with the pluralists, and political power with elitists. This further detracts from the definitional distinction, and the use of the terms for the study of politics. In this study, the term political influence refers to the ability to affect the policy-making process, though there clearly exist varying degrees of influence. Political power refers to the ability to secure a desired outcome. Political power requires influence, though influence does not imply power. There are of course a great number of variables available to theorists of political influence and power, and thus in addition to the substantial differences of opinion which exist, there are many fine distinctions prevailing. However, for present purposes groups of theories will be discussed in order to illuminate broad theoretical watersheds.

The first group to be discussed have been called 'the early elite theorists'. (Giddens, 1974, p.x). This group, epitomised by C. Wright Mills and Floyd Hunter, argued that political influence is exercised by a governing elite who manipulate the democratic framework in order to enhance their position of dominance within society. They also argued that the masses do not really participate in decisions which impinge upon them, as electoral processes are irrelevant to the key economic decision makers. Mills identified what he termed 'the power elite' and stated that

'Whether they do or do not make such decisions is less important than the fact that they do occupy such pivotal positions: their failure to act, their failure to make decisions, is itself an act that is often of greater consequence than the decisions they do make'. (Mills, 1956, p.4).

Mills also considered that

'The top of the American system of power is much more unified and much more powerful, the bottom is much more fragmented, and in truth, impotent, than is generally supposed by those who are distracted by the middling units of power which neither express such will as exists at the bottom nor determine the decisions at the top'. (Mills, 1956, p.29).

The pluralist school developed because certain political scientists had become dissatisfied with these early sociological elite theories, which, the former suggested, lacked empirical foundation. Pluralists suggested that the study of individual issues provides the only valid means of assessing the extent of political influence. Thus the work of the elite theorists was criticised for making too many unfounded assumptions, particularly regarding the central and single location of power in society. The major advocates and innovators of the pluralist approach, Robert Dahl and Nelson Polsby, argued that if for each issue, key decisions and actors in the decision making process are identified, if all actual behaviour related to that process and the policy outcomes is analysed, it is then possible to locate the most influential, and thus the most powerful group or groups in that particular policy making arena.

The pluralist approach in its most simple form entails certain important assumptions. First, it is implied that interests are synonymous with articulated policy preferences; secondly, that differing interests will inevitably evoke observable conflict (thus accessible for analysis); and thirdly, that the important issues are those which necessarily produce such observable conflict. It is generally held by this school that there is no one inherent distribution of power within the community, rather that

'power may be tied to issues, and issues can be fleeting or persistent, provoking coalitions among interested groups and citizens, ranging in their durations from momentary to semi-permanent.' (Polsby, 1963, pp.3-4).

Dahl did however depart from a conventional pluralist perspective when he conceded that influence may be exercised in a more covert manner:

'A rough test of a person's overt or covert influence is the frequency with which he successfully initiates an important policy over the opposition of others, or vetoes policies initiated by others, or initiates a policy where no opposition appears.' (Dahl, 1961, p.66).

In his Preface to Democratic Theory, Dahl commented that

'if it could be quantified I suppose it would be no exaggeration to say that Mr. Henry Luce has a thousand or ten thousand times greater control over the alternatives scheduled for debate and tentative decision at a national election than I do... It is a reasonable preliminary hypothesis that the number of individuals who exercise significant control over the alternatives scheduled is... only a tiny fraction of the total memberships. This seems to be the case even in the most democratic organisations if the membership is at all large.' (Dahl, 1957, pp.72-73).

This also seems to hint at the exercise of influence at a more discreet level. It poses a problem for the pluralist model of political behaviour, as it revokes the principle that all important issues (either those which are of intrinsic importance or those which would claim the support of large sections of the population) will necessarily appear on the public political agenda. E.E. Schattschneider has stated this more bluntly:

'All forms of political organisation have a bias in favour of the exploitation of some kinds of conflict and the suppression of others because "organisation is the mobilisation of bias". Some issues are organised into politics while others are organised out."(Schattschneider, 1960, p.71).

He thus established the notion that not all political questions actually appear as policy alternatives nor are treated as such (i.e. openly discussed and decided upon). To put it another way, they do not all appear on the political agenda. This prevents the emergence of an element of open conflict among interests (a sure way to draw attention to an issue) and secures an outcome favoured by those who prefer no policy change. 'The scope of a conflict can be most easily restricted at the very beginning.' (Schattschneider, 1960, p.4). This hinders the involvement in the issue of those who may favour such a policy change.

Peter Bachrach and Morton Baratz have adopted and advanced the ideas of Schattschneider specifically in order to criticise the pluralist approach, which they suggested

'takes no account of the fact that power may be, and often is, exercised by confining the scope of decision making to relatively "safe issues" .... and that the pluralist model provides no objective criteria for distinguishing between "important" and "unimportant" issues arising in the political arena.' (Bachrach and Baratz, 1962, p.948).

They argued that power is also exercised when individuals or groups

'create or reinforce social and political values, and institutional practices that limit the scope of the political process to public consideration of only those issues which are comparatively innocuous to (those individuals or groups concerned).' (Bachrach and Baratz, 1962, p.952).

Bachrach and Baratz proposed that the political agenda is not synonymous with all potential issues; rather the agenda is subject to the control of those who exercise power, and are thus able to exclude issues which may be contrary to their own interests. Hence the concept of 'non decision making' refers to this means of limiting 'the scope of actual decision making to 'safe issues'.

Steven Lukes however, was concerned that a further dimension of power could not be taken account of by the Bachrach and Baratz thesis. Whilst he agreed with their criticism of the pluralist school, Lukes argued that Bachrach and Baratz also inhibit their own model by placing it within a context of 'observable conflict' (i.e. that employed by the pluralist school). He pointed out that

> 'Just as the pluralists hold that power in decision making only shows up where there is conflict, Bachrach and Baratz assume the same to be true of non decision making.' (Lukes, 1974, p.19).

In other words, for Bachrach and Baratz, a conscious and verifiable decision is still required to make a non decision: it is simply a calculated attempt to prevent the emergence of political conflict. Lukes therefore suggested in addition to the pluralist and elitist views of power described above, a third dimension of power, which takes account of the exercise of power that operated 'unconsciously' through the bias of the system or organisation. He took Bachrach and Baratz to task, by arguing that

> 'Moreover the bias of the system is not sustained simply by a series of individually chosen acts, but also, most importantly, by the socially structured and culturally patterned behaviour of groups, and practices of institutions which may indeed be manifested by individual's inaction ... the power to control the agenda of politics and exclude potential issues cannot be adequately analysed unless it; is seen as a function of collective forces and social arrangements.' (Lukes, 1974, pp.21-22).

Lukes argued that conflict is not a necessary prerequisite for the exercise of power. This dimension of power is thus somewhat reminiscent of Gramsci's notion of ideological hegemony:

> 'The hegemony of a political class meant for Gramsci that that class had succeeded in persuading the other classes of society to accept its own moral, political and cultural values. If the ruling class is successful, then this will involve the minimum use of force.' (Joll, 1977, pp.21-22).

To borrow Lukes' phrase, there exist three dimensions of power. The first arises when important issues necessarily produce open and observable conflict, and the second occurs when those with control of the agenda, may consciously decide to render a question a 'non issue'. The third dimension presents itself when 'non issues' are the product of the unconscious bias of the political system or organisation.

Thus far we have seen the developing recognition among students of politics that issues vary in their salience. Those contributing to the debate about the nature of power and the manner in which it is exercised, have necessarily drawn upon issues. Pluralists have done so in order to demonstrate that each individual issue is characterised by different power relationships. Elitists have done so in order to demonstrate that some questions do not attain sufficient status to become subjects of open discussion and so are not susceptible to policy change. These diverse studies have depicted different types of issue, distinguished by the salience these achieve within the political system. Further, they have provided simple illustration of the relationship between the salience of an issue, and both the nature of the policy making process and policy outcomes; themes which are also central to the present study. It is not contended here that the three views described are in any way mutually exclusive, rather that they account for different conditions under which issues exist. The debate on power has given rise to the recognition of dramatic differences in the salience of issues which will be built upon in the course of this study in order to probe further the dynamics of political issues.

The approaches to political issues discussed above have each been harnessed in order to meet particular theoretical objectives, which are of course perfectly valid in their own right. In giving prime attention to different levels of salience which issues achieve, it is easy to pass over the important questions of how and why issues change from one level of salience to another, and how these changes are identified.

In attempting to refine our approach to different levels of issue salience, Matthew Crenson recognised that a problem in defining issues is that of distinguishing the 'passing recognition of a problem and the idle discussion of it by a few citizens, from a "political issue". (Crenson, 1971, p.30). The concept of the agenda has become important in attempting to define issues. This is first because some definitions of political issues are founded upon their appearance or non appearance upon a formal legislative or executive agenda. Such a course was adopted by the pluralists discussed in the previous section.

In the context of American community politics, Crenson, in considering at what point an embryonic issue becomes an agenda item, contended that only when

'advocacy or opposition has made an appearance among community leaders, will we say that a topic has taken its place on the local political agenda. Both advocacy and opposition are signs that at least a few local leaders seriously desire some authoritative action on a given issue. The subject has therefore become an issue.' (Crenson, 1971, p.30).

This is in contrast to what Crenson termed a 'non issue'. This however tends to induce only a two dimensional view of issues, and in any case, Crenson does not provide an explanation of what he means by 'advocacy' or 'opposition', who are to be considered 'community leaders' and what constitutes a 'serious desire'.

Cobb and Elder attempted to advance the use of the concept of an agenda, by distinguishing the Formal agenda from the Systemic agenda: the former applying to business specifically under consideration of decision makers, and the latter to issues

'that are commonly perceived by members of the community as meriting public attention and as involving matters within the legitimate jurisdiction of existing governmental authority.' (Cobb and Elder, 1975, p.125).

Whilst this distinction draws attention to the fact that the policy makers' and the public's estimation of worthy issues may differ, the criteria suggested for verification were unfortunately vague.

The distinctions made between embryonic and developed political issues, and between the formal and systemic agenda are useful in as much as they draw attention to the diversity of stature among political issues. Problems of verification do, however, remain. Having recognised that issues are subject to different levels of attention and accorded different status by different groups, this study will abandon the issue/non issue and the on/off agenda dichotomies. This is because dichotomous approaches disguise the infinite range of status which an issue can achieve. Indeed, the issue/non issue distinction may impose unnecessary restrictions to the form of analysis which the advocates of such a dichotomy may wish to advance. For instance, it would fail to account for an issue which definitionally could be said to be on the agenda, but captured neither extensive executive nor public attention. This is not a pedantic point. It may be the case that a particular question of intrinsic importance is recognised as a policy alternative, but for some reason remains only a 'muted issue'. Thus the issue/non issue distinction does not enable recognition of questions whose agenda status is ambiguous. Secondly, it cannot account for shifts in the status of an issue, only the transformation from a non issue to an issue and back again. This may render analysis blind to important features of the process of policy making.

Crenson himself did recognise that issues vary in terms of the attention and activity they attract, and asserted that 'the greater the number of civic leaders who take positions, the bigger the issue.' (Crenson, 1971, p.31). Whilst this sounds almost naive, it does provide a step in the right direction. It implies the existence of a continuum or spectrum. Such a notion is to be preferred to the simple dichotomies outlined above, and which too often dog academic discourse on political issues. This study assumes a spectrum of salience, upon which issues could be placed for comparative purposes. At one end of this spectrum would be the classical non issue, about which there is no debate at all, and at the other end, the type of issue which dominates the policy making machinery, public opinion and the other political actors in the system (the press, political parties, interest groups, etc.)

The study of public opinion is of some use here. It provides a means of comparing issues in terms of salience as ascribed by samples of the electorate. It should be noted though that this task is most easily performed among issues which do acquire a certain degree of public status, and more difficult among those which do not. However, it should be considered significant if an issue does not become the subject of any public opinion poll, as this provides at least a nominal gauge of its low level of salience at a popular level, if not at an elite level.

It is the changes in popular perceptions of issues which led Anthony Downs to study the environmental issue in the United States. He addressed himself to the following questions:

'What has caused this shift in public attention? Why did this issue assume so high a priority among our domestic concerns? And how long will the American public sustain high intensity interest in ecological matters?' (Downs, 1972, pp.38-39).

He suggested that a cycle was in operation which was characterised by high levels of public interest followed by boredom with the major issues. Downs' work on the environmental issue is particularly useful in demonstrating that issues vary in terms of the amount of attention accorded to them, and that this is related to broader political factors. His assertion that issue salience changes in cyclical patterns is however less tenable. Indeed Downs does not seem to have been entirely convinced by it himself. At one point he suggested that 'This issue-attention clycle is rooted both in the nature of certain domestic problems and the way major communications media interact with the public: (Downs 1973, p. 63). He later qualified this: 'Not all major social problems go through this issue-attention cycle. Hence I make no claim that this phenomenon is universally applicable in analysing how our society perceives and deals with major problems. (Downs 1973, p. 66).

The relationships between the factors contributing to the public's evaluations of political questions are undoubtedly complex. The two main points should be noted at this stage; first, that issues do vary in terms of the public's interest and estimation of their importance. Thus this study will adopt the concept of a spectrum of salience. Secondly, such popular evaluations can, at least at a general theoretical level, be traced to the influence of other actors and processes in the political system.

ISSUE ANATOMY

It has been suggested earlier that political scientists have failed to come to grips with the concept of the changing anatomy of an issue. What efforts have been made to distinguish the changing character of questions, other than those founded upon the technically separate, but related notion of their salience? It should be recognised

15

that distinctions of sorts are always made among issues. For instance, the question of whether to provide financial incentives for private firms to create jobs in areas of high unemployment is seen as qualitatively different from that of giving these same incentives across the country as a whole: but on what basis are such distinctions made? Often these are the product of inferences drawn by those who have an interest in a specific policy question, and based upon partisan assessments of alternative solutions. Political scientists have attempted to distinguish issues in terms of the location of the decision making process (e.g. central or local, legislative or executive), or in terms of the sphere in which the issue lies (e.g. economic, political, educational or moral), or in terms of those directing attention to the question (whether sectional groups, promotional groups, or political parties, etc.) Whilst the validity of such categorisations is recognised, they nevertheless only tell us about how an issue is handled or processed and which groups take an active interest in them. Such classification of issues does not help in the task of identifying the anatomy of a question and its different constituent parts. This section will proceed by examing studies which tackle the concept of issue salience and its relevance to the policy making process, but which also build upon this concept of salience in such a way as to suggest further dimensions of issue change.

Robert Lieber in his work on British politics and European unity attempted to identify different degrees of politicisation. (Lieber, 1970). For this purpose he adopted a threefold measure. His first variable was the type of government ministry responsible for handling the issue. The premise here was that 'economic' departments like the Board of Trade are more likely to encourage a consultative process with sectional groups than the more 'political' ministries such as the Foreign Office. Thus if the latter type were handling the matter, this would be indicative of a higher level of politicisation.

The second variable he used was the extent to which the major political parties overtly champion or denounce the issue, thereby lifting it out of the exclusive province of sectional interests and further politicising it. His third test was the extent of the response of the broader public to the question, as expressed through promotional group activity, public opinion findings, press coverage and the attention paid to the matter in by-elections.

Clearly, the notion that issues change is central to the

Lieber model. Indeed, his purpose was to illustrate that the role of sectional groups in British European policy making declined between 1956 and 1967 due to the issue's politicisation,

'that is by an increase in the perception and treatment of European unity as a matter of major national importance rather than as a relatively specialised or economic question.' (Lieber, 1970, p.10).

Thus Lieber, building on the concept of changes in issue salience gave emphasis to changes in the particular sorts of group involved with the issue, which in turn provided a measure of politicisation. Clearly the anatomy of an issue cannot be totally divorced from the changing circumstances of the policy making process (e.g. the varying balance of interested parties). However, if the notion of an issue's anatomy is to be viable, it must be construed in terminology other than that of political handling; otherwise anatomy would be rendered synonymous with the changes wrought in policy making, and not as an identifiable consequence (and feedback effect) of such changes.

William Solesbury, (1976), accepting the point that issues arrive and then fade, was concerned with issues which may not have been resolved, yet do not command such political attention as they once did. He pointed out that agenda and media space are finite, and concluded from this that issues (or their advocates and opponents) are involved in a form of competition.

'Most ideas underlying issues arise as a by-product of the more everyday concerns of institutions principally directed to other ends: that is, in research centres, interest groups, executive agencies, political parties.' (Solesbury, 1976, p.382).

The more important question thus is not where do issues originate, but 'what gives them force?' Solesbury continued to argue that

'Issues finally evoke responses from Governments when they have become powerful enough to capture public resources, when they become the subject of political debate, when they come to dominate the media, when organisations grow around them and when they begin to be used to gain influence and money.' (Solesbury, 1976, p.383).

He also contended that in addition to requiring association with a well placed organisation, issues also require legitimacy in order to command attention. He suggested that certain qualities may enhance their degree of attention. This point constitutes a step towards the recognition of the relevance of the study of an issue's anatomy. Solesbury stated that one means of acquiring legitimacy is if the issues

> 'bear some degree of compatibility with the dominant system of values. The distinctions (among issues) lie in the level at which that compatibility may be established.' (Solesbury, 1976, p.387).

Thus the composition or character of the issue has an important impact on the outcome. Solesbury pointed out that once an item had acquired agenda status, and action had been taken towards its consideration by executive bodies, there exists a multitude of alternatives: a simple yes or no dichotomy does not exist in reality. Just as an issue presents policy implications which are potentially other issues (hence issues within issues), so certain elements of an issue may be recognised without full attention being paid to other of its implications.

In their discussion of the political agenda in Britain, Joan Stringer and J.J. Richardson began by stating that

> 'The way in which a problem is defined will greatly influence the decision about the best policy to adopt. Ill-defined or mis-defined problems will almost certainly lead to failure.' (Stringer and Richardson, 1980, p.23).

The notion that groups and individuals define issues in certain ways constitutes a development of the idea touched on by Solesbury that issues are ascribed qualities. Stringer and Richardson examined the issues of Britain's drug problems, air pollution, atmospheric lead levels and crime levels as examples of questions which did not acquire political issue status. This, they argued, was because the questions were not defined in such a way as to appear as problems. Whether for conspiratorial or for more innocent reasons, these issues were excluded from wide consideration as political issues. In some circumstances, e.g. in the case of confronting poverty in Britain, Stringer and Richardson argued that the government response is not to tackle the root causes of the problem, but to treat the symptoms, thereby removing the issue from the political agenda and simultaneously giving the impression that remedial action was effective. They asserted that

> 'Thus much of the "stuff of politics" is concerned with the emergence, non-emergence and <u>definition</u> of "problems". And, as governments become increasingly overloaded, we might expect them to pay even greater attention to the possibility of handling indicators in such a way as to define problems out of existence.' (Stringer and Richardson, 1980, p.29). [My emphasis.]

They used the examples of the statistics concerning Britain's strike record, the definition of the heavy lorry problem and statistics relating to Civil Service numbers as instances where the governments chose to redefine problems by management of official statistics. A similar point which they took up was that of the selection of indicators of policy performance, arguing that governments are in a position both to justify and prove effective their policy solution, irrespective of their palliative's <u>real</u> effects. This was illustrated with reference to figures published on the numbers of unemployed in the country, the financial cost to the country of maintaining high level unemployment and the variables employed in the calculation of the Retail Price Index.

Inclusion of this notion of issue definition within the study of the policy making process seems apposite and is consistent with the concept of an issue's anatomy. An issue is attributed a set of characteristics, which may or may not be an accurate reflection of the 'real' problem.

What precisely is meant by the term issue anatomy? It is used to describe what other writers have more loosely referred to as issue definition or issue presentation. It is defined here as the prevailing characterisation of an issue within a political system; a specific composition of themes in a particular political context. Of course different characterisations of an issue may prevail in the various arenas within the political system, but this does not undermine the concept. It does require that careful research is conducted in order to identify which combination of a number of competing characterisations constitutes a prevailing anatomy. Indeed, that some characterisations of issues are out of step with the prevailing anatomy of the issue is itself of interest to students of politics, as the anatomy of an issue is itself a consequence of factors of political influence and political power, and thus is also

19

subject to change.

More recent studies have pointed to the possibility that the anatomy of issues may impinge upon policy outcomes. Concluding his study of the politics of mass housing, Patrick Dunleavy stated that

'... changes in central government policy or the national local government system cannot be seen as the results of specific professional, industrial, or local authority initiatives aimed at influencing national policy, important as these were. Rather, these interests affected policy in much more diffuse ways, <u>by creating and sustaining a climate of opinion in the public housing apparatus favourable to high rise and by constraining Ministry policy change within narrow limits.</u>' (Dunleavy, 1981, p.177). [My emphasis.]

Similarly Arne Leemans (1983) in a paper on Dutch sea defences, demonstrated that the environmental groups in Holland had a significant effect on prevailing values, which in turn affected the terms of reference of the debate about sea walls and had significant policy consequences.

Several other works have also identified the importance of an issue's anatomy (although they do not use this term) for an understanding of the policy making process. Four such studies appeared in a recent collection of interest group studies (Marsh, 1983). Wyn Grant outlined how, since the issue of the Green Pound had been politicised in British politics it

'ceased to be viewed as an agricultural issue and was seen more as a prices issue or an economic policy issue or as a question concerning Britain's general relations with the European Community.' (Grant, 1983, p.139).

He pointed out that as this change in perception took place, the dominant role of British farming organisations in this policy area was undermined. Similarly, studies on small promotional groups; the penal lobby (Ryan, 1983), the anti nuclear lobby (Ward, 1983) and the Child Poverty Action Group (McCarthy, 1983) indicated that despite the outsider status of these organisations and their lack of specific policy successes, they have had a significant underlying impact on terms of reference and sub issues employed in debate in the respective policy areas by those with more control over policy outcomes. McKay and Cox have suggested that the nature of Britain's Urban Aid Programme 1968-1976 was a function of urban inequalities being perceived as a consequence of individual social welfare problems, rather than as a feature of structural economic change: 'it is indisputable that ideas about the nature of poverty and urban society played a crucial role in determining the shape of the Urban Programme.' (McKay and Cox, 1978, p.504).

On what basis is the claim made for the adoption of the concept of issue anatomy? It is evident that any issue consists of a number of identifiable components. This is clear from the fact that government, press, political party and interest group documents invariably make such distinctions within a single issue. This is for two main reasons. First, an issue may logically encroach on several discernible branches within the system. Secondly, for the purposes of easy handling and communication it is deemed pragmatic to divide an issue into its political, economic and social implications, for example. That the different features of an issue are interconnected is not disputed, but the fact that actors, commentators, and students of politics do make such distinctions is considered significant and useful.

A question arises; at what point can a component of one issue be defined as a separate issue? Ultimately such a problem requires an inductive response, whereby a definition of an issue can be given, and this subjected to critical scrutiny. In the present study, any theme which contributed to the debate on the issue of Britain's participation in European economic integration is deemed a component of this issue. Of course, if a study of British farming policy in the early sixties was to be conducted, certain themes characterising the present study might be prominent, and perhaps would be labelled the 'European component' of the agricultural question. That issues overlap is not denied. It is argued though, that the association of a group of themes with a core issue is defensible.

Evidence would suggest that the components of an issue brought to the attention both of political actors and the general public may vary over time. Clearly the issue of Commonwealth immigration has changed in nature over the last thirty years. At the time of its encouragement it was seen as an almost natural consequence of Britain's role at the heart of the Commonwealth, and as an opportunity to fill certain jobs in the health, transport and postal sectors. Later, however, questions of inner city ghettos, racial friction, rising unemployment, and a cultural swamping of Britain by foreigners who the country could not support, came increasingly to dominate the matter.

What significance does this notion that issues change in terms of their anatomy have for an understanding of the policy making process? It is because changes among the important components of an issue do not take place in a vacuum, independent of other actions and actors in the system. Individual components are maximised or minimised by interested groups, whether consciously or unconsciously, in order to best advance their own case. The ability to succeed in promoting one view of what an issue consists of, at the expense of other views (whether by overt or covert means), is surely as important an asset as the ability to influence the salience an issue achieves on the political agenda. This consideration of the changing anatomy of an issue should be included in the broader study of the policy process.

At first one might assume that the fact that one component should receive particular prominence during a period of time, was solely compatible with a pluralist explanation. This would be argued along the lines that the most powerful groups concerned succeeded in promoting this component (being conducive to their policies and aims), in competition with other aspiring groups, who, whilst promoting other components, did not succeed in achieving such a level of prominence for them. However, the case may not be as simple. It may be, just as an issue's existence on a political agenda may be subject to control, that certain components of an issue could consciously or unconsciously be restricted from a full discussion. Thus, to amend Bachrach and Baratz (1962, p.948), power may be exercised when an individual or group creates or reinforces social and political values and institutional practices that limit the scope of the political process to public considerations of only those components which are comparatively innocuous to them. Similarly, to adopt the Lukes (1974, p.21-22) thesis, it may be the bias of the system itself which prohibits the open discussion and consideration of components which may threaten the group, class or collective systemic forces concerned. All this is not to deny that the predominance of one component over another may include elements of a pluralist explanation. Rather, the intention is to show that the implications of an issue's changing anatomy are relevant to all three of these 'views'.

2 European economic integration 1945-1963

The purpose of this chapter is to provide an account of European economic integration from 1945 until 1963. Initially it will deal with the immediate post-war efforts both at cooperation between countries and at integration of features of their economic, political or social systems. The second section will discuss the publication of the Schuman Plan and the subsequent creation of the European Coal and Steel Community in 1952. The chapter will then outline the attempts at further European integration during the mid nineteen fifties, firstly in the form of the unsuccessful European Defence Community, and secondly in the formation of the EEC in 1957. The fourth section will examine developments in the wake of the inception of the EEC. Britain, having been left outside the EEC, initially attempted to create a loose trading organisation of most west European countries (the Free Trade Area), in order to avoid a split between the EEC and non members. When this failed, Britain and other non-EEC countries formed the European Free Trade Association, which was essentially a cooperative rather than an integrative organisation. Following a short account of the nature and progress of the EEC in the fifth section, the chapter will conclude by outlining the events surrounding the first British application for EEC membership.

Immediately after the end of the Second World War, a considerable amount of rhetoric was spoken about world federalism and European unity, though little was achieved in either sphere. However, the general, if short lived world federalist atmosphere was of importance in locating the origins of the formal and informal movements towards European integration. The decision of the San Francisco Conference in 1944, to retain the system of national sovereignty in the constitution of the United Nations was a great disappointment to the federalists, though for many of them it made a form of west European unity even more imperative, particularly in the face of the perceived political threat from the east and of the task of economic reconstruction.

Towards the end of the War in July 1944, resistance regimes of several occupied European countries [1] drafted a resolution stating that

'Federal union alone can ensure the preservation of liberty and civilisation on the continent of Europe, bring about economic recovery, and enable the German people to play a peaceful role in European affairs.' (Kitzinger, 1967, p.29).

Similarly, and with hindsight more significantly, the Governments of Holland, Belgium and Luxembourg concluded a convention in 1944 for the establishment of a Customs Union when peace resumed - Benelux. This was revised in 1947, and a programme of full tariff harmonisation was set in motion which was successfully completed by 1958. It was Churchill who gave greater impetus to this development with a highly acclaimed speech at the University of Zurich in September 1946. He argued that

'If we are to form a United States of Europe, or whatever name or form it takes, we must begin now.' (Kitzinger, 1967, pp. 33-37).

Churchill suggested that France and West Germany should lead such a re-creation of Europe for 'justice, mercy and freedom'. He implied that Britain was above such an organisation, because he did not think Britain needed to be involved economically, and assumed that Britain's traditional world status was not destined to whither:

'Great Britain, the British Commonwealth of Nations, mighty America, and I trust the Soviet Union ... must be friends and sponsors of the new Europe, and must champion its right to live and shine.'

Having delivered this speech, Churchill founded and promoted an organisation known as the United Europe Movement, to work for the achievement of this end. Statesmen of many European countries joined, and a conference which the Movement organised in 1948 at The Hague led to the formation of the Council of Europe in the following year.

Whilst the policy of the new British Labour Government followed that of its Conservative and Coalition predecessors in attempting to maintain the balance of power in Europe, it did not advocate a swift movement of integration of nation states, as suggested in Churchill's speech. (The policy of the British Government will be more fully explored in Chapter 4.) Rather, the new Foreign Secretary, Ernest Bevin, laid emphasis on inter-governmental cooperation.

The general fear of an aggressor in Europe obviously contributed to the feelings of the need for cooperation among states, and Bevin instigated the Anglo-French Treaty (1947) providing reciprocal guarantees against renewed German aggression. The Anglo-French Treaty was soon followed by the Brussels Treaty Organisation of 1948, comprised of Britain, France, the Netherlands, Belgium and Luxembourg. This was initially devised as a security measure against a resurgent Germany. However, it was soon thought that any military threat would be more likely to come from behind what was becoming popularly known as the Iron Curtain. This perception was instilled by the atmosphere created by the Berlin Blockade of 1948, the Hungarian coup of the same year, and the refusal of the USSR to permit her satellites to participate in the negotiations concerning Marshall Aid. Consequently the Brussels Treaty Organisation was superseded by the North Atlantic Treaty Organisation (NATO) in 1949 [2]. This signalled the culmination of a fairly rapid process which had served to drive a wedge across Europe. From this point onwards, there was really no possibility of close economic cooperation between, let alone integration among the countries east and west of the Iron Curtain.

The Council of Europe was also formed in 1949 and became a forum for debate among west European countries. Its statutes were sufficiently broad to accommodate both those who desired to progress towards federalism in Europe and those who preferred a system of inter-governmental cooperation.

Turning to economics, the devastation that had been inflicted on the economies of mainland Europe was a crucial factor in influencing future developments. It was not just the political value of the nation state that was under question in Europe at this time, but also the efficacy with which national strategies could promote economic recovery and growth. The Marshall Aid programme, gratefully accepted by west European countries, was itself instrumental in encouraging discussion of economic unification. One of the guidelines established by the Marshall Plan was that the programme should be a joint one: this required some measure of discussion and agreement among the beneficiaries. Hence, in 1947, the Committee of European Economic Cooperation met in Paris to prepare a report on the best method and pattern of distribution of the aid. This Committee was transformed into the Organisation for European Economic Cooperation (OEEC) in the following year, and continued to coordinate the work of the Marshall Plan [3]. The OEEC in turn set up the European Payments Union in 1950, which provided a debt cancellation system in Europe, to avoid any scramble for gold and dollars.

Alongside this story of cooperation and agreement however, lies another story of disagreement concerning future aims and palliatives for the economies of western Europe. The talks surrounding the administration of the Marshall Plan in Paris in 1947, brought to light a fundamental difference of opinion. The Americans suggested that the recipient countries should form more than a simple organisation for economic cooperation; something more on the lines of the Benelux experiment. This idea was particularly attractive to the French and Italian delegations. The French proposed that

'the present division of Europe into small economic units does not correspond to the needs of modern competition, and that it will be possible with the help of customs unions to construct larger units on the strictly economic plane ... that it (France) is ready to enter into negotiations with all European governments who share these views who wish to enter a Customs Union with France and whose national economies are capable of being combined with the French economy in such a way as to make a viable unit.' (Cabinet Papers, (47), 260).

The British, who assumed the role of senior participants by virtue of being undefeated in the War and by being close allies of the USA, were opposed to the idea. Consequently the OEEC terms of reference matched the British preferences and contained no mention of supranational economic controls.

However, integrationist views could not be totally stifled; The Hague Congress of 1948 had provided a mass forum for European statesmen to discuss the suitability and practicality of varying degrees of greater unity: the only major government not to be represented was that of Britain. The Congress called for political and economic union, a European Assembly, and a Court of Human Rights. Five months later an umbrella group, the European Movement, was founded in order to unite such organisations as the European League for Economic Cooperation (1946), the United Europe Movement (1947), the European Union of Federalists (1946), the Socialist Movement for a United States of Europe (1947) and Nouvelles Equipes Internationales (a Franco-Belgian Catholic Movement, 1947).

At a governmental level, the French continued to make initiatives for some economic integration among nation states. Exchanges took place between the French and the Belgian Governments, culminating in an announcement that they

> 'hoped to use the Brussels organisation (i.e. the Brussels Treaty Organisation, the forerunner of NATO) as a sort of official nucleus for further action in integrating Europe'. (Zurcher, 1958, p.31.)

THE CREATION OF THE EUROPEAN COAL AND STEEL COMMUNITY

Frustrated by consistent British reluctance to support proposals implying anything more than inter-governmental cooperation, the French Government made a unilateral proposal in May 1950 (Cmnd 7970,1950). This became known as the Schuman Plan after Robert Schuman, the French Foreign Minister, although it has been generally acknowledged that the scheme was chiefly inspired by Jean Monnet (Commissar General of the French National Economic Plan). This announcement was timed to occur a couple of days before a meeting of American, British and French representatives, who were to discuss the 'German Question'. The essence of the Schuman Plan was that a peaceful united Europe was impossible without the 'elimination of the age old opposition of France and Germany'. In order to eliminate this antagonism, the French proposed

> 'to place Franco-German production of coal and steel as a whole under a common authority, within the framework of an organisation open to the participation of other countries ... this would lay a true foundation for their economic unification.'

In order to encourage growth in these sectors the 'movement of coal and steel between member countries would immediately be freed of all customs duty'.

The phrase 'supranational authority', which was to become infamous in the British debate on the issue, was not actually mentioned, and the method of government was outlined as follows:

> 'Management of the scheme will be composed of independent personalities appointed by Governments on an equal basis. A chairman will be chosen by common agreement between Governments; its decisions will have executive force in France and Germany, and other member countries. Appropriate measures will be provided for means of appeal against the decision of the authority.' (Cmnd 7970, 1950, p.5).

The British response was somewhat lukewarm, and eventually the decision was made to decline the invitation to participate in the talks. The main reason given was that the British Government was unwilling to make a prior commitment to a scheme whose terms of membership was unknown. Belgium, Italy, West Germany and Luxembourg all immediately responded favourably, as did the Netherlands, although she expressed some reservations regarding the principle of supranational authority. Exchanges continued for about three weeks between France and Britain, but these did not bring about a change of heart by the British Government. However, events were moving more quickly on the continent, and by the 3rd of June 1950, France, West Germany, Italy and the three Benelux countries issued a joint statement outlining their

> 'determination to pursue a common action for peace and European solidarity, economic and social progress'... and ... 'their immediate objective the pooling of the production of coal and steel, and the institution of a new high authority whose decisions will bind [them]'. (Cmnd 7970, 1950, p.14).

These countries met in Paris later in the same month, to begin negotiations on the French proposals. The treaty establishing the European Coal and Steel Community was finally signed in Paris on the 18th of April 1952. The original French proposals, particularly regarding the government of the community were subject to some modification, largely due to Dutch pressure. Rules of considerable detail were laid down in the Treaty to govern the High Authority, and a Council of Ministers was created to which the High Authority had to refer for various types of decision, thus providing a safeguard for national economic interests.

The return of a Conservative Government in Britain in October 1951, did not bring about a radical change in Britain's European policy. This came as a great disappointment to many Europeans who had expected such a policy reversal due to the Conservative advocacy of British participation in the Schuman Plan when in Opposition. No effort was made by Churchill's Government to veer from established British policy. Once the ECSC became firmly established, Britain did however acquire Associate status with the Community, which was ratified by the House of Commons in February 1955. This enabled the British Government to receive information on the progress made by the ECSC, without making any commitment or contribution to its work.

THE EUROPEAN DEFENCE COMMUNITY AND THE EUROPEAN ECONOMIC COMMUNITY

Ideas for a European army had been aired since the end of the War, particularly within the European Movement, but due to concerns about the consequences of re-arming Germany, these had not been developed seriously. It was the outbreak of the Korean War in 1950 which brought matters to a head. Fears of a Soviet threat intensified, and there was a certain amount of American pressure on the west European countries to pull together and present an adequate deterrent to the Soviet Union.

Once again it was Monnet who took the initiative, proposing to the French Government that a limited re-arming of West Germany under the supervision of a European Defence Community would both advance European union and provide an essential component of a European defence plan. These ideas were formalised under the title of the Pleven Plan (after the French Prime Minister), and were given initial approval by the French Assembly in October 1950. The success of the Pleven Plan in even getting thus far was largely due to the achievements of the ECSC in generating Franco-German cooperation. The Plan included proposals for a European Defence Minister responsible to the European Assembly, a European Defence Council of Ministers and a single European Defence budget.

Britain and the countries involved in the Schuman Plan negotiations were invited to consider membership of the EDC. The Labour Government declined to participate in the Plan but approved of it for continental countries. Although Churchill had advocated such an idea when in Opposition, he too refused to participate when he took office in 1951, but offered to give support to the scheme. The other Governments gave it more sympathetic consideration; the legislatures of West Germany, the Netherlands, Belgium and Luxembourg had approved the EDC plans by early 1954. However, by this time Italy and France were both undergoing considerable domestic instability, and ironically it was from Paris that the death knell for the EDC was sounded. The final vote on the Pleven Plan in the French National Assembly coincided with the advent of a Gaullist-Radical coalition led by Pierre Mendes-France, and the fall of the French-held Dien Bien Phu to the Viet Cong. The debate in August 1954 was dominated by Communist and Gaullist anti-German feeling which won the day: the EDC Plan was rejected by the country which had originally sponsored it. Uwe Kitzinger put the defeat of the EDC down to four factors:

'it would resurrect the German Army; it would destory the army of France; it would affect French political sovereignty; and it would imply an Economic Community for which the French economy felt unprepared.' (Kitzinger, 1962, p.13).

Kitzinger also pointed out that German re-armament could not have been the single decisive factor for the National Assembly as this was incorporated in the Western European Union (WEU) proposals, sponsored by Britain and passed by France later in the same year.

Britain was undoubtedly relieved at the failure of the EDC, and happy to propose the WEU; a distinctly less federal alternative. This plan was adopted by Britain, France, the Brussels Treaty powers, West Germany and Italy, and came into operation in 1955. It provided for gradual West German re-armament, to be controlled by the other member countries. In the same treaty, West Germany was recognised as a nation state and admitted to NATO.

Despite the failure of the EDC and its replacement by the more functional WEU, the energy of certain federally inclined politicians had not abated. J.W. Beyen, the Dutch Foreign Minister, redrafted some of his earlier proposals concerning a common market for a wide range of products, backed up by a greater degree of political union. In December 1954, the ECSC's Common Assembly called for a working group to be set up to examine possible extension of its sphere. This was followed up by an inter-governmental convention to prepare further steps of integration. Proposals were issued by the West German and Italian Governments calling for progress in this direction, and by Benelux, suggesting that a new stage of integration could be achieved primarily in the economic field.

Thus the leaders of the Six came together at Messina in June 1955, with the intention of re-launching the European idea in the atomic energy and economic fields. (Our concern is primarily with the latter.) The resolution adopted by the delegates at Messina drew extensively upon ideas put forward by the most integrationist of the participants, the Benelux countries. However, considerable dexterity was used in wording the resolution, in order to avoid offending the less federally inclined. The broad objective was agreed:

'a united Europe by the development of common institutions, the progressive fusion of national economies, the creation of a common market and the progressive harmonisation of social policies.' (Cmnd 9525, 1955).

In the details that followed, transport, power, production and atomic energy were included as sectors which could be improved on a united front. The objective specified was of a European Market without customs duties and other such obstacles to trade. The creation of a European Investment Fund was envisaged to finance industrial developments. It was also considered essential for the member states to begin the harmonisation of social policy, particularly regarding working conditions. At the end of the resolution there was a clear invitation to Britain, as a member of the WEU and an associate of the ECSC, to take part in the deliberations. The Messina Conference also established a committee of governmental delegates under the chairmanship of Paul-Henri Spaak (the Belgian Foreign Minister) to prepare items for discussion at a future, more conclusive conference.

The Spaak Committee, as it became known, worked speedily, and produced a report by April 1956, which was presented to the foreign ministers of the Six at Venice in the following month. It was soon agreed that the Spaak Report could be used as the basis for negotiation and indeed, it came to constitute the underlying philosophy of the Treaty of Rome. Whilst delegates of the Six remained fairly united throughout the Committee proceedings, this unity of purpose did not extend to the British representative whose status had been restricted by the British Government to that of observer rather than delegate. Similarly, when the foreign ministers of the Six met in September 1956 at Nordwijk, the British Foreign Minister declined his invitation to attend. Essentially, Britain wanted a free trade area rather than a customs union, and preferred to make use of the existing OEEC apparatus rather than create new institutions. At a further meeting of the Spaak Committee, the British representative, Robert Bretherton (a permanent official from the Board of Trade), made it clear that the British Government could not take a definite position on the proceedings so far, but that the British Government would have difficulties participating in a common market. At this point Bretherton withdrew from the Committee; Britain made no other contribution to its work, but in withdrawing, permitted a greater unity of purpose among the remaining participants.

The drive towards a settlement in early 1957 was not only hastened by the absence of Britain and the common aim of the six countries involved. The imminence of elections in West Germany, the vulnerability of Mollett's Government in France, the impact of the Suez crisis, and the fears deriving from the developing British interest in a broader free trade area all gave the negotiations an air of urgency. Thus on the 25th of March 1957 two Treaties of Rome were signed, the first concerning the European Economic Community and the second, Euratom. The first treaty stated that the EEC

> 'shall have as its task, by establishing a common market and progressively approximating the economic policies of Member States, to promote throughout the Community a harmonious development of economic activities, a continuous and balanced expansion, an increase in stability, an accelerated raising of the standard of living and closer relations between the States belonging to it.' (see Sweet and Maxwell, 1972).

Thus the Six were now clearly content to pursue their own economic goals, using the method they considered best. In contrast, Britain had not considered such forms of economic organisation appropriate for her needs, and increasingly became interested in the idea of a broad European economic cooperative scheme.

THE PROPOSED FREE TRADE AREA AND THE EUROPEAN FREE TRADE ASSOCIATION

As the movement towards further integration of the ECSC countries took place during 1956, members of the British Government, whilst hardly considering participation in this process as a policy alternative, were at least aware that the extent of the centripetal forces within the Six posed the possibility of British isolation in western Europe. It was at the instigation of Britain that the OEEC set up a working party in July 1956 to study the possibilities of closer relationships between the emerging customs union of the Six and the other OEEC countries. However, it was clear from a press statement by Peter Thorneycroft (President of the Board of Trade) and Harold Macmillan (Chancellor of the Exchequer) that, should a free trade area emerge, food, drink and tobacco would, on British insistence, be excluded from any general tariff reduction and that in times of balance of payments difficulties, a country would be able to reassert import restrictions. These sentiments could hardly have appealed to the Six who were engaged in negotiations for a more comprehensive reduction of tariffs between member countries. Nevertheless in November 1956 the British Government formally decided to go ahead with a scheme for a European free trade area.

From 1957 until 1959, Britain sought to create an economic organisation which was more far-reaching than the OEEC, though still founded on an inter-governmental pattern. The British Government first circulated a memorandum to the OEEC countries, which, whilst meeting with domestic approval, cut little ice among the Six. (Cmnd. 72, 1957). It was ambiguous on the point of future harmonisation of economies, stated that agriculture should be excluded, and did not deal with the question of institutions. It should have been no great surprise to Reginald Maudling (Paymaster General 1957-59, with responsibility for the free trade area negotiations) that no progress was made. The Six preferred their own arrangements and deadlock ensued, which was further cemented by the advent of General de Gaulle as President of France in May 1958. He considered that France would gain more from membership of an economic community which excluded Britain.

Thus by summer 1958, the idea that non-EEC European countries should form their own trading organisation was being mooted. It was becoming increasingly obvious during the free trade area talks that these other OEEC members were developing a united approach to the problems: they held a common preference for low external tariffs and for the retention of control over their own economies and external commercial policies. It was the respective industrial organisations rather than the governments of these other countries which gave impetus to the idea of an independent agreement. They published a discussion document on the subject, Free Trade in Western Europe. The respective governments concerned took up these suggestions and signed the Stockholm Convention in July 1959, establishing EFTA in November of that year (Cmnd. 823, 1959). This provided for expanding markets for non-agricultural goods, and did not infringe the neutral status of those countries who desired it. [4]

THE EARLY YEARS OF THE EEC

The EEC came into operation in 1958 heralded by the successes of the ECSC. Although the coal production of the Six increased by only 4 per cent between the years 1952 and 1956, it did appear that other economic benefits were being reaped. In the same period, steel production increased by 40 per cent and the internal steel trade doubled between 1952 and 1954 alone. Exports of steel rose from 7.3 million tons in 1952 to 11.7 million tons in 1957. The advent of cheap oil power in the late 1950s meant that the coal situation, which had been so poor as to necessitate American imports, was changed into one of a coal surplus.

The Treaty of Rome established four institutions to hold together and administer the EEC: the Council of Ministers, the Commission, the European Parliament and the Court of Justice. The Commission was designed firstly to ensure that the Treaty and legislation passed by the Community was implemented. Secondly, it was made the executive agency of the EEC, which entailed the responsibility for the formulation of legislative proposals (administrative decrees). Also the Commission was empowered, within limits laid down in the Treaty, to make its own decisions and issue regulations. It was given power to scrutinise such things as tariff quota and the role played by national governments in their own economy in order to ensure their consistency with the law of the Community. Finally, the Commission was entrusted with the management of the financial affairs of the EEC.

The Council of Ministers, representing the national governments of member countries, was designed to safeguard national interests. Initially it was permitted only to respond to proposals from the Commission, and not initiate changes in the Community of itself. If it acts unanimously the Council could override the Commission, though if the Commission is in agreement with a majority of the Council of Ministers, the minority within the latter was expected to give way. In practice of course, the relations between these bodies has not been so straight forward.

The Parliament, consisting originally of members appointed by the national Parliaments of the Six, was designed not to reflect national loyalties, but those of political groupings. Whilst in some respects the nature and work of the Parliament changed in later years, its central functions remain the same; the control over the work of the Commission, including its dismissal, and the scrutiny of the Commission's legislative proposals, prior to their submission to the Council of Ministers. The Court of Justice originally consisted of seven judges appointed by agreement between the member governments, and was given the task of ensuring that the implementation of Community law is correctly conducted.

With the exception of provisions for gradual abolition of tariffs between countries, and the target of a common external tariff, few specific instructions were given within the Treaty of Rome: the objectives were of a more general nature. Thus considerable initiative rested with the Commission - a title preferred to High Authority (used in the ECSC), reflecting diminishing enthusiasm for supranational overtones. Its task was to reconcile the often conflicting interests, which had been bypassed by the Treaty. The decisive power to accept or reject the Commission's proposals still rested with the Council of Ministers.

The early years of the EEC coincided with periods of relatively fast economic growth in the member countries which encouraged them to reduce tariffs more quickly than might otherwise have been the case. The first reduction of 10 per cent was made after the first year of operation. Also, in 1960, it was decided to explore the possibility of implementing a common agricultural policy. Agreement was reached by 1962 to institute a transitional period for such an agricultural policy.

Discussions had also been conducted, and broad agreement reached, on progress towards a closer political union, and on extending the Community's purview into cultural, foreign and defence matters. In 1958 a joint system of social security for migrant workers was agreed; two years later measures designed to enable the free movement of capital among the countries, and rules against discrimination in transport were published. In the same year the European Social Fund commenced operation with an annual budget of £30 million. At the end of 1961, the European Investment Bank had provided £120.5 million in loans, and legislation for free movement of business and services had been approved.

No doubt attracted by the achievement and successes of the EEC, Denmark, Ireland, Norway and the United Kingdom all applied for membership of the Community in 1961.

THE FIRST BRITISH APPLICATION FOR EEC MEMBERSHIP 1961-1963

The period during which this application for EEC membership was made coincided with a considerable if not comprehensive reappraisal of British attitudes to the question of participation in the movement towards European economic integration at influential and popular levels. The reasons for this reappraisal on the part of those within the Government and of those outside, are of course difficult to assess, and probably varied from one individual or group to another. Certainly a combination of factors acted upon the leadership of the Government. Although the Conservatives had enjoyed power since 1951 and Macmillan had been Prime Minister since 1957, there was some evidence of failure on the international stage. It was becoming clear that the Conservatives were presiding over the decline of Britain's world status.

The Suez failure of 1956 most poignantly symbolised this theme, but other significant developments under Macmillan's leadership gave further substance to fears concerning Britain's reduced role in international affairs. Indicative of this was the failure of Maudling's efforts at bridge-building in Europe: Britain had proved unable to restrain the Six from furthering their own unification by her attempt to form a wider European economic grouping. The abandonment in 1960 of Blue Streak, Britain's independent nuclear deterrent, not only left Britain more dependent upon the USA, but was also a rude reminder of her inability to equal the economic and technological resources of the new superpowers. If Britain could not compete as one of the superpowers, Macmillan considered that she could at least play the role of mediator between the USA and the USSR. However, this attempt also proved futile when the 1960 Paris Summit, designed to bring an end to the Cold War, was ended by the shooting down of an American spy plane by the USSR. This failure was cited by Sir Philip de Zulueta (Macmillan's Principal Private Secretary at the time) as the most important milestone in the conversion of the Prime Minister to the belief that Britain should join the EEC. (Charlton, 1981)

Britain's demise as a world power was underpinned by her recurrent domestic financial problems. Stimulation of economic growth by successive Chancellors, Derek Heathcoat-Amory and Selwyn Lloyd, brought with it a balance of payments deficit, pressure on the pound, and the consequent imperative to deflate the economy. The fundamental inability of Britain to attain steady growth contrasted sharply with the successes of EEC members who were simultaneously enjoying increases in trade, capital investment and living standards.

In addition to the problems of comparative economic weakness, and a declining world role, there was a third factor of concern to the Government. A major plank in British foreign policy had been her leadership of the Commonwealth countries. Indeed a considerable proportion of Britain's international trade had been carried out with her ex-colonies. However, Commonwealth countries increasingly looked elsewhere for political support, and in some cases for military support, and were tending to diversify their trading links. The entry of many new African and Asian members to the Commonwealth profoundly changed its traditional appearance of an old white man's club. This shift also caused the persistence of the South African apartheid policy to be viewed differently, and the fact that Macmillan was unable to prevent the departure of South Africa from the Commonwealth was seen as a particularly serious failure in the eyes of many British Conservatives.

In view of Britain's poor fortunes in the three areas

outlined, it is no great surprise to learn from Lord Butler that Europe had become a major premise in Macmillan's forward thinking. (Butler, 1971, p.235) Thus, despite having been instrumental in the formation of EFTA in 1959, the British Government was not content to remain politically and economically separated from the Six. By 1960, Britain was beginning to attempt to repair relations with France and West Germany, which had been somewhat frayed since the breakdown of the free trade area talks. The overtures of rapprochement took the form of ministerial visits, and use of the forum provided by the WEU. In January 1960, an OEEC Special Conference was held, which produced at least an appearance of cohesion among the countries concerned, if nothing tangible. Later in the same year EFTA set up a special study group to investigate further possibilities of bridge-building between itself and the EEC countries. Selwyn Lloyd (then Foreign Secretary), speaking at the Council of Europe in January 1960, said

> I believe we made a mistake in not taking part in the negotiations which led to the formation of the Coal and Steel Community. (Camps, 1964, p.278)

Similarly, in June 1960, John Profumo (Minister of State at the Foreign Office) gave further indication of a new British attitude at the Assembly of the WEU:

> I can say however, that the British Government, without regard to all that has happened in the last few years, will certainly be ready to consider anew the proposal that Britain should join Euratom and indeed the European Coal and Steel Community as well. (Camps, 1964, p.290)

Over the next year, the British Government gave consideration to membership without any explicit commitment until July 1961, when Macmillan announced the Government's intention to open negotiations for membership of the EEC. He had just reshuffled his Cabinet appointing Edward Heath as Lord Privy Seal with special responsibility for the European negotiations, and a negotiating team was formed. However, because the Six gave priority to discussing the next stage of their own integration, talks were only at an exploratory level until April 1962. The period of negotiation from April until August 1962 appeared very productive, and contributed to the British expectation that a settlement might be made in spring of 1963. Despite Monnet's advice to Britain to join and settle the details afterwards, the British Government felt that they were not in a position to do this. It was thought that the agriculture lobby, and EFTA and Commonwealth relationships would not permit such a move as there was the danger of creating a split within the Conservative Party, over these three themes. Thus the negotiators were obliged to produce a package covering all points of commercial detail. This was a task which the Spaak Committee, when preparing the Treaty of Rome, had avoided. The Conservative Party later claimed that provisional agreement had been reached in the following spheres:

African and Caribbean Commonwealth Countries: free access for their raw materials and tropical foodstuffs. India, Pakistan and Ceylon: a comprehensive agreement for their manufactured goods and free access for Indian and Ceylon tea. Canada, Australia and New Zealand: free entry for wool and jute, special attention to New Zealand's exports and a reasonable temperate foodstuffs pricing policy. United Kingdom Agriculture: transitional arrangements for the United Kingdom and that the Community would adopt the practice of an Annual Review. (Conservative Party, 1964, p.467)

However, Duncan Sandys (Minister for Commonwealth Relations, 1960-64) commented after the breakdown that

no outline agreement had been reached on horticulture... little progress had been made on sugar, although a precise agreement on the status of the Commonwealth Sugar Agreement was clearly a 'must'. Arrangements for the other EFTA countries, one of the major preconditions of United Kingdom entry into the EEC, had not been defined. Most important of all a satisfactory agreement over the future of New Zealand exports of agriculture produce was still a very long way off. (Butterwick and Rolfe, 1968, p.78)

In the end, however, it was not simply the minutiae of negotiating and bargaining that was the undoing of the British application. On the 14th of January 1963 General de Gaulle, having consolidated his personal standing in French politics with the referenda of 1961 and 1962, announced that the British were not yet ready for membership of the EEC. Whether this was because Britain was too slow in making concessions to the Six, (and implicitly, France) or simply because it suited de Gaulle to exclude Britain from the European developments, is a matter of debate. Despite some criticism from the other five members of the EEC, de Gaulle's statement signalled the end of the first British application for membership of the European Economic

Community.

NOTES

[1]   These represented Czechoslovakia, Denmark, France, Italy, the Netherlands, Norway, Poland, Yugoslavia and the anti Nazi group in Germany.

[2]   This saw the addition of Canada, Denmark, Iceland, Italy, Norway, Portugal and the USA.

[3]   This was comprised of Austria, Belgium, Denmark, France, Greece, Iceland, Ireland, Italy, Luxembourg, the Netherlands, Norway, Portugal, Sweden, Switzerland, Turkey and the UK.

[4]   The member countries were Austria, Denmark, Norway, Portugal, Sweden, Switzerland and the United Kingdom.

3 The analysis

Harold Lasswell suggested that the study of politics can be advanced by 'quantitative analysis of political discourse' (Lasswell, 1966, p.247). It is in this belief that content analysis was employed in the present study. This method of analysis has previously been adopted for a variety of purposes, ranging from exploring the cultural differences reflected in the songs and literature of various nations to the differences which characterize the language behaviour of schizophrenic and normal persons (see Holsti, 1969). Bernard Berelson asserted that

'content analysis is a research technique for the objective, systematic and quantitative description of manifest content of communications' (Gerbner et al, 1969, p.10).

It is this notion which has encouraged social scientists to use content analysis to increase their understanding of international relations. For example North, Brody and Holsti used it to assess the importance of individual decision makers as spokesmen for their culture:

'A feasible approach to the behaviour of nation states, therefore, is to concentrate on attributes of those relatively few individuals in any given government who make foreign policy determinants and commit the nations to a course in international activity' (Gerbner et al, 1969, p.30).

Thus content analysis has been used to take note of different cultural perceptions of international events, in terms of the differing views of who did what, how they did it, to whom they did it and the consequences of that action. These findings would be given additional sophistication with such types of quantitative scales as the number of statements, their length and intensity.

Content analysis has not, however, been fully exploited for an understanding of the nature of political issues within a particular system, nor in assessing their implications for the study of policy making. The present study departs from the more orthodox content analysis by attempting to use the method to depict an aggregate perception of an issue. This consists not simply of 'who has done what' etc., but of which themes are attributed to an issue at any one time, and the relative significance attached to these.

A study by Brookes, Jordan, Kimber and Richardson (1976) on the growth of the environmental issue in British politics provided an attempt to probe at the anatomy of that issue. Their intention was to trace its development and salience, and to examine whether increased attention had been paid to certain component problems. A content analysis of The Times was conducted to ascertain what changes had taken place in the twenty year period from 1953 to 1973. Thirteen categories were produced which covered what the authors considered to be all aspects of the environmental issue (e.g. Air Transport, Air Pollution, Road Transport, Foreign). Six sample years were chosen, and from these twelve sample issues of the newspaper were selected for scrutiny. As well as highlighting changes in the salience of the issue, the analysis revealed considerable variety in the proportional coverage of individual component topics. For instance, there was a decline of interest in planning matters over the period, with a corresponding increase in the roads topics. Whilst the authors did not posit a general theory for the increase in importance of the issue, they concluded that

'The level of mass media coverage is, however, one index (however crude) of the public significance of individual issues and is thus worthy of serious consideration. In this context, despite its inherent limitations, content analysis research provides a more accurate basis for issue evaluation than impressionistic assessments or speculation' (Brookes et al, 1976, p.253) (My emphasis.)

THE CASE STUDY

The case study used to demonstrate the usefulness of the
issue anatomy and salience concepts for our understanding of
issue change is the question of British participation in the
process of European economic integration between 1950 and
1963. The main data base for the study is the Hansard
record of House of Commons debate on the question, and a
content analysis was utilised to depict the issue's changing
anatomy over four sub periods. (The content analysis method
will be outlined in a following section.)

What precisely is meant by the European question and what
makes it suitable for the sort of study envisaged? For
present purposes the European question between 1950 and 1963
is comprised of the British relationship to the process of
economic integration among the six western European
countries who came to form the ECSC in 1952 and the EEC in
1957. Whilst these organisations differed in some respects,
they have been merged into this same question because
membership of both required a measure of sacrifice of
sovereignty in specific areas of the national economy and a
certain amount of pooling of economic resources. Thus, this
excluded debate on the European Army for instance; which
whilst concerned with some measure of supranational
authority and pooling of military resources, did not require
pooling of economic resources, nor did it have such direct
economic implications as the ECSC and the EEC. Similarly,
unless debate on the Free Trade Area and the European Free
Trade Association touched on the EEC alternative, it was not
included in the analysis. These former organisations had no
such requirements for pooling and central administration of
sectors of the economy. It is obviously the case that
membership of the EEC entailed additional commitments to
those of the ECSC, and indeed, membership of the EEC in 1962
implied a different set of requirements for Britain than
would have been the case in 1956. The minimum terms set out
above are however common to the issues of British membership
of both organisations over this period. This position would
only have been invalidated had the terms of British
membership been less stringent at the time when Britain was
not deliberately excluded from the creation of the ECSC and

the EEC. During the years 1950-57 when these were formed, successive British Governments were officially and specifically invited to participate in the Schuman Plan (1950), the ECSC (1952), the Messina Conference (1955) and the Spaak Committee (1955-56, which led to the Treaty of Rome and the creation of the EEC). It should also be emphasised that the purpose of the study is neither to bemoan nor justify British policy over these years. It is rather, by way of analysis of the issue's changing anatomy, to throw further light on the policy making process.

Having established the parameters of the issue, what makes it suitable for the sort of study envisaged? Firstly, it was expected that during the period 1950-1963, the issue would prove to be subject to considerable variations in salience, and that this would permit contrast of the issue at times of high and low stature. Secondly, it was thought that the issue would be characterised by varying policy preferences, which might have had a bearing, not only upon salience, but also upon the anatomy of the issue. Linked to this point was the fact that the issue did not neatly and consistently divide the two major parties. It was thought that at most times during the period concerned there would be individuals within the Conservative and Labour Parties who might differ from the point of view expressed by their Party leaders on the issue. This would imply that activities and expressions of view on the issue need not necessarily be a function of adversary Parliamentary politics. Finally, the European question was, irrespective of its salience at any one time, of great intrinsic importance. Whilst superficially a foreign policy matter with ramifications for the country's pattern of international relations, it also possessed significant implications for domestic economic, political, and social life. Though these were not necessarily recognised in Britain during all of the years concerned in this study, the impact of the issue upon the participating countries illustrates its potential importance for Britain. Indeed the European issue has preoccupied every British Government since that of Macmillan, it has been a continuing item of debate among and between the political parties, and it was the subject of the first (and hitherto, only) United Kingdom Consultative Referendum.

It is clearly not possible to systematically measure and aggregate all depictions of an issue's anatomy over a number of years: research, as well as politics, may be described as the art of the possible. Thus a body of material was required which could be deemed broadly representative of all the public debate about the European question over the years specified. The constraints of what was accessible and feasible with study time limits were also taken into account.

The study of public opinion was considered unsuitable, as it usually only provides information on policy preferences and issue awareness: depictions of an issue's anatomy are difficult to extract from such data. In any case, public opinion findings are not normally available for muted issues. Use of the press might appear to be more fruitful for the intended purposes as more or less continuous data is available and press reports are ideally suited to content analysis techniques. Problems do exist however. Which papers should be examined, given that they vary, not only in broad political outlook and more specific issue preferences, but also in their style and approach to news? ·That one thousand words should be devoted by a popular daily to an issue may be less significant than a thousand words on that issue in, for instance, The Times, but how can this significance be accounted for in the study? Also circulation figures vary enormously: can the depiction of an issue by a paper with a three million readership be three times as important as the depiction of it by a paper with a readership of one million? Further, there is the problem of attributing a paper's depiction of an issue to either the editor, the journalist or to their perceptions of the readers' likely views. Whilst public opinion findings and the study of press coverage of the issue undoubtedly contribute to an understanding of its anatomy, they have limitations for producing a defensible characterisation of it. In the light of these considerations debate on the issue within the House of Commons was chosen as the object of analysis.

The Hansard record of debate is of course easily accessible, and is presented in a uniform style over the period concerned. Thus each column of reported speech contains more or less the same number of words. Further, the Hansard record is well indexed, thus indicating instances of debate on the European question, and also indicating the periods when little or no such debate took place. Clearly though, the choice of data to be studied cannot rest solely on the technical merits and availability of one particular alternative. Practicalities aside, can the Hansard record of Parliamentary debate be considered in any way representative of the overall estimation of this issue? This question will be discussed at two levels; firstly with respect to the nature of the House of Commons,

45

and secondly regarding the specific treatment of this issue by the House.

Firstly then, is it tenable to assume that views expressed in the Commons can be construed to some extent as representative of a broad range of popular and informed views? The House of Commons has been described as

'a football stadium, where the crowd may cheer or boo, but have only limited influence on the game' (Ryle, 1977, p.14.)

Ryle argued that because of the electoral link between the public and the M.P.s, and by virtue of the public nature of parliamentary proceedings, the House of Commons is, in the words of Lloyd George, 'the sounding board of the nation', and, emphasising the role of the individual M.P.:

'His are, of course, the constant ears and eyes of the House. With varying degrees of success he measures public opinion in his constituency, or within his social, professional, business, industrial or otherwise specialist community, or he acquires relevant knowledge and briefing by reading the Press and specialist journals. Or he is briefed by pressure groups or experts. And to varying degrees he conveys this opinion, this information and these views to the House. He thus articulates the anxieties of the people' (Ryle, 1977, p.15.)

The comment could be levelled that far from transmitting public opinions, M.P.s create them. If this view was accepted, it would still not detract from my case: the House of Commons' debates could be broadly described as illustrative of a range of popular opinions. In fact, it would be naive to subscribe wholeheartedly to a single directional flow of opinions within the political system. Whilst it is undoubtedly the case that politicians contribute to the shaping of public beliefs, the reverse is also true. David Judge, in trying to explain the reluctance of M.P.s to adopt a system of functional specialisation, concluded that Members were afraid of losing their broad representative role. Judge cited the remarks of David Steel M.P. as typical:

'I have no great inclination to be highly specialised, but if I had, my constituents would soon stop it. They write to me on every subject under the sun and they expect me to take an interest in an enormous range of subjects. Consequently I do so' (Judge, 1981, p.203.)

For clarification, it is not being argued here that the House of Commons' decisions are necessarily representative of public policy preferences, nor that interests are proportionately represented within the House. What is suggested however, is that the House of Commons does provide a forum for a wide range of views to be expressed, and that this does bear some relation to wider debate of an issue.

It could be argued that attention to the parliamentary debate would lead to the analysis ignoring the interest group/civil service relations which J.J. Richardson and A.G.Jordan, for example, have argued are central to the process of policy making and yet take little notice of Parliament:

> 'Many 'key' parliamentary issues are in fact symbolic gestures to satisfy the government's parliamentary majority who are effectively ignored in more central matters. Even with these issues one cannot credit Parliament with initiating them. They usually have extra Parliamentary origins' (Richardson and Jordan, 1979, p.41.)

Such a view is not incompatible with the use made of Parliamentary debate in this study. It is not held that the Hansard record should necessarily be considered representative of the views of those involved in such functional relations, but representative of a range of public views on the issue. Indeed, any contrasts and comparisons which can be made between the anatomy of the issue as represented by Parliamentary debate and views on it in the more private consultative machinery, may provide clues as to the extent of the relevance of public debate for the policy machinery and policy outcomes.

It is arguable that the Hansard record may not be totally representative of views and beliefs held in the Commons, if either the Speaker or the Leader of the House acted perversely. In the case of the Speaker, this could be due to a bias in the calling of Members to speak. In the case of the Leader of the House, this could be due to bias in the timetabling of Parliamentary business. There is however no evidence to substantiate such claims. In any case, the Opposition does play a role in timetabling, and the provision of Supply Days enables matters to be raised outside the specified business of the government. Finally, those responsible for the ordering of Parliamentary business

do not necessarily have any control over <u>what</u>
<u>is actually said</u>.

The objection could still be raised that, even if this were
supposed to be the case, it may not be in practice:
Parliamentary debate may still be unrepresentative of public
debate. It could be argued that the nature of the two party
system is such that only a narrow range of views are heard
within the Commons. This argument would carry particular
weight with respect to the period dealt with in this study
when the two party system was at its strongest (Drucker,
1979). However, studies of the major British political
parties have consistently indicated that they are not single
political entities, but rather broad alliances spanning wide
range of opinion and belief. The Labour Party has been
described as being made up of 'factions' and the
Conservative Party of 'tendencies' (Rose, 1964). This is
more representative of the range of public opinions than the
illusion that political opinions fall into one of two blocs
as represented by the Conservative and Labour Parties. It
should be acknowledged here that the extent of party
cohesion does vary considerably from one issue to another.

Having conducted a content analysis on instances of House
of Commons debate regarding the European question, what use
can be made of the findings for the study of policy making
in Britain? It is intended that the findings should be used
first to simply discover the extent of changes in the
salience and anatomy of the issue. Secondly the findings of
the Parliamentary salience and anatomy of the issue can be
examined alongside evidence of the evaluations and opinions
of it among groups and organisations within the political
system. This would be with the object of ascertaining the
extent to which the Parliamentary findings were
representative of the variety of the evaluations and views
within the political system, and the relevance of this for
an understanding of policy making. It is not envisaged here
that simple one to one relationships can be found to explain
a particular set of findings for salience and anatomy.
However, it is expected that the Parliamentary findings will
bear some relation to the wider activity and beliefs within
the system, and that they will be susceptible to some form
of explanation. Perceptions of an issue do not take place
in a vacuum, and whilst the processes of the creation of
beliefs and their reinforcement are undoubtedly so complex
as to preclude a positivist account, it is expected that a
student of politics can make some informed observations to
account for the stature and anatomy of an issue in a certain
period. The analysis of activities and beliefs related to

the European question will centre around different organisations and groups, however, the adequacies of a group explanation for the changes in the standing of the issue will also be considered.

One problem envisaged at this stage is that of the variations in the availability of sources from one organisation to another, and in the case of government records, from one period to another. (Only the very first years covered by the study fall outside the thirty year rule.) Whilst such problems should be acknowledged they do not necessarily undermine the value of the project: perfect knowledge of even the immediate past is always elusive. The comment that 'The scientist has no other method than doing his damnedest' (Kaplan, 1964, p.27) applies equally to the student of politics.

The attitudes towards the issue by successive governments were examined and, where official records are not available, recent historical studies and memoirs have been relied upon. This is also the case for the Whitehall departments. The records of party conferences were available, and constituted a useful source on party views. Other publications of the main parties, in addition to biographies, memoirs and historical accounts, provided useful source material.

The evaluation of and views about the issue by sectional interest groups was also the subject of examination. Here documentary evidence was more variable. The records of some trade unions during the period were found to be well catalogued and comprehensively preserved, whilst others were incomplete if not decimated. Fortunately, the records of the National Union of Mineworkers and of the Iron and Steel Trades Confederation, who were among the most relevant unions with regard to the European Coal and Steel Community, were well preserved and available. The Trades Union Congress records were easily accessible. The records of the Federation of British Industry and of the Association of British Chambers of Commerce were used as illustrative of British business views, and the National Farmers' Union records as representative of the views of farmers in England and Wales. In the cases of all this range of sectional groups, evidence was found of their functional relations with Whitehall departments, and this has been drawn upon in addition to their more public pronouncements.

The records of promotional organisations related to this issue posed the biggest research problem. Only the European Movement had maintained a fairly complete record of its business. Publications of various groups were particularly difficult to track down. Contemporary press reports of such groups' activities and sentiments often provided a useful back-up source. Selected newspapers were also scrutinised to draw out their varying evaluations and views of the issue.

It was considered that all of the above mentioned organisations and groups might have some impact upon the salience and anatomy of the issue as depicted in the analysis of the Parliamentary debate. This question was explored with special attention being paid to the instances of depictions of the issue divergent from those deduced from the content analysis.

The role of public opinion in the policy making process is particularly difficult to assess, with the central problem of whether to ascribe to public opinion the position of function or cause of, for instance, Parliamentary views. It would however be foolish to opt for one description of the role of popular opinion at the expense of the other. Clearly, in liberal-democratic systems particularly, political leaders have at least a marginal sensitivity to public opinions which might have an impact upon their own electoral prospects. Equally, a main source of political views held by the public is the reported speeches of political leaders and press coverage of, and comment upon, political events. Where findings were available for public opinion, they were drawn upon in the second stage of the analysis. The findings of this 'second level' of research will be set against the content analysis findings for the individual periods in subsequent chapters.

THE METHOD OF ANALYSIS

The Hansard sections which have been analysed are only those that constituted a record of House of Commons debate on the European question as defined [1]. Parliamentary questions were excluded from the analysis, because, although they can be used as a measure of issue salience, they do not provide such opportunity to delve into the anatomy of the issue. In any case, these are often directly inspired by members of the government. The data has been divided up into four sections for the purpose of comparison - P1, P2, P3 and P4. P1 lasts from 8th May 1950 (the date of the Prime Minister's announcement of the Schuman Plan to the House of Commons) until the 2nd August 1951 (the dissolution of the Commons

prior to the 1951 General Election). P2 begins on 31st
October 1951 (the opening of the new Parliament under the
Conservative Government), and lasts until the 21st February
1955 (the end of the debate of Britain's associate status
with the ECSC). P3 lasts from the beginning of the Messina
Conference in June 1955, when the Foreign Ministers of the
ECSC countries announced that they intended to seek means of
achieving a greater degree of economic union, and invited
Britain to join them, until the end of 1960, thus including
the time of the creation of EFTA. P4 lasts from 1961, the
beginning of the period during which the Government was
known to be reconsidering its EEC policy, until de Gaulle's
veto of British EEC membership in January 1963.

One caveat should be added at this point, although it
concerns a problem which is encountered in many such studies
and is never accompanied by a totally satisfactory solution.
This concerns the methodology of enclosing a period of
months and years and interpreting it as a single entity:

'Unlike dates, periods are not facts. They are
retrospective conceptions that we form about past events,
useful to focus discussion, but very often leading
historical thought astray' (Trevelyan, 1944, p.92.)

The anatomy of any issue is almost certainly bound to alter
in some small detail over a period of a month, thus the
depiction of an issue's anatomy over, say, twenty-four
months must remain only an aggregation. Similarly, the
placing of a transitional month in one group of years rather
than another can only be on the basis of common sense. It
is historical and political departures that provide frames
for time; whether the formation of a European body, the
election of a new British Government, or a recognisable and
critical shift in policy of a major actor within the British
political system. It is to be expected that each of these
would have potential impact upon the salience and anatomy of
the issue.

An SPSS computer programme was utilised for storing and
analysing the Hansard material. As the object of the
analysis was to provide both quantitative and qualitative
contrasts of the issue within several distinct periods, it
was necessary to devise appropriate units of measurement and
description.

Many content and analysis studies have used a sentence, or
a word as the main unit of measurement. In this study a
more flexible method was preferred, which, while requiring

more thought and deliberation at the record taking stage, does have certain advantages. Holsti suggested than an alternative unit of measurement to the grammatical type, is that of using a 'theme': a single assertion on a subject (Holsti, 1969, p.116.) Adopting his approach, a self contained statement made in debate was used as the initial unit of measurement. Each statement was labelled with one of twenty or so 'Components'. Issues are clearly composed of several sets of implications and consequences for various different facets of political, economic, and social life. Speakers cannot embrace in the space of a comparatively short verbal delivery, all elements of the European question. Instead they select one or several themes which they wish to explore, or utilise in their argument. A range of components was drawn up on the basis of several pilot studies of the data (see Table 1.)

A statement was deemed to end when a new component of discussion was introduced. Thus, a statement may have consisted of a single phrase, a sentence, or several paragraphs. Record could be then made of the number of occasions on which the different components were raised in each period. This however, took no account of the amount of attention each component received when raised. So, a further means of measurement has also been employed. When a component was mentioned, the number of Hansard columns it occupied was also recorded.

It was considered desirable to acknowledge in the analysis the difference between a simple statement of belief and a carefully constructed, well illustrated justification of a policy preference. A detailed and precise depiction of the variety of 'depths' of argument is elusive. However, a simple dichotomous variable has been provided which goes at least some way towards achieving this end. Each statement was examined to ascertain whether or not it was 'substantiated'. Substantiation simply means that the statement contained some self-explanation or justification of an argument, in contrast to a statement which constituted a mere declaration of belief or policy preference. This dichotomy draws on Abraham Kaplan's distinction of 'substantive' terms from 'notational' and auxiliary terms: 'substantive terms remain fundamental' (Kaplan, 1964, p.49.) What was needed, was a uniform method of identifying such substantive statements. The method chosen was that of asking of a statement, is its conclusion explained and does it answer the question how or why a belief is held? Thus statements which contained an attempt at clarification as to why certain beliefs and policy preferences were held were

TABLE   1

COMPONENTS USED IN ANALYSIS OF THE EUROPEAN QUESTION

Sovereignty	Political Perceptions
Defence	Britain's Historical Traditions
Broad Utility of Unity	Commonwealth (General)
Commonwealth (Specific)	Third World
Wider Trade Commitments	Economic Implications
European Economy	Commercial & Industrial Stability
Economic Alternatives	Agriculture
Regulations	Welfare
Trade Union Affairs	Employment
Popular Opinion	Nature & State of Negotiations
Party Scoring	Other

deemed substantive. For example, if an M.P. stated that British entry into the EEC would detract from Britain's trading benefits with the Commonwealth, this statement would be recorded as unsubstantiated. If however, he added that, for example, this was because the EEC external tariff system was incompatible with the system of Imperial Preference, it would be recorded as substantiated.

A problem of partisanship could obviously arise at this point: what one person may consider to be a 'substantiation' may be rejected by another as inadequate or inaccurate. A statement was deemed to have been substantiated if the speaker is considered to be intending and attempting a justification, irrespective of whether such explanation is considered by the analyst to be politically or economically valid. As with many such studies however, ultimately such judgements have to be entrused to the analyst, and the results treated with some caution accordingly.

It may be asked what relevance this has to the present study? The above 'how/why' test of a statement constituted an attempt to distinguish a greater 'depth' of discussion from simple sloganising, or statement of belief. This was on the premise that debate which involved an effort to provide such explanations was qualitatively different from that which did not: a distinction which is intrinsically interesting, and also which permits a further level of analysis. In order to provide substantiation for a statement, the speaker will necessarily have to provide some means of illustration or explanation. Thus each component has been further broken down into 'Points of Detail'. These were recorded if and when a statement had been substantiated. The list of points of detail within each component has been provided in Appendix 1.

It might at first appear that there is some duplication of the points of detail (details) among the different components. This does not however constitute a transgression of the content analysis axiom that all categories should be mutually exclusive. Rather, the allocation of details among components was simply to acknowledge that, for instance, the question of threatened British isolation, as a consequence of not taking part in the European developments could arise in a number of the components: i.e. defence (component 4: point of detail 5 – see Appendix 1), Britain's historical traditions (5:1) and economic implications (11:8). These are obviously different points as they bear the quite distinct emphases of defence, tradition, and economy.

In addition to being able to make these relatively fine distinctions, it was felt that for comparative purposes especially, it would also be of advantage to introduce somewhat broader categories for describing the anatomy of the issue. To this end all points of detail have been regrouped under the headings of 'Policy Aspect' and 'Geographical Focus'. The three policy aspects are 'Political', 'Economic' and 'Social'. The Political aspect refers principally to factors relating to and consequences of entry for government, for the European and World international relations, Britain's role in the international system, defence and the desirability of different forms of international cooperation. The Economic aspect includes factors relating to and consequences of entry for different spheres of the British and Commonwealth economies (from agriculture to industrial investment), perceptions of the economies of the European communities and their likely appropriateness for Britain's economic needs. The Social aspect consists principally of consumer, welfare and trade union matters. The precise make-up of each aspect is laid out in Appendix II.

The geographical focus (or focus) variable simply enables distinction between the three different geographical areas of interest specified: Britain, Europe, and Extra-Europe. That covered by the label Britain comprises of those items deemed to be of specifically domestic interest. Europe refers in the present study to western European considerations, and for the most part relates to the countries of the Six and of EFTA. The Extra European focus includes all other areas and those points of detail which are of a more general nature, applying to no one particular geographical area. The exact distribution of points of detail among these three focuses is presented in Appendix III.

It is also possible to stratify the categories of aspect by those of focus. Those details which refer to British Political matters can be distinguished for instance, from those referring to British Economic or European Political considerations. These further units are termed Spheres, and are listed in Appendix IV.

It should be noted that the components of the state of the negotiations and party scoring do not feature here as they do not directly pertain to perceptions of the European question. However, they have been recorded in the content analysis as they provide further data on the issue's anatomy in each period. Party scoring refers to the occasions when a speaker made use of debate on the European question to make an attack upon political opponents (within or outside his party) or to uphold the views and activities of his allies. The state/nature of the negotiations, similarly does not refer to the actual issue, but to perceptions about the stage or process of inter-governmental activity related to the issue.

In addition it was also considered desirable to provide some means of verifying any policy preference for which each component and detail was utilised. Thus any changes in overall policy orientation and in the specific treatment of individual themes could be identified. All components and details labelled 'For' refer specifically to those which favoured, on varying terms, full British membership of either the ECSC or the EEC. Clearly the exact terms of membership, whether for external tariffs, investment policies etc., or with regard to the steel industry, agriculture, etc., were negotiable. A statement for required the willingness to enter on the terms practically thought available. The label for also included cases where the statement was used to denounce an argument against if it is apparent that in doing so the speaker was advocating a positive European alternative. All statements which were critical of Britain's membership of the Six, or advocated an alternative path for Britain (e.g. a Commonwealth Free Trade Area, a wider European Free Trade Area) in preference, were labelled 'Against'.

Alternatively a component may not appear to be specifically for or against a policy option. This could be because the speaker was genuinely unsure of where he stood on an issue, or because he was preparing the ground, in order to make his preference clear in due course. Equally it could be because the remark made did not directly impinge on the question in hand. This particularly applies to the nature and state of the negotiations and party scoring components. In all these cases the component or point was labelled 'Neutral'.

A certain amount of vigilance was necessary at this part of the coding as on occasions various M.P.s waxed eloquent, for instance, on the benefits of a united Europe, but nevertheless indicated an unwillingness to comply with one of the necessary fundamental conditions of membership which developed as the integration of the Six continued. Similarly, M.P.s may have only been referring to association with the Six, or the establishment of a body such as the

Western Europe Union or the Free Trade Area based upon no more than inter-governmental cooperation. These did not require the economic and political commitment embodied both in the ECSC and the EEC.

As the method of analysis and concepts employed may not have been previously encounted in their present use, there follows a short summary.

1. Speeches were divided up into statements, which were identified by one of twenty or so components (e.g. sovereignty, Commonwealth, agriculture.) See Table 1.

2. Statements/Components were measured by a simple addition of the frequency with which they occurred, and by the number of Hansard columns they occupied.

3. Statements were deemed to be substantiated if they answered the questions how? or why?

4. Those statements which were substantiated were given further identification (i.e. in addition to component) of one or more points of detail. See Appendix I.

5. Points of detail were grouped in terms of their policy aspect, or whether Political, Economic, or Social. See Appendix II.

6. Points of detail were also grouped according to geographical focus, whether Britain, Europe or Extra Europe. See Appendix III.

7. The categories of policy aspect and geographical focus were cross tabulated, in order to identify spheres. See Appendix IV.

8. Components and points of detail were all labelled according to their policy preference, whether for, against, or neutral regarding British entry into the ECSC and the EEC.

An example of how the analysis was conducted is provided in Appendix V.

The expectation that the issue would vary in salience over
the four periods was confirmed as illustrated in figure 1.
In P1 over ten times as many columns were devoted to the
issue as in P2.   In P4 however, it clearly exceeded both of
the earlier periods: by over two times in the case of P1
and by over twenty times for P2.   The number of references
made to the European question in P3 was so small as to
preclude any content analysis of it during this period.   The
significance of this will be discussed in Chapter 6.

It cannot strictly be inferred from these figures that a
magnitude of, say over 1.7 per cent (the case of P4), is an
absolute measure of high salience of an issue.   This is
because no other data is available for other issues in these
periods.   For the purposes of the present study however, it
is sufficient to say that comparatively, the issue in P4 is
one of high salience, in P1 of moderate salience, and in P2
of low salience.

It is to be expected that to some extent the levels of
attention to an issue will vary, as other matters of
Parliamentary business come and go.   Nevertheless it must be
acknowledged that the differences illustrated in figure 1
are very large.   Obviously, the question of EEC membership
would have been relevant to more sectors of British society
than membership of the ECSC, although the central question
of Britain's relationship with European economic integration
was essentially the same.   This may account for a higher
proportion of attention to the issue in P4.   Even if this
were a fully satisfactory explanation, it does not help to
explain the vast difference between P1 and P2, nor the
absence of debate in P3 during which the issue would
potentially have had a broad sectoral application, as it did
in P4.   The issue was treated as of great importance during
P1 and P2 by the countries which did come to constitute the
Six.

Figure 2 depicts the varying proportions of policy
preferences, indicating that those against declined from P1
to P4.   However, the çorollary (which might have been
expected) that statements for would increase, did not take
place.   In P1 policy preferences were comparatively evenly
divided, whilst in P2 and P4, neutral statements dominated.
Figure 3 illustrates the different levels of substantiation
over the three periods, suggesting that statements in P2
were subject to the lowest degrees of justification, and

FIGURE 1

DEBATE ON EUROPEAN QUESTION AS A PERCENTAGE

OF TOTAL PARLIAMENTARY DEBATE

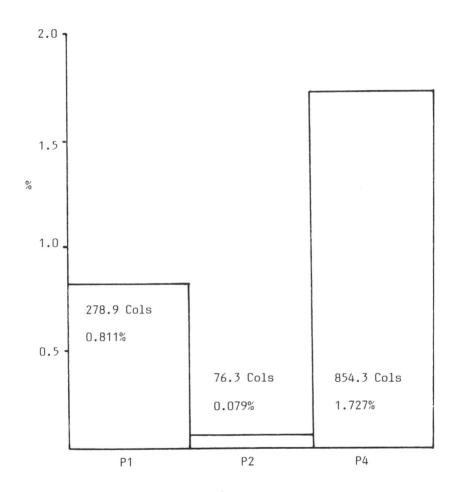

FIGURE 2

PERCENTAGE OF STATEMENTS MADE FOR, AGAINST OR NEUTRAL

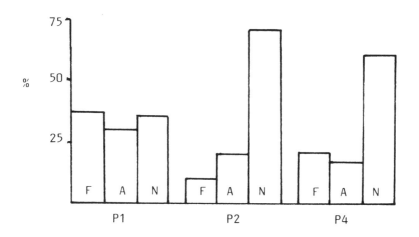

FIGURE 3

PROPORTION OF STATEMENTS SUBSTANTIATED

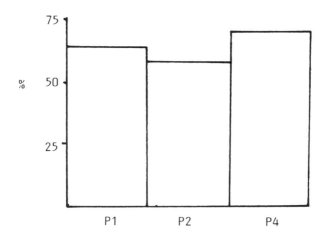

implying a low degree of exploration of the subject.

It might have been expected that the more attention each individual component received, the greater the level of scrutiny it would be accorded. The correlation coefficients between these two sets of variables are too weak to confirm this - indicative of weak relationships in all three periods. It is possible that it was felt that matters which warranted greater attention were already well understood, and thus did not require a high level of explanation. An alternative conclusion is that components which appeared important - by virtue of the degree of the attention they received - did not achieve the degree of substantiation they may have warranted, and were simply 'banners' which speech makers felt it necessary and expedient to wave.

Figure 4 compares the changes in aspect from P1 to P4 [2]. The most notable feature of figure 4 is the increase in the importance of the Economic aspect over the three periods. It doubled in stature from P1 to P4. This is mirrored by a decline in the proportion of the Political aspect from P1 onwards. In P1 it achieved 20 per cent more attention than any other aspect from P1 onwards. In P1 it outweighed even the combination of the Economic and Social aspects. Its dominance was significantly reduced in P2, and by P4 it was exceeded by the Economic aspect, although it still accounted for a 42 per cent share of all details. The Social aspect only exceeded 10 per cent of the total in P2, and received a particularly low level of attention in P1.

Figure 5 depicts the distribution of the three different geographical focuses in each of the three periods. Once again there is considerable evidence of changes of the emphases of debate. The European focus dominated both P1 and P2, although in neither case achieved an overall majority of points occupied by this focus. The patterns for the other two focuses are, however, very different. Whilst in P1 they were both around the 30 per cent mark, in P2 there was a 12 per cent increase in British concerns and a 20 per cent drop in Extra European matters. Although the latter focus accounted for only 9 per cent of all details in P2, in P4 it became the most important of the three. In this period, however, there was a more equal distribution of details with only 7.5 per cent separating the British and the Extra European focuses.

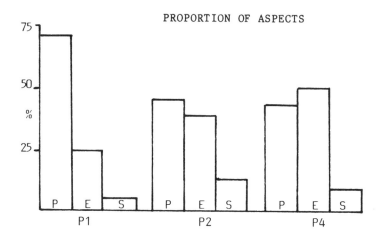

FIGURE 4

PROPORTION OF ASPECTS

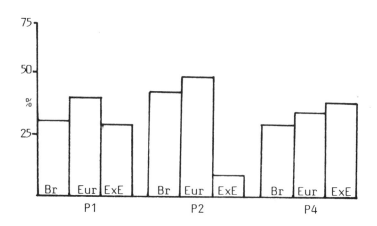

FIGURE 5

PROPORTION OF FOCUSES

62

Having made several broad observations in order to highlight overall changes in the salience and anatomy of the European question, the following chapters will give rather more detailed attention to the individual periods, elaborating upon the above findings, seeking to explain them and to assess their impact.

NOTES

[1] The types of debate potentially included were from any of the following:

a. Debates on the Address to the King/Queen in reply to the King/Queen's speech.

b. Government Motions (excluding Supply), including Motions on Reports (e.g. of Royal Commissions, Select Committees, White or Green Papers.)

c. Opposition Motions (excluding Supply.)

d. Adjournment Motions (excluding Supply) including debate on Ministerial Statements. (Whether immediately after the statement or in a debate arranged as a consequence of the Ministerial Statement.)

e. Supply Motions - Opposition Motions
                    - Adjournment Motions
                    - Government Motions
                    - Motions relating to Reports from Select Committees.

f. Private Members' Bills and Private Members Motions in Government time. (See Lidderdale, 1976.)

[2] It should be noted that this graph is based upon aggregation of points of detail, as opposed to components, and therefore does not employ the same units used in figures 1 to 3. This applies to all graphs illustrating aspect or focus.

4 P1: The Schuman Plan in British politics

It is intended in the following chapters to posit explanations for the particular features of the Parliamentary anatomies and statures which occured in P1, P2 and P4. In addition an account of the issue in P3, for which no Parliamentary content analysis was possible, will be provided in Chapter 6. Secondly assessment will be made of the extent to which the Parliamentary characterisation of the issue matched the debate on it which took place outside Parliament, and whether the nature of the Parliamentary debate was of any relevance in the resultant policies. To this end the periods will be considered individually, with a brief resume of the main features of the anatomy and salience of the issue noted in Parliamentary debate, followed by analysis of the significance and character accorded to the issue by the respective governments, their civil servants, the three major political parties, sectional groups, promotional groups and the press. In the chapter where a group or organisation is first encountered (most usually in this chapter), additional discussion is provided on its general role within the policy-making process.

It will be recalled that the stature of the European issue in P1 was described in the previous chapter as moderate, accounting for slightly under 1 per cent of all Parliamentary debate during the period concerned. Secondly, in comparison to the other periods, it was shown that a

singularly high degree of partisanship was displayed by
M.P.s regarding this question, with the party scoring
component accounting for over one third of all statements
made. Turning to policy preference, P1 was characterised by
the highest proportions of statements both for and against:
a combined total of 65 per cent with by far the lowest share
of neutral statements for any period. The level of
substantiation was moderate, standing mid-way between those
noted for P2 and P4.

Excluding the components of party scoring and state of the
negotiations, the Political aspect clearly dominated the
issue's anatomy, accounting for 70 per cent of all points of
detail (figure 6). The Economic aspect constituted a 24 per
cent share of the details: a significantly smaller
proportion than in either P2 or P4. As in the other two
periods the size of the Social aspect was relatively small,
amounting to 5 per cent of the points of detail. In this
period the Social aspect was also small in absolute terms,
with only ten details.

The distribution of points of detail among the three
focuses was somewhat more even than that among aspects, with
the British and Extra European focuses each receiving a 30
per cent share of the points of detail, and the European
focus accounting for the remaining 40 per cent.

Within the Political aspect, European points of detail
accounted for almost half of the total. These were
primarily devoted to the need for and the means of achieving
a strong and united Europe, and to questions of defence and
security. Secondly, emphasis was given to the methods of
government and administration of a community of the type
proposed. The Extra European focus occupied about one third
of the points within the Political aspect, and this sphere
was dominated by the subject of the Commonwealth. Such
questions as whether Commonwealth relations would be
adversely affected by British participation in the proposed
community, and the degree of loyalty owed by Britain to her
former colonies were regularly raised. International
security also figured prominently, although in this case,
the relevance of a British role in Europe was considered in
a world-wide context of defence against communism.
Discussion within the British Political sphere only
accounted for 18 per cent of the details, and hinged upon
the concept of sovereignty. Questions concerning the impact
of European participation upon British Parliamentary
sovereignty, and independent economic planning, were of most
importance.

FIGURE 6

SUMMARY OF ASPECT AND FOCUS P1

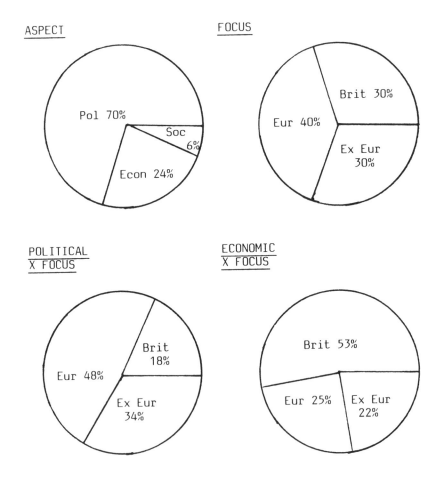

The Economic aspect when stratified by focus was dominated
by British concerns, which accounted for over half of the
total details. These were concentrated on the impact of
entry upon the British coal and iron and steel industries,
and secondly, on the prospects of economic isolation from
mainland Europe. The European and Extra European focuses
each accounted for over 20 per cent of the Economic aspect.
The European Economic sphere was almost exclusively taken up
with the varying perceptions both regarding free trade and
economic planning within the proposed community. The Extra
European matters were mainly related to Britain's trading
ties with the Commonwealth, and the economic future of the
latter should Britain participate in the Schuman Plan.
There were not sufficient details within the Social aspect
to enable further classification other than to note their
emphasis upon British factors.

The foregoing has provided a synopsis of the issue in P1,
in terms of its salience and its anatomy. The purpose of
this chapter is to provide some account for these features,
by ,exploring the context in which the issue was discussed
and the contributions of those groups and organisations with
an interest in the issue, and by assessing the extent to
which the Parliamentary anatomy was representative of wider
debate. More specifically, then, what explanations could be
levelled for such findings as the domination of the
Political aspect and the comparatively lowly position of the
Economic aspect? Secondly, within this overall pattern, it
was noted that whilst the Political aspect was predominantly
characterised by the European and Extra European focuses,
over half of the details within the Economic aspect were of
the British focus: can this feature be accounted for?
Thirdly, can the peculiarly high degree of partisanship
illustrated by the stature of the party scoring element, and
the high proportion of statements indicating a positive
policy preference (i.e. for or against, rather than neutral)
be ascribed to particular contemporary political forces? In
drawing these themes together the question of the relevance
of the salience ,and anatomy of the issue in P1 for the
decision not to participate in the Schuman Plan will be
considered. Discussion of the issue in P1 will also pay
some regard to the issue of European economic unification
prior to the announcement of the Schuman Plan as this
provides a setting for the study of British responses to
this French initiative.

This section will concentrate upon the aims of and the constraints upon the Labour Cabinet with respect to the European issue. It will examine the policies of the Government and its depiction of the stature and anatomy of the issue both in its rather nebulous pre-Schuman stages and, more importantly, during the period after the announcement of the Plan. Attention will be given to the standing of the issue within the Cabinet, and this will be compared with the success of the Cabinet in influencing the evaluations and depictions of the issue within the broader Labour Movement. Finally, the Parliamentary salience and anatomy of the issue will be compared to the findings for the issue within the Cabinet and other elements of the Party.

The Labour Party was heralded into office in 1945 with one of the biggest Parliamentary majorities in British history, and a mandate to carry out a programme of social and economic reconstruction. This included the nationalisation of key sectors of the economy, such as the coal, electricity, transport, gas, iron and steel industries, and a series of social reforms in the education, health and social service sectors.

Despite the continued war-time levels of taxation, the economic crisis in 1947, the persistence of rationing, and gloomy balance of payments figures, the Government believed that Britain would be able to solve her economic ills herself, provided that policies of economic intervention and public ownership were judiciously applied. It is thus not surprising that, whilst Britain engaged in international defence agreements, she was less interested in economic palliatives which required the merging of sectors of her economy with those of neighbouring competitors. Ernest Bevin, the Foreign Secretary, had played a key role in planning and administering Marshall Aid, and even though Britain had been in receipt of such financial assistance, the Government held that Britain was a world power, distinct from her defeated neighbours who also benefited from American finance. Not only was the proposed coal and steel community viewed as unnecessary for an economy of Britain's potential strength, but also it would necessitate compliance with supranationally made economic decisions, which might contradict a British Government's economic strategy: an obvious anathema to those believing that 'the nationalisation of the "commanding heights" of the British economy would enable a socialist government to pursue a policy of indicative planning within a mixed economy' (Sked and Cook, 1979, p.31).

In foreign affairs, Bevin followed a fairly traditional policy. The maintenance of the balance of power came to mean the containment of communism rather than the sustenance of Franco German equilibrium. However, Britain's reaction to the perceived communist threat was couched rather differently than that of mainland western Europe. The latter countries, especially France and Italy, feeling strategically vulnerable, and more open to internal instability, were eager to close ranks. British foreign policy, however, presented a picture of an impregnable island of great power status, by virtue of her support from the Commonwealth and her immutable ties with the USA. The preoccupation of the Labour administration with wider foreign questions (eg Palestine, India, NATO) diverted attention from questions of Britain's role within Europe, as opposed to her balancing role from outside Europe.

From early in 1947 the French Government had expressed interest in some form of economic association with Britain. The French Prime Minister, Leon Blum, sent a representative to Britain to discuss the question of economic coalition either in isolation, or within a broader European framework. The British response was not enthusiastic. In Cabinet, the President of the Board of Trade, Sir Stafford Cripps, 'hoped we might avoid early discussion of these general issues with members of the French Government'. He wanted Britain to make her own economic decisions first. The Cabinet only expressed a willingness to discuss France's economic problems with the French Government. (Cabinet Minutes, 2 (47), 6.1.47.)

Later that month the Cabinet discussed a memorandum from the Foreign Secretary; 'Proposal for a study of the possibilities of close Economic Cooperation with our Western European neighbours'. It discussed the idea of closer economic ties in western Europe sympathetically, but was more hesitant about a customs union:

'Such a step would need the most careful consideration. It raises great practical difficulties connected with the position of the Dominions, and the status of the respective colonial empires: moreover, for its successful working over any length of time, some measure of concerted industrial and commercial planning with other members of the union would be necessary.' (Cabinet Papers (47) 35, 18.1.47.)

69

The document offered two broad alternatives: a full customs union, and an economic regime falling short of this between the United Kingdom and (a) Metropolitan France, (b) the French Union or (c) western Europe as a whole. Bevin spoke of the obvious political advantage, of either model, but was less sure of the economic advantage to the UK. Both Cripps and the Chancellor of the Exchequer, Hugh Dalton, emphasised the priority of an international trade organisation, rather than one involving a few countries. (Cabinet Minutes, 13 (47), 28.1.47.)

In 1948 the question of a European economic organisation was over-shadowed by the more immediate concerns of defence: the Treaty of Dunkirk and the Western European Union both constituted diplomatic victories for Bevin. Nonetheless Britain was considering some form of economic union. A Cabinet memorandum presented by Bevin and Cripps outlined policy for the forthcoming Paris negotiations on European economic unity. Its overriding theme was that Britain should be closely linked with European economies, without weakening her connection with the Commonwealth. The paper gave the impression that a European economic union was both to be expected and welcomed. Whilst potential threats to Commonwealth trade were recognised, it was anticipated that Britain would be able to influence the proceedings so as to avoid these. It was agreed in discussion that there was

'no alternative to a policy of full support for closer economic cooperation in western Europe, and that this policy should be adopted on the assumption that it would be maintained even at the cost of considerable changes in the economic structure of the United Kingdom and some loss of the advantages which we now enjoyed over other European countries. (Cabinet Minutes, 20 (48), 8.3.48.)

However, in contrast, Bevin informed the Cabinet in the following year of

'excessive readiness to endorse superficially attractive proposals, paying too little heed to the practical implications ... we must be aware lest the Assembly (of the Council of Europe) should be used as a means of putting political pressure on us in such organisations as the OEEC.' (Cabinet Papers, 49 (200), 10.10.49.)

This provides a clear indication of the increasing difference of opinion between Britain and other west European countries as to how European integration should proceed. As discussed in Chapter 2, the 1948 Paris negotiations had been an important watershed, at which the incompatibility of the British and other European plans came to light. It also became clear that Britain would not be able to dictate the course of any west European economic settlement. Thereafter Bevin portrayed European economic integration as impractical: a tactic commonly used by opponents of full British participation in Europe.

Bevin and Cripps (now Chancellor of the Exchequer) presented a further paper to the Cabinet entitled 'Proposals for the Economic Unification of Europe', to encourage the Cabinet to settle its views on the question, as it had become known that France, Italy and Benelux were contemplating closer economic union. It recommended that Britain should not run risks which might imply

'i) Loss of Her Majesty's Government's responsibility for the budgetary and credit policy and for the management of reserves.

ii) Hindrance to our own efforts to reach and maintain equilibrium between the dollar area and the sterling area: we cannot sacrifice opportunities for dollar earning (or dollar saving) in order to make it easier for other European countries to earn or save dollars;

iii) Opening to European decision the size of strategic dollar earning and dollar saving of United Kingdom industries.

iv) Materially affecting the system of Imperial Preference.' (Cabinet Papers, (49) 203, 25.10.49.)

This paper, which effectively distanced the British Government from European aspirations of economic unification, was accepted by the Cabinet, and became its effective policy.

Having outlined the changing views of the Cabinet members towards European economic integration prior to the Schuman announcement, we should consider the extent of their success in advancing these within the broader Labour Party. Clearly, it would not have been to their advantage for radically different perceptions of the issue to predominate therein. Constitutionally the Party is not led by the leaders of the Parliamentary Labour Party, but by the National Executive Committee (NEC), elected by various sections of the Labour Movement. However Lewis Minkin noted that

> 'It is true that there has always been a tendency when the
> Party formed a Government for "the Platform" to take a
> firm grip on the proceedings; the status of the Party's
> leaders rose, trade union leaders shared the general
> feelings of loyalty to the Government, agenda management
> tightened. This had been true of the Party during both
> Labour minority Governments. The existence of a majority
> Labour Government brought out these features with added
> strength. Ministers personally dominated the NEC and the
> Government's claims and needs were always given first
> priority by a body which adopted the role of 'hand maid'
> that it had played for the MacDonald administrations.'
> (Minkin, 1980, p.24.)

During the late 1940s the Cabinet's perceptions of the
European issue did differ significantly from those of some
others within the Labour Movement. For example, George
Orwell stated that 'I cannot imagine it (socialism)
beginning except through the federation of the western
European States.' (Orwell, 1947.)

More specifically, R.W.G. Mackay, a backbench M.P.
criticised the British delegation at the Paris Conference
for saying that Britain could not cooperate in a customs
union. He advocated an economic union in which states were
no longer independent and argued that a west European
federal democracy was the best method of achieving peace and
freedom, and the best solution to the German problem. He
pointed out that Britain's world position had changed and
that Europe could become as powerful a force as the USA and
the USSR. (Mackay, 1948, pp 104-109.) On this basis, Mackay
and a small group of other Labour M.Ps and activists
followed Churchill's lead in trying to accelerate European
economic integration.

However, the Party leadership's response to the United
Europe Committee (UEC) set up by Churchill in 1947 proved to
be an important indicator of future Labour attitudes. At
the 1947 Party Conference it was asked why the NEC had made
no statement on the UEC's formation. Dalton replied that a
statement printed in the Daily Herald indicated that the
NEC'did not like this new organisation being supported by
any persons connected with the Labour Party.' He added
that a letter had been sent by the NEC to all those showing
'collaborationist tendencies'. The letter's principal
thrust was party political:

'The NEC came to the conclusion that while it is
desirable to encourage the maximum cooperation between
the nations of Europe it should be clear that an
organisation led by Mr. Churchill is not likely to
stimulate such cooperation at the present time.' (Labour
Party Conference, 1947, p.107.)

The letter argued that Europe's future was dependent on the
success of the United Nations, and on strengthening
collaboration between the USSR, the USA and Britain;
clearly assuming continued world power status for Britain.
It also symbolised the differences of opinion between the
Party hierarchy and the small group of forty-one individual
members who were prepared to follow Churchill's lead and
defy their Party leadership by attending the Congress.

The conflict within the Labour Party over European economic
integration was evident in two contradictory policy
statements on the subject in 1948. A memorandum submitted
by the British Labour Party to the European Socialist
Parties' Conference on the European Recovery Programme (in
March 1948), stated that

'The economic integration of Europe is a revolutionary
aim; it must be recognised and exploited as such. The
necessary redirection of national thinking cannot be
maintained unless European unity is presented as a
dynamic new ideal.' (Labour Party Conference, 1948,
p.222.)

In contrast, a Labour Party pamphlet on the Western Union,
argued specifically for a gradual movement towards political
and economic unification, and for a need to keep feet on the
ground and 'avoid tempting mirages.' (Labour Party 1948.)
This pamphlet, which was primarily for domestic consumption,
considered European unification to be something only
achievable in a piecemeal fashion.

Further contradictions on the question of Britain's role in
Europe were exposed at the 1948 Party Conference. Fenner
Brockway, a backbench M.P., proposed a resolution which

'urged the Labour Party to cooperate with the European
Socialist Parties in practical steps to achieve the
United States of Europe (including the establishment of
supranational agencies to take over from each nation
powers to allocate and distribute coal, steel, timber,
locomotives, rolling stock and imports from hard currency
countries) in complete military independence from the USA

and the USSR.' (Labour Party Conference, 1948, p.172.)

This motion was not actually opposed by the NEC and was accordingly accepted by Conference. However, in summing up for the NEC, Dalton made so many qualifications to the resolution that it became clear that Brockway's proposal would not be undertaken by the Government. Dalton emphasised the role of the OEEC in the Recovery Programme, and the successes of the representatives of the member countries (thus approving of the functional rather than federal approach.) He stated that

'You should begin, not with conclaves of chatter-boxes but with functional advances by Governments who have the power to make their decisions operative ... I am wholly for the practical British functional approach rather than for any theoretical federalism.' (Labour Party Conference, 1948, p.177.)

This was clearly in direct contradiction to the aims of the resolution, but this tactic of not expressly opposing the resolution avoided any risk of further serious Party division, yet it enabled the Government and NEC to put forward their views on the matter. When Dalton referred to European federalism or supranational authority, it was in such terms as 'lifting our eyes towards the high mountains', and he warned that collaboration would mean losing full employment, social provision and economic security in Britain. At the same conference a motion to refer back the NEC recommendation that Party members should not participate in the United Europe Committee, was easily defeated. Again Dalton summed up on behalf of the NEC, arguing not on the merits of the issue, but on the 'quasi-fascist' nature of the Committee (a reference to Conservative and Christian Democrat participants), thus ignoring the high level of European socialist participation (Labour Party Conference, 1948, p.119.)

The NEC did not initiate debate on the question of European economic integration in the late 1940s: when others drew attention to it, the NEC particularly through Dalton, was able effectively to defuse controversy within the Party. This was achieved principally in two ways, first by emphasising the political complexion of many who were prominent in the cause of European unification, and second by asserting that if integration were to take place it should be gradual.

The Schuman Plan itself was not discussed in Cabinet until about three weeks after it was delivered to the Government. Despite this delay, the issue was subsequently accorded greater attention. A Committee of senior ministers was set up to maintain contact with the European developments. Also the responsible ministers (Bevin, and during his illness, Kenneth Younger) made regular reports of diplomatic exchanges in the ensuing months.

Turning to the anatomy of the issue in Cabinet, we have seen how it was indicated that, as the Government became more suspicious of the European developments, prior to the Schuman Plan, and how the portrayal of European economic integration shifted, giving greater emphasis to problems of economic management inherent in the attendant loss of national sovereignty. Similarly, after the Schuman Plan was announced, the Cabinet became preoccupied with questions of a prior commitment to a supranational authority and the pooling of resources. The initial reaction of Herbert Morrison, who was acting Prime Minister during Attlee's illness, was somewhat dismissive. When given the news in a London restaurant, he is reported to have said 'It is no good, we cannot do it, the Durham miners won't wear it.' (Donoghue and Jones, 1973, p.481.)

After preliminary consultations with the French the British Government issued a memorandum indicating that the United Kingdom could not accept a commitment to pool resources or set up an authority with certain sovereign powers as a prior condition of joining further discussions. However, recording a meeting with the French Ambassador, the Minister of state for Foreign Affairs (Kennth Younger) reported that after he had clarified the British position, the Ambassador

'found my (Minister of State's) explanation reassuring since it seemed to him that our reservations would not in any way limit our effective participation in the discussions.' (Cmnd 7970, 1950.)

However, he also reported that due to a French desire for a 'prior commitment', agreement as to terms on which Britain could join the talks had not been possible. At a Cabinet meeting on the proposals the main points of discussion were:

(i)   the bulk of popular opinion as reflected in Parliament and the Press would support the Government

(ii)   the risk that America might construe rejection as opposition to European Union

(iii) that an attempt could be made by the Foreign Secretary to slow down the French plans

(iv) a suspicion of an underlying French motive being to cut their own defence costs

(v) whilst other countries had accepted the French proposals with reservations, the British were not in a position to do so, for fear of exacerbating relations further (the implication being that Britain had exhausted the French fund of goodwill)

(vi) Britain's Commonwealth commitment made the circumstances different for Britain: there would need to be prior consultation with the Commonwealth anyway.

The Cabinet agreed that

(i) the United Kingdom Government should not participate in the Plan

(ii) that the Minister of State should suggest to the French a ministerial meeting of the countries concerned to discuss the proposals

(iii) that an announcement should be made explaining Britain's attitude (Cabinet Minutes, 34 (50), 2.6.50.)

A memorandum was sent to the French, declining participation in the talks, with emphasis on the problems involved in the prior commitment to submit British resources to a high authority (Cmnd 7970, 1950.)

At a later Cabinet meeting it was agreed to reject the idea of supranationality, although some integration of west European coal and steel industries was not opposed in principle. It was however clear that the Cabinet were still taking the European developments seriously. Discussion included reference to the questions of administrative and political control of the community, and which financial arrangements would be most beneficial and a Committee of ministers was appointed to investigate further (Cabinet Minutes, 38 (50), 22.6.50.) Its report urged that Britain should press her own proposals, and reiterated the objection to supranationality and participation in a federal scheme. British membership of such a body as Schuman proposed would depend on its constitution; most particularly that there be a chain of responsibility to the respective ministers. The Committee also suggested that Britain should resist 'any proposals that Commonwealth preferences should be modified as a result of the United Kingdom joining the new body.' (Cabinet Papers, (50) 149, 4.7.50.)

A further report on the defence implications emphasised the importance of Britain's Commonwealth and Extra European allies. Again, implications of supranationality for domestic programmes were questioned, and the desirability of domestic military self sufficiency asserted. In contrast, it was also noted that should Britain participate in the scheme, she would be enabled to influence the operation of authority (Cabinet Papers, (50) 154, 1.7.50.) In addition a report on the Commonwealth implications of the integration of west European coal and steel industries had been requested from the Secretary of State for Commonwealth Relations. He reported that

'I think that the Commonwealth countries would look askance at any departure from our present policy of combining our responsibilities as a member of the Commonwealth with support for the development of European unity, and would probably react sharply to any "integration" of our economy into that of Europe in any manner which they regarded as prejudicing their vital interests.' (Cabinet Papers, (50) 153, 3.7.50.)

Nevertheless he did think that, given adequate safeguards, most Commonwealth countries would look favourably on the United Kingdom being associated with such a scheme. Two annexes were provided, the first giving details of the Commonwealth iron and steel industries, and the second outlining High Commissioners' reports on Commonwealth attitudes. It is interesting to note that only New Zealand supported Britain's refusal to participate in the scheme. The South African Government was critical of her refusal, and the Canadian Government though Britain over-cautious. There was no evidence that the Australian Government had given detailed consideration to the matter and the Governments of India, Pakistan and Ceylon expressed no opinion.

In summary, the depiction of the issue among Cabinet members concentrated primarily upon the political ramifications of the Plan, notably the prospect of having to make a prior commitment to a supranational authority and the pooling of economic resources. In addition, some attention was given to the Commonwealth and defence implications of the scheme (by way of reports to Cabinet), and passing references were made to the possible impact of the scheme upon British industry. There was no attempt in Cabinet to address questions of a European economic nature, nor were any of the political advantages for Britain of participation in the scheme elaborated upon.

How then did the Cabinet handle the issue within the broader Party forum? Given the Cabinet views on the Schuman Plan, and their opposition to British participation, it was clearly in their interests to discourage discussion of themes which might invite a more favourable response.

No attempt had been made by the Party leadership or Cabinet spokesmen to introduce the issue to the 1950 Party Conference, although the NEC did publish a document, European Unity on the subject in 1950. A motion was debated to reject European Unity, which was swiftly and easily defeated after a short speech by Dalton. Thus the pro-European activists failed to raise the salience of the issue within Conference: the only salient reference to the Plan was European Unity. What perspective on the issue did this document portray? It opened unequivocally:

'The Labour Party's attitude towards problems of European unity, as towards all other problems of domestic or foreign policy, is determined by the principles of democratic socialism and by the interests of the British people as members of the Commonwealth and of the world community.'

The pamphlet continued to outline the relevance to the European question of the principles of democratic socialism, of Britain's economic problems and of the Commonwealth and Sterling Area. It argued that a supranational authority was undesirable and that a community based on a free market economy would not be able to provide a better distribution of manpower and resources. The notion that a united Europe could become a third world force was also rejected. From the British point of view this was justified on the grounds that she had to work at least as closely with the Commonwealth and USA as with Western Europe. It was also argued that western Europe would have to work closely with the USA on economic and strategic matters. Turning to a different tack, it was asserted that the constitutional changes proposed should require the approval of each country's electorate. It argued that it is the responsibility of sovereign governments to control the basic industries of coal and steel, as these were the key to full employment in each country. The fear was expressed that private industrialists would exploit the community for their own financial interests. In conclusion, the document opposed the creation of a European parliament with legislative powers, preferring the maintenance of the Consultative Assembly of the Council of Europe. By the end of the document the emphasis had shifted from the question of British participation in the Schuman Plan to the general threat to European democracy of unemployment and the lack of social justice, and the commitment of the Labour Party to fight against these.

In the short debate which took place on the motion to support European Unity as well as the brief proposing and seconding speeches by representatives of constituency parties, contributions were made by William Blyton M.P. (a member of the delegation to the Council of Europe) and Hugh Dalton. The themes of Blyton's speech were the good record of Britain on European unification, the threat of federalism, and the desire for international agreement without a supranational authority. He concluded by attacking the Tories and pointing to the strength of Communists and Christian Democrats within the French trade union movement. Dalton's speech echoed these themes at greater length, with particular emphasis on the need for full employment in Europe above anything else.

European Unity certainly constituted the most detailed consideration given by the Party leadership to the question of European integration. The most substantial objection to British participation was that of her wider international role. Secondly, political and economic perceptions as to what the Schuman Plan entailed, were of importance. The former included concerns as to the nature of the decision-making process within the proposed community (British democratic socialism was contrasted with supranational authority), and fears about being dominated by anti-socialist groups. The latter were based upon concern as to the consequences for economic stability. Thus the themes assigned in Cabinet to the issue prevailed within the Party forum. How then did the Parliamentary salience and anatomy of the issue compare with the evaluations of the Cabinet and others in the Labour Movement. The Government succeeded in defeating the Opposition motion of 26th of June 1950 and in carrying almost all of their own Party. (Hansard, Vol. 476, col. 1909, 26.6.50.) From the number of Labour M.P.s known to favour European unification, only Mackay publicly criticised the Government, arguing that economic integration of Europe provided the best means of increasing standards of living and of increasing exports. He asserted that there was no thought among the Europeans of excluding the

Commonwealth from the Plan, and he concluded by contrasting the economic weakness of individual states with the possibilities for strength in unity.

Several Labour M.P.s who had previously shown European sympathies (e.g. M. Edelman, H. Hynd) pointed to the threats of supranationality and of cartels, which, they asserted, distinguished the Plan from the United Europe which they had hoped for. Others (e.g. G. Lang and L .Hale) said nothing. Unless they wanted to speak but were not called, presumably they either found the Government line convincing or thought the matter not of such importance as to warrant disregarding the whip.

The Government's response to the Opposition attack was led by Sir Stafford Cripps. Having asserted the need to protect the iron and steel industries for the sake of the British and Commonwealth economies, he explained that there was no realistic possibility of British participation in the Plan. He argued that were the Conservatives in office, they would not commit the country to such a course, as the French were not willing to reconcile points of difference, and that participation in the talks would constitute acquiescence to the federalist principles of Schuman. In response to a question on the negotiability of the points of difference, he put it that supranationality was not up for discussion, and he rejected the notion of a west European political federation. The Labour Government, he argued, saw Britain's Commonwealth role, Atlantic ties and world power status as precluding such a departure.

Attlee, closing the debate, declared that the British Government had a good record on European unity, but the Schuman Plan introduced new considerations; it was not international but supranational, and national safeguards were incompatible with supranationality. Whilst Cripps had introduced economic considerations, the overall impact of the two front bench speeches was indomitably political. The Government drew most attention to the requirement to make a prior commitment to supranationality and the possibility of losing control of key sectors of the economy; an emphasis hardly designed to stir up great enthusiasm for the Plan.

The contributions made by Government spokesmen to the Parliamentary debate which was subjected to content analysis, have been isolated and examined in order to contrast the anatomy of the issue ascribed by this group with that overall. As Government front bench spokesmen only accounted for 15 per cent of all points of detail made in

Pl, there is no serious problem of duplication of data here.

The distribution of points among the policy aspects in the speeches of Government spokesmen was broadly similar to that overall. As might be expected, substantial differences were detected in the case of policy preferences, with Government speeches all against, or neutral, in contrast to the 37 per cent proportion of those for in the overall findings. The Government spokesmen, in common with the aggregate for all other contributors to the debate, devoted about half of their total points of detail to party scoring.

In summary, the leadership of the Labour Government had tried to avoid conflict within the Labour Party over the European question. Party unity had been more or less preserved by use of party scoring and an emphasis on gradualism. A measure of the success of this approach can be gauged by examining the extent to which the arguments of those who favoured a full British role in European economic integration achieved prominence. After the announcement of the Schuman Plan, as there was virtually no formal debate on it within the Labour Pary, only the views inherent in European Unity achieved any prominence. Further, the views of the issue expressed by Orwell (the coupling of socialism and European integration), Mackay (the contribution of integration to peace, and the third force notion) and Brockway (the opportunity to act immediately to unite Europe and gain independence from the USA and USSR), achieved no prominence at all within the anatomy of the issue derived from the Parliamentary debate. In contrast, themes emphasised by the leadership enjoyed prominence. The depiction of the issue within Cabinet work and discussion gave emphasis to worries over prior commitment to pooling and any loss of sovereignty, to the Commonwealth (despite the lack of express views by the Commonwealth countries) and to defence (particularly the American partnership). These themes were prominent in the House of Commons' anatomy of the issue. The main emphases in Labour Party circles prior to the Schuman Plan were of party scoring, Britain's wider role and cooperation as preferable to federalism and supranationalism. They were all prominent in the Parliamentary anatomy of the issue, as were themes evident in European Unity, such as supranationalism, Britain's broad economic and employment needs, the needs of the Commonwealth and wider foreign policy considerations. Finally, the themes promoted by Government spokesmen in the House of Commons, in contrast to those mentioned by Mackay, were broadly coincident with those which prevailed overall.

In so far as access allows, this chapter and those devoted to P2, P3 and P4 will assess the salience and anatomy of the issue within Whitehall circles. This, however, is not to equate Whitehall with promotional groups or political parties, as its work reflects something of the views and preferences of ministers as well as of civil servants, prominent sectional groups as well as, in the case of the present study, foreign governments. Finally, Whitehall is not a unitary organisation. The individual departments develop attitudes reflecting their own traditions, the preferences of their senior civil servants and ministers, and the prevailing priorities of the respective issue communities. The role of Whitehall departments in policy formation is usually highly significant, being relied upon for experience and expertise in their respective areas of specialisation. Not all students of British Government would characterise the power of Whitehall over ministers as that depicted in the BBC series Yes Minister, but there is general agreement that Whitehall enjoys a unique position in defining policy alternatives. The analysis of the issue within Whitehall is included in the present study to enable comparison of the salience and anatomy derived from Parliamentary debate with the actual work of and attitudes within the governmental bureaucracy.

Prior to the announcement of the Schuman Plan, most relevant Whitehall representatives had become disenchanted with the prospect of economic union on the lines proposed by the more federally inclined continentals. The London Committee, (the team of civil servants working at the Paris Conference, 1947), concluded that, given British economic interests, the political difficulties of adjustment and the strategic implications (all implying loss of British sovereignty),

'it is not in our interests to encourage the idea of a European customs union of which the United Kingdom would be a member and that in any case a general Western European customs union is out of the question as a matter of practical politics.' (European Economic Cooperation Committee of Ministers, 31.7.47.)

One of the few senior British civil servants sympathetic to integration, Sir Edmund Hall-Patch (Deputy Under Secretary Foreign Office 1946-48) wrote a minute in August 1947 stating that 'there is a well-established prejudice in Whitehall against a European customs union, it goes back a long way and is rooted in the old days of free trade ... The Board of Trade is overstating the case against it. One of the most potent arguments is that we have to choose between a European customs union and the Commonwealth. However, that may be, the Board of Trade have successfully blocked for two years our efforts to look at these proposals objectively.' (Charlton, 1981.)

When Jean Monnet visited London in 1949 to discuss economic unification with the British Government, Edwin Plowden (Chief Planning Officer, The Treasury, and Chairman of the Economic Planning Board 1947-53), who attended these meetings, wrote to the Foreign Office officials for policy guidance. Their reply stated that pre-eminently Britain's relations with the USA were most important. (Charlton, 1981).

Roger Makins (Assistant Under Secretary 1947-48, Under Secretary 1948-52, Foreign Office), who was singled out by his colleagues as one who 'pooh poohed' European aspirations, stated that there was a fear of America becoming isolationist if Britain got over-involved in Europe. Simultaneously Britain felt under some pressure from America to throw her lot in with Europe: this was a source of considerable resentment in the Foreign Office, and probably cemented its allegiance to the Commonwealth. In addition, Saville Garner (Assistant Under Secretary 1948-51, Commonwealth Relations Office), spoke of the Foreign Office viewing the Europeans as unreliable and liable to communist subversion, but the Commonwealth in contrast, was seen as loyal. (Charlton, 1981.)

Not only did British officials appear to oppose any European economic integration, but such an alternative was not posed as a major one: the issue did not enjoy high salience among them. Oliver Franks (British Ambassador in New York, 1948-52) said that integrationist views simply did not carry much weight in Whitehall (Charlton, 1981). The main emphases attributed to the issue were the Commonwealth, the American partnership, British autonomy in economic and defence matters, and less federal alternatives to a customs union.

The announcement of the Schuman Plan did not appear to precipitate a shift in Whitehall opinion. Con O'Neill (of the Foreign Office) stated quite simply that the Foreign Office did not think the ECSC a 'very significant development at that time'. (Charlton, 1981). However, a committee of British officials was appointed by the Prime Minister to report on the proposals.

It was chaired by the Permanent Secretary to the Treasury, and included a wide range of senior officials: the Chief Planning Officer to the Treasury, (Plowden) and senior officials from the Foreign Office, the Board of Trade, the Ministry of Fuel and Power, the Ministry of Defence and the Ministry of Supply. Only three weeks elapsed betweeen the appointment of the committee and its report. It is thus likely that their consideration of the question remained within the prevailing economic and political assumptions. Indeed, the committee was instructed to report on the effects of a purely European scheme (i.e. excluding Britain) and one which included Britain, assuming present policies of a planned economy, full employment etc., on the general economy of the Commonwealth and Sterling Area, and on defence. The report asserted that the economic arguments for staying out or going in were 'inconclusive either way', but that the main issue was really 'political - was this a step towards the federation of Europe?' It concluded that Britain could not commit herself irrevocably to Europe either in political or economic terms, unless the extent of the commitment could be measured. Thus, whilst describing the issue as essentially a political one, the committee felt unable to advise British participation due to their inability to assess the full implications. The committee added, somewhat ironically, that by declining membership Britain should not be prevented from participation at a later stage. This rather implied that the officials assumed that Britain would be likely to have her own way in European matters (Cabinet Papers (50) 120, 2.6.50.)

A further report dealt with the impact of a hypothetical coal and steel community upon Europe. There was little on its implications for the British economy, but great detail on the economic situation of the time, including figures of British and European coal and steel production, and their respective dependence on imported iron ore. An attempt was made to estimate the impact of tariffs, quantitative restrictions, preferential tariffs and the elimination of government subsidies. The report cited the National Coal Board's fear that British inclusion in the Plan would mean a loss of flexibility and a decline in the UK's bargaining strength vis-a-vis non-members. It was thought that membership would threaten the steel industry, due to the availability of cheaper European imports. In contrast the point was made that non-participation denied Britain easy access to the European markets, though no estimate of the loss of potential exports was made, nor was the point elaborated upon.

The Treasury Economic Planning Board also contributed to the report, concluding that there were economic and political advantages of international regulation of iron and steel. However, it recommended that the United Kingdom should prefer a governing body with advisory as opposed to mandatory powers. This report was particularly against a governing authority with control of wage and labour conditions.

Despite the appointment of the Whitehall committee by the Cabinet, the Schuman proposals do not appear to have been considered as significant by most senior members of the bureaucracy. The approach to the Plan was on its relationship to existing British practice, rather than how British policies might be adjusted to accommodate the Schuman proposals. The depiction of the issue within Whitehall appears to have been largely similar to its Parliamentary anatomy, with emphasis on the virtues of a functional rather than a federal approach, the Commonwealth, and Britain's world role. Whilst acknowledgement was made of the advantage of access to European markets should Britain participate, this possibility was not further explored.

Although, as demonstrated, Cabinet ministers laid stress on the European Political sphere in Parliament (which was reflected in the overall anatomy), the Whitehall committee did investigate specific implications for the British coal and steel industries. Little attention was given to the wider economic consequences of the scheme; and the subsequent formation of the ECSC does not appear to have been envisaged.

Thus it could not be claimed that in Pl the Parliamentary anatomy of the issue differed significantly from that in Whitehall: even the somewhat disparaging attitudes towards the Europeans occurred in both places. The salience of the issue within Whitehall was divorced from the requirements of party politics, and was more a function of a moderate level of Cabinet concern for information on the scheme. It does not appear that any great impetus existed among civil servants to promote the issue, as proved to be the case ten years later.

THE CONSERVATIVE PARTY

The fact that the Conservative Party was in opposition during this period had a clear bearing on its pronouncements and policy on the European issue. Having less formal responsibility than the Government, it was able to give the appearance of being all things to all men, and thus adopt several incompatible policies. Secondly, being in opposition encourages that party to oppose Government policy often regardless of its content. Thus, despite the primacy normally given to the Commonwealth and Britain's world role by Conservatives in this period, in the Parliamentary divisions in Pl, they opposed the Government's refusal to take part in the Schuman Plan discussions.

During this period it seemed that the motive force of Conservative opinion towards Europe was less a function either of historic Conservative principles, or of a conscious Party re-appraisal, and more the product of the views of one man, Churchill. He set the pace in thinking and action for integration in Europe by virtue of his elevated position among world statesmen, and despite losing the 1945 Election, he was still a popular Party leader, and was thus largely responsible for the Europeanisation of post war Conservative thinking.

In his celebrated speech at the University of Zurich in 1946, he spoke of the tragedy that Europe, with its great civilisation, should have been dogged by 'that series of frightful nationalistic quarrels', and urged a 'United States of Europe', to prevent the repetition of disaster and destruction (Kitzinger, 1967, pp.29-33.) Churchill intimated that Britain, due to her greater status, would not be involved directly, but when he subsequently formed the United Europe Committee, he seemed to intend that Britain should be a major protagonist. Despite the obvious lack of political and economic specifications in his scheme, 'details were neither asked for nor provided.' (Hene, 1970, p.47.) Those were still optimistic days and so perhaps for Churchill particularly, a detailed plan was inappropriate.

In his address to the 1947 Conservative Party Conference, Churchill linked the British Commonwealth, the fraternal association with the USA, and European Union, as all being vital connections for Britain. In this precursor to the three interlocking circles theory, he put European union on a par with the two factors which, paradoxically, came to be of such importance in the preference of both major parties to remain outside European economic collaboration, which 'sincerely hopes that the Governments of the U.K. and other Empire countries taking part in the International Conference on Trade and Employment, will not enter into tariff agreements with any foreign country, which will hamper their freedom of action, or weaken the existing system of Imperial Preference.' (Conservative Party Conference, 1947, p.67.)

This clearly was much more in the mainstream of Conservative thinking at this time. Thus, the Conservative Party appeared to be in the vanguard of the movement towards European unity, without modifying its historic commitment to the Empire and Commonwealth. Resolutions passed at Party Conferences in the ensuing years indicate that Conservatives thought Britain was able to maintain three sets of ideals and commitments simultaneously: to the USA, the Commonwealth and Europe. One delegate pointed out that the situation was analogous to promising to meet the demands of both the Jews and the Arabs in Palestine – this comment went unheeded however. For example, in one speech Harold Macmillan M.P. placed emphasis on European and Commonwealth relations. In the case of the former he asserted that 'politically, the abandonment of Europe brings World War Three closer.' He proceeded to combine both groupings, arguing that 'Commercially, we need large markets to be rich, which both the Commonwealth and Europe provide. (Conservative Party Conference, 1949, p.63.)

Thus, prior to the announcement of the Schuman Plan, the issue of European integration remained in the forefront at Conservative Conferences, largely due to the role of Churchill and other prominent Conservatives within the European Movement. However, the depiction of the issue as one which complemented Britain's relations with the Commonwealth and the USA betrayed certain ambivalence. There was virtually no consideration of the economic implications, and the issue appeared to have little relation to Conservative thinking on industrial matters. The 1947 Party statement on industrial policy made no mention whatsoever of Europe, rather it stated that

'The principle of granting Preferences, which has been the lifeline of our Commonwealth and in particular, of our Colonies, must be preserved. (Conservative Party, 1947, p.21.)

In many policy statements, the interpretation of European unity clearly pertained specifically to defence matters:

economic collaboration was not considered, indicative of tacit approval of the Government's attempts to stimulate inter-governmental cooperation as opposed to integration.

It is instructive to contrast the somewhat ambivalent nature of the issue (in terms of salience and anatomy) in Conservative policies for British consumption, with a speech made by Robert Boothby, M.P., a representative of the Conservative Party at the Consultative Assembly of the Council of Europe in 1949:

'I said that absolute State sovereignty was one of the principal causes of evil in the modern world, and that the only solution to this problem lay in some merging or pooling of national sovereignty. We must coordinate our monetary and fiscal policies. We must plan investment in our basic industries on a European scale, and encourage specialisation. We must also negotiate reciprocal trade and payment agreements on a preferential basis. This would require the establishment of a number of permanent functional European authorities. But it would also require frequent and major decisions of policy, and therefore, unless we established at the same time an executive international political authority, the functional authorities would be powerless, because they themselves could not decide policy, or give the necessary orders.' (Boothby, 1978, p.218.)

Whilst it should be added that Boothby was a greater advocate of wholesale European integration than Churchill and Macmillan for instance, this does illustrate that in Europe, the British Conservatives continued to make rhetorical commitment to European integration, causing Europeans to expect a Conservative Government to show greater commitment than it actually did after 1951.

The Schuman Plan and the subsequent Government reaction provoked considerable activity on the part of the Conservative Party leadership, who initiated two debates and a number of Parliamentary questions on the matter. However, at the 1950 Conservative Party Conference there was hardly any mention of Europe at all. The main foreign policy motion passed at the 1950 Conference included the statement that 'Conference ... re-affirms the need for an unfettered policy of mutual cooperation for the whole Commonwealth and Empire.' (Conservative Party Conference, 1950, p.32.) Such a sentiment hardly augured well for European economic collaboration. Thus, for the Conservative leadership, the issue was essentially a Parliamentary one. It is likely that difficulties would have arisen if membership of the Schuman Plan was advocated at Conference where Commonwealth loyalty ran so high. In keeping with the low salience of the Schuman Plan at the 1950 Party Conference, it received no mention whatsoever in the 1951 General Election Manifesto.

As suggested above, the issue was of importance in Parliament. The Conservatives combined with the Liberals to argue that the Government take part in the talks. Anthony Eden, proposing a motion, argued that the Schuman Plan was a movement for peace and could not, for that reason, be allowed to fail. He suggested that the supranational element was not central to the Plan, and that involvement with it need not be at the expense of Commonwealth relations, adding that Britain should be leading such developments, not divorcing herself from them. (Hansard, Vol. 476, col. 1153, 26.6.50.)

Edward Heath, making his maiden speech, pointed out that British interests would be represented in the deliberations of a high authority, and also suggested that there was risk to Britain's long-term economic interest should she stand outside the scheme. Both Heath and Eden said that the Commonwealth were not opposed to the scheme. Only one Conservative M.P., E.A.H. Legge-Bourke, expressly disassociated himself from the Party line. He sarcastically confessed to not being a federalist and that he did not endorse the Schuman Plan. Whilst he thought that Britain should play a lead in Europe, he saw her first loyalty as to Crown and Commonwealth. It is possible that these views were not propounded by other Conservatives because the motion was likely to fail and thus it could have been assumed that the subject would "go away". Alternatively they were unaware of, or preferred to ignore, the implications for Commonwealth policy should Britain join, and choose to remain loyal to the Party leadership.

Churchill, closing for the Opposition, was sharply critical of the Government, denouncing their 'one party' attitude to Europe, their inability to get on with the French, and their decision to reject a proposal, the mechanics of which they did not know. He asserted that Britain could influence events, if she attended the talks: a course which he said the USA and the Commonwealth were encouraging. Sounding almost like a federalist he claimed that 'For the sake of World organisation we would even run risks and make sacrifices.' (Hansard, Vol. 476, Col. 2160, 26.6.50.)

In conclusion, it seems certain that, were it not for the preferences of the Conservative Party leadership, the issue would not have achieved such salience within the House of Commons. There is no evidence that there was great pressure from the Conservative backbenchers or indeed from the Party outside Parliament to advocate British participation in the Schuman scheme. The handling of the issue by the Conservative leadership was very much in keeping with the political climate of the months between the 1950 and 1951 General Elections: the issue was used as a stick with which to beat the Government. The second debate initiated by the Opposition was specifically critical of the remarks by John Strachey, (Minister at the War Office) about the Schuman Plan. This further contributed to the high profile of the party scoring component. (Hansard, Vol. 477, Col. 1153, 11.7.50.)

The effect of the Conservatives upon the anatomy of the issue was less clear cut, mainly because their very policies towards Europe were unclear. Conservative preoccupations with Britain's wider role - the three circles - were evident in the issue's anatomy, yet this theme was also advocated by Labour. Certainly the themes developed in Boothby's 1949 speech did not loom large in the overall anatomy: where they did occur it was with the opposite policy preference. Elsewhere, there was little formulation of a coherent Conservative policy towards European economic integration. In Parliament it was generally considered by Conservatives that a British presence was a good idea and in the interests of her world role. This was normally expressed within the Political aspect. The theme that it would not be in Britain's economic interests to be outside the European developments (as suggested by Edward Heath) did not figure largely in either Conservative thinking or in the overall anatomy of the issue. It could well have proved difficult to advocate expressly the placing of the British coal, iron and steel industries under the aegis of a supranational authority, when the Party was engaged in criticism of the Government's nationalisation of them. Thus, the control of these industries by European bureaucrats may have been considered by many to be incompatible with the Tory theme of 'setting the people free'.

THE LIBERAL PARTY

During the War the Liberal Party had enjoyed the prestige of being represented in the Coalition Government, however, in the 1945 General Election it suffered heavy losses and only twelve M.P.s were returned. This precipitated a period of considerable disarray, with members and supporters being pulled in two opposite directions: towards the Labour and Conservative Parties. In the 1950 Election only nine Liberal M.P.s were returned, and 319 out of 475 candidates lost their deposits. Thus in the eyes of the electorate and by virtue of the British electoral system, it appeared that the Party of Gladstone, Asquith and Lloyd George was of little relevance to the post war issues and problems.

The Liberal Party had consistently claimed throughout the period immediately after the War, to be the only British party committed to European unification. In 1947, at the Liberal Party Conference, a motion was passed on European unity:

'The Liberal Party considers that steps can and should be taken towards the unity of Europe by the method of functional approach. International organs for European transport and other economic purposes should be constituted at the earliest possible moment embracing such European countries as are willing and ready to participate.

It trusts that such agreements may ultimately lead to a confederation of all European states within the framework of the United Nations.' (Liberal Party, p.1.)

The method of unification – functional – was in line with that advocated by the other main political parties, but the aim of such measures – a confederation of European states – did appear to be more unequivocal than those of the Labour or Conservative Parties. At their Conference in the following year, the Liberals again discussed the matter, although on this occasion it was in the context of world affairs and urged

'That there should be an emergency policy designed to secure immediate and effective cooperation between the countries of Western Europe, and a long term policy designed to bring into being a federation of Europe; that the emergency policy should establish forthwith a council of Western Europe ... to lay down the broad lines of common action; that the Council should have power to set up permanent international staffs to coordinate the social, economic, and defence policies ... that the necessary staffs should act under the direction of the council of Western Europe, and should be in continuous session; that the long-term policy should be to create a

91

democratic federation of Europe, with a constitution based on the principles of common citizenship, political freedom, and representative Government, including a charter of Human Rights;

That such a federation should have defined powers with respect to external affairs, defence, currency, customs, and the planning of production, trade, power and transport; and that to achieve this objective, the governments of the states of Western Europe should take steps to convene, as soon as practicable, a constituent assembly composed of representatives chosen by the Parliaments of the participating states, to frame a constitution for such a federation.' (Liberal Party, pp 1-2.)

Certainly the overriding aim was political 'to save European Democracy' and create 'a democratic federation of Europe'. That the economies and social provisions of the participating countries should be merged was also explicit. There was also a clear pointer to a supranational authority of sorts, with its own independent staff, under the direction of a European legislative body. This was clearly a radically different policy from those advocated by the two major parties. This was not an isolated sentiment throughout the period , prior to the announcement of the Schuman Plan, the issue of European economic integration was distinct within the Liberal Party both in terms of salience and anatomy. The issue was considered sufficiently important as to occupy regularly its Assembly and the Council. Whilst within the Labour and Conservative Parties the issue and especially the political ramifications were to some extent fudged, the Liberal Party laid stress on the federal theme, explicitly advocating supranational agencies. Whereas the Commonwealth and Colonies were seen by the Liberals as reasons for caution in Britain's commitment to Europe, they asserted that no incompatibility need exist.

After the announcement of the Schuman Plan, the stature of the issue continued to be high within the Liberal Party. The Council of the Liberal Party was quick to respond to the Schuman initiative, claiming that the proposals

'are to be welcomed on political, economic and strategic grounds, and should be examined by His Majesty's Government in a sincere effort to find means by which this country can participate in the operation of the scheme.'

The rider was added that Britain should

> 'ensure that it will not be a restrictive cartel but a stimulus to European efficiency and the well-being of the workers and consumers.' (Liberal Party, p.3.)

Nevertheless, it was thought that the presence of Britain at the talks was a necessary prerequisite to finding a way in which Britain could play a part in the Plan. At the Assembly of the same year, the belief was reiterated that there was no clash of interests between the participation of Britain in Europe, and her Commonwealth obligations. Indeed the Assembly declared that it

> 'welcomes the Schuman Plan and deplores the refusal of the British Government to join in the discussions in which this country might have played a constructive part.' (Liberal Party, p.4.)

The 'semi-isolationist' attitude of the Labour Government also came in for criticism. The urgency with which the Liberal Party treated the issue contrasts markedly with the Government's handling of the matter. The former considered it a major issue, whereas the latter saw it as having little relevance for this country.

Liberal M.P.s, most notably the Leader Clement Davies, made some effort to press their views within Parliament. The themes which they presented to the debate were of European unity as a means towards world peace without threatening the Commonwealth. It was asserted that economic integration would provide favourable economies of scale and encourage modernisation of industry. The Liberals also argued both that the living conditions of the workers and the prospects for the maintenance of full employment would be enhanced by economic unity. Obviously wary of the adverse associations of the term 'federalism', they argued that there was no imminent danger of this, and equally, that such difficulties could be overcome by negotiation.

In the debate specifically on the Schuman Plan, Davies seconded Eden's motion. He gave emphasis to the above themes, and in addition, castigated the Government for not taking part in the Schuman discussions, stating that the talks were in accordance with the implications of the Marshall Plan, agreed by Britain, America and the Continental countries. Thirdly, he accused the British Government of wielding the Commonwealth as an objection at home, without actually presenting it to the six participating countries as an item for negotiation.

It was clearly the case that the Liberal Party attached a
great deal more importance to the questions raised by the
Schuman Plan than either the Labour or Conservative Parties,
and than indicated in the analysis of debate in the House of
Commons. The cynic might suggest that this was pure
opportunism by a declining Party desperate for distinctive
policies, and it is indeed true that the incompatibility of
a customs union with the Liberal tenet of free trade, and
the problems of simultaneously meeting the needs of
Commonwealth and continental economies, were not fully
explored. However, the commitment of the Liberal Party to
European integration both prior to and after the Schuman
Plan suggests that the issue's salience within the Party
during Pl was not a flash in the pan. Despite this
attachment to the issue, the fact that in Pl this issue was
shortlived, even within Parliament (and as already suggested
it was primarily a Parliamentary issue) is indicative of the
Liberals' comparative inability to push the issue to the
fore. Equally the Liberals' depiction of the most
noteworthy features and characteristics of the question was
also out of step with that found in the overall anatomy of
the issues. Such themes as the contribution that
participation in the Schuman Plan would make to British
industrial modernisation and efficiency and the benefits to
workers and consumers did not achieve any status outside the
ranks of the Liberal Party. Indeed that Liberals had to
dwell on denying the clash of European and Commonwealth
interests is indicative of a failure on their part to
communicate what it was that they thought the issue was
really all about. Their influence in this matter was
minimal.

TRADE UNIONS

The experience of the War, its aftermath and the return of a
Labour Government in 1945 were together instrumental in
producing a period of trade union support for Government
economic policies. This even extended to the acceptance of
a Government wage restraint policy until 1950. The shift in
the role of trade unions from that of the 1930s was perhaps
best summarised by Walter Citrine (General Secretary of the
TUC 1926-46) at the 1946 Trades Union Congress, where he
asserted that the trade unions had 'passed from the era of
propaganda to one of responsibility.'

At the same time, the trade unions were either involved in decision-making on major economic issues, or were content to tolerate the policy of the Government. The trade union movement at this time was preoccupied with certain internal questions, such as the role of Communists within unions and the problems posed by the new emerging service sector and white collar unions for the balance of power within the TUC. The only TUC concerns for Europe were with regard to the practicalities of economic recovery. In the TUC declaration on the European Recovery Programme and Trade Unions, emphasis was on the relief afforded by the Marshall Plan rather than European unity per se. To this end, an OEEC liaison office was established in Paris to facilitate close relations on recovery matters, and to stimulate specific action where necessary. There is little evidence of trade union interest in European integration prior to the Schuman Plan. However, at the 1950 Trade Union Congress, a resolution was moved by R. Edwards (President of the Chemical Workers Union) seconded by R.H. Edwards (National Union of Vehicle Builders):

> 'Congress welcomes the initiative embodied in the Schuman Plan for the coordination of European Coal, Iron and Steel, and urges the British Government to participate in the discussions on the clear understanding that a) The Schuman Plan must not be a restrictive cartel b) There will be a progressive improvement in the Trade Union consultation which will be guaranteed on a national and international level and c) Existing machinery for collective bargaining will not be interfered with. Congress is of the opinion that further European cooperation is desirable for the Chemical and other basic industries.' (TUC Report, 1950, p.397.)

In his opening remarks, Edwards said that the policy of uniting Europe and her basic industries had long been the traditional policy of the British Labour Movement. He saw it as a contribution to world peace, with Europe acting as a third force. He also argued that the end of trading restrictions would be in the interests of world trade. Summing up, he claimed that the European economy was going bankrupt, and that Britain should share what she had with her neighbours: the alternative was an American-dominated Atlantic community, and the Schuman Plan presented the best means of ending the Franco-German conflict.

Speaking on behalf of the General Council Arthur Deakin (Secretary of the TGWU) criticised the motion, first because the conditions of membership were unknown, and second because of the threat of economic control being ceded to a supranational authority. The motion was easily lost at the vote.

The urgency attached to the issue by the Chemical Workers was not reflected in the general work of the TUC or its leadership. The themes raised in the former's motion, notably of representation of labour in a European plan, the benefits of participation for British industries, and the need for Britain to share its economic benefits with her neighbours, were not representative of broader TUC opinion. At home and abroad the TUC leadership adopted the Government's view of the Schuman Plan, emphasising the prospect of a supranational authority. It is likely that without the Chemical Workers' Union motion, the matter would not have been discussed at Congress.

Two individual unions with an obvious potential interest in British membership of the ECSC were the National Union of Mineworkers (NUM) and the Iron and Steel Trades Confederation (ISTC). Neither appeared to devote great attention either to the notion of a customs union, as discussed in the late 1940s or, more specifically, to the Schuman Plan.

The Schuman Plan did not formally occupy the NUM'S time or resources at all. One reference which did occur at the 1950 Congress was made by a J. Hammond (Lancs.), who congratulated the Union's President for not doing as French, Belgian and German trade unionists had done in rushing in and giving sanction to the Plan which would lower wages and conditions of British miners. The Chairman added that the NUM had made no verbal contribution to the broader debate because nobody knew exactly what the Plan was. The only evidence of the General Secretary's (William Lawther) views on the matter was when he was quoted as asking the somewhat rhetorical question of would the high authority be in a position to reduce the British miners' living conditions? (Daily Herald, 16.6.50.)

The quarterly reports of the ISTC indicate that there was no consideration whatsoever of European economic integration in general or the Schuman Plan in particular. However, the union journal, Man and Metal did give some attention to the Schuman proposals. In a leading article on the matter in June 1950, it was argued that the proposals had 'an air of unreality, particularly in relation to our own position.' (Man and Metal, Vol. XXVII, no.6, 6.6.50), and continued by questioning whether the equalisation of living standards of

European workers in the coal and steel trades was possible. It also questioned the impact of membership of such a community upon the balance of payments, and concluded that the Government could make no advance commitment. Although the harmonisation of industrial and social policies was seen as a valid aim, the Schuman Plan was not seen as an inappropriate vehicle to achieve it.

The Schuman Plan was discussed in the column of D. Llewellyn Mort (an ISTC sponsored M.P.) The issues of equalisation and supranationality were his main themes:

'As the strength of the unions and pressure groups vary, equalisation could only be brought about by the act of a Central Authority; in other words, it would be imposed from the top.' (Man and Metal, Vol. XXVII, no. 6, 6.6.50.)

The low salience of the issue noted within the NUM and the ISTC, was reflected in other major British trade unions. The only mention of the Schuman Plan in the records of the Transport and General Workers' Union was when the General Secretary addressed the General Executive Council on the subject. He emphasised the demand by the continentals for a prior commitment to the principles of federalism. The journal of the Amalgamated Engineering Union during the relevant period gave no mention whatsoever to the Schuman Plan.

In summary, the European question enjoyed a much lower status within the trade union movement than that noted within the House of Commons. Such views as there were, seemed predominantly compatible with Government policy, which was in effect no change of policy. In consequence, no trade union activity was necessary to impress any distinct policies upon the Government, the press or public opinion. The themes of supranationality, terms of membership (implicitly unfavourable), and the effects upon wage and living standards, prevailed when the issue was raised. The subjects presented by the Chemical Workers' Union, of the more attractive implications of economic unification and the positive role for unions therein failed to gain the attention of others discussing the issue in a formal trade union context.

BUSINESS

The organisations used to illustrate business opinion in the periods to be studied are the Federation of British Industry (FBI) and the Association of British Chambers of Commerce (ABCC). The FBI was formed in 1916, with positive Government encouragement, to represent the broad interests of industry. Thus it became a forum for, and an aggregator of, business opinion. The scale of FBI involvement with government policy-making greatly increased during, and in the wake of, the Second World War, with the more interventionist policies of the Coalition and the Labour Governments.

The ABCC is a very different organisation, founded in the mid-nineteenth century and constituting a loose confederation of local chambers of commerce. Its role is somewhat weakened by its attempts to represent the often divergent interests of traders and industrialists. Also some of the larger constituent chambers are powerful enough to secure government attention in their own right – causing some resentment among smaller members.

Prior to the Schuman Plan, the FBI showed some interest in the integration of west European economies. It submitted a memorandum for Cabinet consideration in 1947 entitled, 'Industry and the Way to Recovery'. The discussion of European collaboration opened by pointing out the extent to which Britain was economically dependent upon the Commonwealth, but it argued that all European countries faced import problems and a possible consequence of this would be import restrictions throughout:

> 'We believe that the approach towards economic collaboration in Western Europe transcends in importance the narrow and shortsighted concept of national interest ... We therefore urge, that all possible steps should be taken to indicate the desire of the United Kingdom to arrive at a basis of collaboration with the nations of Europe. Serious consideration should be given, even at the risk of some under-employment this winter, to making a good start with the export of coal to Europe, as an indication of the genuineness of our wish to collaborate, and as a tangible means of assisting the economic recovery of those countries that form a large part of our traditional markets.' (Cabinet Papers, 47 (52), 5.9.47.) (FBI's emphasis)

This suggested that for economic reasons alone collaboration with Europe would be a sound investment for British industry. During the Paris Conference, the Overseas Policy Committee thought that 'the regulation of the volume of the imports between European countries would have greater practical consequences than minor adjustments to tariffs which could only benefit the national revenues. Once the permanent lines of European cooperation had been fixed, then we could fit the Empire into the system.' (FBI, Overseas Policy Committee, 5.5.48.)

Whilst the importance of the Empire was noted, this minute presented an interesting reversal of the traditional and prevailing British priorities, suggesting that the accommodation of the Empire could be built on to a European agreement. This enthusiasm for European integration was reiterated in a document on European recovery:

'The trouble was that few people appeared to appreciate that the general form of industrial and commercial life of the future was at issue. That the country has to face a reformulation of traditional ideas, habits and technique if it is to pull through... Anything in the nature of a European Customs Union would also be regarded as a step in the direction of this common European integration of effort by enlarging the area of freer trading.' (FBI, European Recovery Programme, 1948.)

The ABCC gave less attention to the subject and were initially more cautious than the FBI on the question of a Western European Customs Union:

'The subject was extremely complicated and many obstacles would have to be overcome before a European Union became a practical possibility. There was for instance, the question of tariff nomenclature. Further matters which would have to be dealt with would include the basis of assessment of duties and dutiable values. The Committee agreed that to express a hurried opinion on the practicality of a European Customs Union would be most unwise.' (ABCC, Overseas Committee, 7.4.48.)

Having detected FBI enthusiasm for European economic unification, it is something of a surprise to find no discussion of the Schuman Plan at a committee level in the FBI. The caution already shown by the ABCC was evident at the announcement of the Schuman Plan:

'The (Overseas) Committee felt that Britain could not easily remain outside this Treaty, for it was recognised that we were committed to some form of European Unity, but that care should be taken to ensure that our

Dominions and Colonies had been consulted at every step.'
(ABCC, Overseas Committee, 2.5.51.)

It appears that the ABCC was so cautious and equivocal as
not to express any further opinion on the matter. The
International Chamber of Commerce (ICC) sent a delegation to
the General Affairs Committee of the Council of Europe, and
expressed favour in the creation of a single European
market, with freely exchangeable currencies and some
economic, political and social coordination in order to
increase productivity and raise purchasing power. The
disadvantages of any large scale economic adjustment were
recognised, though it was thought that these could be
reduced if the union were carried out in careful and
controlled stages. (The Times, 24.3.50.)

Despite the views of their international counterpart, the
ABCC failed to express a firm policy on European economic
integration, before or after the Schuman Plan. Either their
interest was not aroused by the subject or they were content
with Government policy. In contrast, initially at least,
the FBI displayed considerably greater awareness of the
schemes under discussion in Europe, and a greater propensity
to address them. They made it clear in their Cabinet
memorandum of 1947 that they saw commercial advantages to be
gained from a form of economic collaboration with western
Europe. However, it was possibly assumed that Britain would
to some extent hold the strings of such a development, and
thus could afford to make some short-term sacrifices 'as an
indication of the genuineness of our wish to collaborate.'
Thirdly, there was something to be lost should such a scheme
not operate: 'a possible consequence of... import
restrictions through-out' and something to be gained from
its success: 'a tangible means of assisting the economic
recovery of those countries that form a large part of our
traditional markets.' These themes were not however in
evidence at the time of the announcement of the Schuman
Plan. As in the case of the trade unions, it is likely that
British business had no quarrel with Government policy on
the question. Thus they made no attempts to exploit
available functional channels regarding the issue nor to
publicise any contrary perceptions that they held.

PROMOTIONAL GROUPS

The term promotional groups is used here to denote
organisations formed to promote or oppose a specific cause,
in this case British participation in European economic

integration. This distinguishes them from the trade union and business organisations which exist primarily to protect and advance their members' interests. This distinction draws upon the work of Potter (1961),and Kimber and Richardson (1974), though the latter rightly pointed out that groups belonging to one category may bear certain characteristics of the other. Grant (1978) thought that a more important distinguishing feature was whether or not groups have 'inside' access to the machinery of government or whether they choose or are obliged to operate 'outside' governmental circles. However, the former categorisation is preferred here, as it pertains to the nature of the group, not its mode of activity, though Grant's observation is clearly to be borne in mind, as it draws attention to an important variable in groups' activity which may bear upon their influence over government policy. This section then, concerns groups with no sectional interest or attachment, but which were formed with the intention of campaigning on the European and related issues.

The first point to note regarding pressure group activity in P1 was the absence of any group specifically organised to oppose British membership of the ECSC. This itself is of significance, as it could be expected that had any potential founders or activists of such groups felt that there was a serious possibility of British entry, they would have organised themselves to oppose it, as happened in P4. It is inferred from this that such individuals were in accord with and had confidence in the Government's approach to the question.

Several groups did exist which were united in a general desire that Britain should play a full role in European unification, but their other policies differed, and they advocated differing means of achieving their goal. These groups joined together in 1948 to form the European Movement (UK Council). The founding members were the British sections of the United Europe Movement, the United Socialist States of Europe Movement, the European League for Economic Cooperation, and the Federal Union. These were joined in the following year by the British Legion and the Christian Movement for European Unity. The United Europe Movement had been established after Churchill's Zurich speech, and the British section was led by Duncan Sandys, Harold Macmillan and Churchill himself. The European League for Economic Cooperation (ELEC) founded in 1946 by the Belgian Senator, Van Zeeland, had the broad aims of advising informed European public opinion of cooperative ways to meet the economic problems of Europe. The Federal Union's ultimate goal was world federalism, but it adopted the democratic federation of Europe as a short-term aim.

At its first meeting, the European Movement UK Council agreed the following aims:

'1) To coordinate activities of British organisations or British sections of international organisations working for the cause of European Union. 2) To organise groups to study the issues of policy involved. 3) To nominate British representatives to the International Council to be created by the International Committee of the Movements for European unity.' (European Movement Minutes, 14.7.48.)

The Movement succeeded in attracting a fairly wide range of support among informed and elite groups. The leaders of the three main political parties became its Presidents, and its Vice Presidents included Victor Gollancz (a left wing publisher), Julian Amery, M.P. (a noted Conservative defender of the Commonwealth) and several Archbishops.

The Movement's campaign was waged at two broad levels. First, efforts were directed at the informed and most directly influential circles, usually in Parliamentary circles, by means of luncheons and conferences. In addition a deputation, led by Churchill and including representatives of all parties, did obtain the opportunity to discuss European economic cooperation with the Prime Minister and Foreign Secretary in 1948. Churchill, introducing their business, stated that the purpose of the delegation was

'to present for the favourable consideration of His Majesty's Government, the resolutions passed at the Congress of Europe... adding that the delegation had endeavoured to maintain the non-party character of the Movement.' (Cabinet Papers, (48) 109, 21.4.48.)

The delegation urged the Government to consider the creation of a European assembly as a means towards political, cultural and economic unification, given that it need not fear supranationality, as any progress would be subject to the control of national governments.

Secondly, the European Movement campaigned on a more popular basis. In 1949 a series of public meetings was held and it was agreed to enrol supporters as well as members, with badges produced for the former. It was also considered that there had been insufficient publicity in Britain of the

Council of Europe. A pamphlet was published on the matter and a letter written to the BBC proposing that more attention could be given to the subject. This suggests that the Movement was dissatisfied with the overall salience of the issue in the country, despite its own efforts. The meeting with Attlee and Bevin did not appear to infect them with the Movement's view that European integration was a matter of the highest priority and which was attainable.

Turning to the depiction of European integration prior to the announcement of the Schuman Plan, the sentiments of the resolution passed at a United Europe Committee rally in 1947 were certainly not representative of wider views on the question:

'in the interests of freedom and peace, the people of Europe must create unity among themselves and together make a positive contribution to the progress of civilisation and world order; and recognising that Britain must play her full part, pledges its support in the forthcoming campaign for a united Europe.' (The Times, 15.5.47.)

In the first issue of the Movement's newsletter, United Europe, Churchill, appealed for all-party support and suggested that a European sense of identification was needed among ordinary people in order to push governments into action. There is certainly no evidence that such identification occurred either among the British 'ordinary people' or Government during these years.

After the announcement of the Schuman Plan, the question of public ignorance of European integration was again raised, indicative of the Movement's failure to have the impact it desired, despite having organised public meetings, at London, Birmingham, Manchester, Brighton, Bristol, Oxford and Edinburgh. This perception of public ignorance was related to the feeling within the Movement that press coverage of the European developments was inadequate (see next section.)

The bitterness with which the political parties contested the Schuman proposals, made it especially difficult for the European Movement to present a united front on the issue. This problem had risen earlier when the Labour Party NEC had publicly advised the Labour members of the Movement not to attend the Congress at The Hague. Then, forty-one Labour members had been prepared to defy the Party line and attend, but in 1950 the inter-party rivalry over this and other issues was such that Labour MPs clearly did not feel able to depart from the Party line. This in turn detracted from the efficacy of the European Movement. Indeed, at the Movement's Council's first meeting after the Schuman announcement, the unprecedented absence of a large number of Labour MPs was noted. At this meeting two resolutions were passed. The first, proposed by Macmillan, was a simple two point statement:

'1) To express the Council's welcome of the initiative of the French Government, and
2) To urge the British Government to play a full part in working out the plan.' (European Movement, Minutes, 25.5.50.)

However, a Mrs. Manning, concerned at the possibility of over-production and a consequent slump, proposed the following resolution which was passed unanimously:

'The UK Council of the European Movement congratulates the French Government upon the proposals made by M. Schuman on its behalf for the unification of the steel and coal industries of Europe, and expresses its strong belief that in the political and economic interests of this country and of Europe, His Majesty's Government should take full and active part in working out a concrete plan for giving effect to M. Schuman's proposal.' (Ibid.)

The Macmillan motion was symptomatic of the Conservative Party view of the issue, which welcomed the Plan, but was hesitant over the likely benefits. The idea of positive economic benefits of British involvement in the Schuman Plan, as expressed in Mrs. Manning's motion, did not figure significantly in the Parliamentary anatomy of the issue.

It could be argued that the organisations within the European Movement did have a small impact on the issue's anatomy, as certain prominent members were MPs who contributed to the debate. Boothby, in the debate of the 26th of June 1950 reminded the House of the consequences of cut-throat international competition in the 1920's, leading to unemployment and the rise of Hitler, and advocated the Schuman Plan as a step towards international economic planning. It was

'the issue of peace or war. We are now faced with the greatest challenge that has ever been made to our Western democratic civilisation.' (Hansard, Vol. 476, col. 2115,

However such views were not among the prominent themes encountered in the overall Parliamentary anatomy of the issue in P1. Some themes of the European Movement's depiction of the issue were also held by Conservative spokesmen, e.g. that Britain could attend the talks and if necessary reserve her position on sovereignty and the compatibility of Britain's Commonwealth and European roles. However, the dual membership of individual leaders and members of the Council of the European Movement may account for this. Even the Movement's slight impact upon the issue's anatomy, as represented by House of Commons debate, was certainly not matched by any effect upon Whitehall or Cabinet thinking: perhaps a function of their limited access to the executive arms of government and their inability to impose their views and interpretations upon the other channels of political communication.

Although the Movement included several notable public figures, it did not really succeed in gaining solid grass roots support, despite the innovation of the supporter status and the various regional meetings. Thus, whilst it had managed to gain the audience of Attlee and Bevin in 1948, it failed to become the catalyst for a national campaign on the issue. Its most successful activities were on an informed/elite level before 1950. The announcement of the Schuman Plan, however, precipitated the division among the major political parties, which in turn undermined the Movement's all-party outlook. The qualms expressed at several of the Council meetings at the insufficient publicity of the issue, present evidence of the Movement's impotence to arouse British sympathy with the aims of the Schuman Plan.

THE PRESS

The role of the press in a political system is of considerable importance; equally it is highly complex. Its importance stems from the central role it plays in communicating views and interpretations of policies. This function is probably of even greater importance in the 1950-1963 period than in later years, as television was only beginning to gain its pivotal position in political communication. The precise role of the press is, however, difficult to unravel. For example, in interpreting news items, there are problems in distinguishing the simple reproduction of a report from a press agency or press release, from the conscious slanting of a news item consistent with the ideology of a paper's editorship or ownership, or thirdly from the expression of a more subconscious bias in the handling and selection of news. Also, a newspaper should not really be conceived of as a monolithic whole due to the varying, and at times competing interests of the owners, the editors and journalists. Thus in the analysis of press coverage of an issue, simple causal explanations may be misleading. Some generalisations are possible in describing the stances of papers for the period in question. The Daily Express was a fairly consistent defender of Empire and Commonwealth interests, which is itself important for an understanding of its anti-European position, and usually it supported the Conservative Party. The Daily Herald was continuously linked with the Labour Party, though had only been owned and fully controlled by the Party during the 1920s. The Daily Telegraph was a consistent Conservative paper for a more elite readership than the Daily Express. The Times, was considered to be an establishment newspaper and in most cases its views were broadly similar to those of the Conservatives. These four papers will provide the main material for analysis in the press section of this and the following chapters.

Generally speaking the salience of the European question in the British press, prior to the announcement of the Schuman Plan, was very low indeed. Only The Times gave consistent coverage of the developments towards European integration, though its attitude to these was circumspect. Even when Churchill formed the United Europe Movement in 1947 The Times expressed caution:

> 'Advocacy of a united Europe, in the present condition of world affairs, must be either platitudinous or controversial.' (The Times, 15.5.47.)

The questions of a united Europe's relationship with the USSR, of defining western Europe, of the method of union to be adopted and of Britain's Commonwealth connections were all emphasised. Similarly, when Britain joined the customs union talks in 1947, The Times gave a guarded reaction, welcoming her participation, but stating that it was recognised that Britain should approach them with caution, being unable to make advance commitments.

In an isolated reference to European integration prior to 1950, the Daily Herald expressed its support for the Government's approach. A strongly worded editorial advised the invited Labour delegates not to attend the Hague

Congress. It argued that attendance would only provide a platform for Churchill and his associates, who desired the 'old order of things.' (Daily Herald, 30.4.48.)

The announcement of the Schuman Plan, the invitation to Britain to take part, and the subsequent rivalry between the parties in Parliament, provoked some change. The issue achieved high stature within the British press during the months of May and June 1950 particularly. Although the Daily Herald accorded very little attention to the European issue prior to the Schuman Plan, for the six weeks following the announcement, the question was given comparative prominence, occupying the editorial columns on ten occasions and its headlines seven times. In the same weeks, the issue occupied the Daily Express editorial columns ten times, and it was also featured in a front page letter signed by Lord Beaverbrook entitled 'The Enemies of the Empire Strike Again' (Daily Express, 26.6.50.) These findings were reflected in the other national dailies.

The coverage by the Daily Herald of the issue laid considerable stress on criticising the opposition parties. One editorial referred to the prevailing Tory and Liberal 'foolery' for advocating British participation in the Plan, and it criticised the threatened supranational body for having authority over crucial aspects of the British economy (Daily Herald, 26.6.50.) Other editorials challenged the Tories to advocate positively a 'European Super Government', and were asked whether they would sign the Schuman Plan as it stood. Suspicions were cast on the motives of the French Government, who were criticised for having sprung a surprise on the rest of Europe, and for being perverse, if not devious, in not giving more details of the Plan.

Criticism of the Schuman Plan by Reynolds News (owned by the National Cooperative Press Ltd, and supported by the Cooperative and Labour Movements) was also based upon the political complexion of those advocating it. One article entitled 'Steel Kings Behind Schuman Plan', argued that such steel barons as Hugenberg, Dinkleback, Thyssen and Krupp, who had backed Hitler, were the real advocates of the Plan (Reynold News, 18.6.50.)

The more elite Labour Party-orientated weekly, the New Statesman and Nation, was also in broad agreement with the Government's policy towards the Schuman Plan although it did concede that

'The junior partner in an Anglo-American alliance may in

fact achieve less real independence than the leader of a European revival and the mediator between the blocs.' (New Statesman and Nation, 7.6.50.0

However, a month later, this hint at a possible advantage of British participation in the movement towards European economic integration had evidently been forgotten, and the Schuman Plan was dismissed as trickery on the part of the French.

The reaction of the more Conservative press to the French initiative was less cohesive. The Daily Telegraph gave a cautious welcome to the Plan, asserting that it was primarily political and only secondarily economic, and that the question of Britain's role would have to be duly weighed (Daily Telegraph, 12.5.50.) A later editorial pointed to the advantages for European security and peace which the Schuman Plan brought (Daily Telegraph, 18.5.50.) On the publication of the Labour policy document on the subject — European Unity – the Daily Telegraph responded with an editorial entitled 'Socialism versus Europe', which was critised for its rudeness and lack of diplomacy (Daily Telegraph, 13.6.50.) The Labour Party was also derided for unwillingness to work with non-socialist countries, and Attlee attacked for his isolationist policy: it was stated that the only other parties opposed to the Schuman Plan were the Communists and diehard Conservatives. Prime coverage was given to the debate in the House of Commons, and the Daily Telegraph broadly agreed with the Conservatives and Liberals and advocated that Britain should follow the example of the Dutch in participating, but reserving final judgement. The policy was described as 'selfish and grasping'. The editorial commented that whilst Labour had won on the vote,

'a powerful body of British opinion rejects the socialist brand of isolationism and is resolved that Britain shall play her full part in consolidating the forces of the free world.' (Daily Telegraph, 28.6.50.)

The Daily Express reacted in a very different manner to the French initiative. Immediately after the Schuman announcement it expressed concern over the possibility of Britain losing her independence.

It was asserted that the Schuman Plan would retard the cause of peace and would drag down Britain's standard of living to that of Europe. In contrast, it argued that hope of peace lay with the strengthening of comradeship with the

Empire and the Commonwealth. The Schuman Plan was described as being born of a jealous French desire for control of Britain's Commonwealth and Empire markets, with the aim of forcing Britain to submerge herself in the European economic system: 'If we lose this struggle for independence, all is lost.' The editorial columns were expressly critical of the Conservative and Liberal Parties for making cause against the Empire and for threatening to lower Britain's living standards. The only criticism of the Government was that its refusal to participate was not couched in sufficiently strong terms. The Labour document European Unity was praised especially for its Commonwealth commitment. Obviously the Daily Express found it difficult to use too strong words in attacking Churchill personally: his European policy was described as 'mistaken for once.' Faith was expressed in Britain's economic independence, as it was stated that she could manage even if America withdrew Marshall Aid. After the Commons defeat of the Opposition motion on the Plan, the Daily Express gave its own epitath

'The Schuman Plan as far as Britain is concerned is dead. And in its death there should be rejoicing.' (Daily Express, 28.6.50.)

The Times gave full coverage of the Schuman Plan, the reasons for its announcement and its likely implications. It stated that French statesmen and experts saw no reason why Britain should not play a full part in the scheme, and the Plan was first described as

'a bold attempt to cut through obstacles in the face of which all efforts in the past few years to coordinate Europe's industrial growth have been fruitless.' (The Times, 11.5.50.)

The implications of the scheme for the French and German economies were discussed, and it was also assumed that the proposals would be attractive to the British steel industry and to the Government, due to the desire for a rational distribution of production, though The Times advocated a careful study of the role of cartels and of the real prospects for economic progress. It can be inferred from its editorials in these weeks that The Times saw British participation in the Plan as important, but express approval was also gven for the British Government's attitude of not being able to make any prior commitments. The reaction of The Times to Attlee's Commons statement on the Schuman Plan was that it revived old doubts about the Government's willingness to cooperate more closely with other European countries, as had the NEC statement European Unity, though an editorial of the previous day stated that there was much good sense in the statement.

In criticising the Government's stance on the Schuman Plan, The Times could not be said to have fallen in behind Churchill. Commenting on his motion to the House of Commons on the matter at the end of June 1950, it was asked whether this was simply a deft move on the part of the Leader of the Opposition, and whether he really ranged himself with the federalists, as might be construed from the tenor of the motion. The paper did however support a British presence at the talks, albeit without full commitment and with full scrutiny of the proposals.

The Manchester Guardian adopted a position similar to that of The Times. It was critical of Britain's absence from the talks:

> 'All our objections boil down to this: that we want to wait and see what sort of high authority it is going to be before we commit ourselves to obey it. They do not mean that we need remain outside the Plan forever.' (Manchester Guardian, 5.6.50.)

However, like The Times, it ultimately approved of the Government's handling of the matter.

Perhaps the paper most sympathetic towards the Schuman initiative was the Economist, which accused the Government of acting as if they were 'inverted Micawbers', waiting for something to turn down. The article agreed with the Government's objections to a supranational authority, but argued that it should realise the underlying sincerity of the French proposals, and should not continually thwart such initiatives. It suggested that it had become difficult to find anyone in Europe, America or in some circles of Britain

> 'who has not been driven to the conclusion that the British Government's desire is to sabotage any moves towards European economic unity, under cover of accepting them in principle... it ought not to have been very difficult to find a formula for acceptance of the French Government's invitation with the qualifications which are assuredly in the minds of the governments that did accept.' (Economist, 10.6.50.)

The Economist concluded that Britain should not be isolationist and should play a more constructive role in world affairs; the implication being that taking part in the Schuman talks would be consistent with this end.

In summary, the issue of European economic integration enjoyed a short-lived but high salience in the press immediately after the Schuman announcement. This was primarily a product of the Parliamentary debate on the question. Only The Times attempted to discuss the issue prior to 1950, and thus readers of other papers had minimum media sources of information concerning the background to the Schuman announcement. When discussing the Schuman Plan, the Daily Herald and the Daily Telegraph both gave considerable attention to criticising their respective party political opponents, which corresponds with the high incidence of party scoring in the Parliamentary debate. Also, the theme of supranationality loomed large in the Daily Herald and the Daily Express: this concept being contrasted with the national freedom which would be lost by participating in the Plan. Three other major themes were developed in the Daily Express depiction of the issue, all of which were prominent in its Parliamentary anatomy: the Commonwealth and Empire, the impact on British living standards, and the threat of European cartels. The Daily Telegraph developed themes which the Conservative Party leadership unfolded, notably the contribution of the Plan to European security and peace, and that Britain could take part in the talks, with the same reservations as the Dutch. These themes were raised in the Economist and The Times. The latter also raised issues for consideration which achieved little status in the Parliamentary anatomy or in other national newspapers such as the benefits both of European industrial growth and of a rational distribution of production.

PUBLIC OPINION

The measurement of public opinion by sample surveys is undoubtedly a difficult exercise, but in a country where there is no institutionalised means of ascertaining popular opinion by referendum (as exists for example in Switzerland), this provides the best technique available. However, two points should be made concerning the way in which such data is handled and interpreted. First, it has been assumed too often that polls give an indication of the opinions of the respondents alone, and insufficient regard given to other possible interpretations. It may of course be that these opinions simply constitute a reproduction of the views which the individuals receive from various media, organisational or personal stimuli. Secondly, both the construction of questions within a survey, and more importantly in the present context, the subjects on which respondents are invited to give their opinions, are themselves reflections of prior judgements, whether by the pollsters or those who hire their services (e.g. political parties or newspapers). Thus the fact that a survey might be conducted at one particular time on for instance the attitudes towards the operation of economic planning, but not on attitudes towards the introduction of an incomes policy, may itself reflect established opinion.

There were no public opinion polls conducted on the questions raised by the Schuman Plan during this period in Britain. This may reflect the importance attached to the issue by Gallup Poll, who were the only public opinion firm operating in the country until 1959. Presumbably it did not consider the issue one which might seriously divide the country: this may or may not have been the product of a conscious decision. The main domestic subject of concern in the polls was nationalization (especially steel). The main foreign issue was the Korean situation. Certainly the Labour Cabinet had assumed that public opinion would support their non-participation in the Plan. The absence of opinion polls in this period indicates that the issue's moderate salience was indeed short-lived and that it had no significant continuing stature in British politics.

DISCUSSION

What contribution have the content analysis of the Parliamentary debate and the foregoing discussion of the responses of various organisations and groups to the issue made an understanding of the issue in P1? The issue was described, on the basis of the content analysis, as of moderate, but short-lived salience. Can this be accounted for? It seems that this feature was largely the product of the activities of the small group of Conservative leaders in Parliament who introduced the two debates mentioned above. With the exception of Attlee's statement to the House of Commons, the Government made no attempt to raise the issue for discussion in the House of Commons, and presumably with loyalty in mind, those Labour backbenchers who had earlier supported a British role in European economic integration were reluctant to embarrass the Government. The issue achieved a very low level of prominence at the 1950 Labour Party Conference. There was no groundswell of feeling towards the issue within the Conservative Party to push the

Parliamentary leadership into taking up the issue. Indeed the latter made no effort to present the issue of the Schuman Plan to the Party. Nor was the issue raised by the British press, who, with the major exception of The Times (and for different reasons, the Daily Express) simply responded to the debate on the matter in the House of Commons on Party lines, rather than conduct probing investigations into the nature and context of the Schuman Plan. The issue was not the product of concerns raised by trade union or business representatives through their functional channels, nor of a popular campaign by interested promotional groups. Irrespective of the sincerity of the Conservative leadership, or of the policy outcome, this episode illustrates that the levels of salience of political issues are not simply within the prerogative of the Government, Whitehall or of sectional groups within British politics. This issue, which might otherwise not have troubled the British public, was brought to its attention by the efforts of the leadership of the Opposition Party. However, the fact that the moderate level of salience of the issue was not sustained suggests that the importance attached to it by such advocates of British participation in the Plan as the Liberal Party, Robert Boothby, MP, and R.W.G. Mackay, MP, was not widely shared, and more particularly, was not shared by the Conservative Party leadership. The latter were content to exploit the issue, but were ambivalent about the merits of the Schuman Plan for Britain.

The high level of partisanship noted within the Parliamentary debate did not appear to be reflected much more widely as the issue was simply not of such importance within for instance the Labour and Conservative Conferences, the business and trade union organisations. That no public opinion poll was taken on the issue, also indicates short-lived salience. This leads one to suspect that the exceptionally high level of statements for and against the issue in Pl was related to the extent of inter-party rivalry prevailing over this and other issues of the time. The February 1950 General Election had left the Labour Government with such a slim majority and it was clear that a second Election was imminent. Thus, Parliamentary politics between February 1950 and October 1951 were more highly charged than might otherwise have been the case. The issue was characterised by a very high level of party scoring. This reflected the preoccupations of the leadership of both Labour and Conservative Parties who were eager to exploit the issue in criticism of their political adversaries. Party political themes were also taken up in the press, most

113

notably in the Daily Herald and the Daily Telegraph.
Together these factors mitigated against a high level of
neutral statements: it became important for MPs to be seen
to be for or against the issue.

The dominant aspect of the issue was the Political one,
with special emphasis on the themes of sovereignty and
supranationalism. This is consistent with the depiction of
the issue by leading members of the Government, who in
Cabinet, within the Party and within Parliament, sought to
air their objections to participation in the Schuman Plan.
The Conservative leadership however did not attempt to steer
the debate on to other topics, but chose instead to denounce
the Government's interpretations of the political
ramifications of the Plan. This was also the case with the
theme of the Commonwealth within the Extra European focus.
Despite the lack of evidence of official Commonwealth
opinion - a report of the Cabinet Committee on Commonwealth
implications, illustrated ambivalence among Commonwealth
Governments (Cabinet Papers (50), 153) - great stress was
laid on this theme by Government spokesmen, and this was
matched in the Parliamentary anatomy.

The Conservatives also dwelt on this topic, by simply
countering the Government's argument and suggesting that
participation was possible despite the Commonwealth. Thus,
the Conservative leadership were singly successful in
raising the salience of the issue, but they did not appear
anxious to emphasise notions of the issue's anatomy, other
than those raised by the Government.

Dissident views of the issue's anatomy did exist, but did
not enjoy wide dissemination. The idea of the relationship
between socialism and federalism, Europe as a third force
(both held by Labour minorities), the contribution of the
Schuman Plan to British industrial modernisation and
efficiency, material benefits to consumers and workers
(views held by the Liberal Party), the representation of
workers within the Plan, the need for Britain to share its
economic benefits (embodied in a Chemical Workers' Union
motion to the 1950 TUC) and the prospect of expanding export
markets for British goods (as raised, but not elaborated
upon, in the report of a Whitehall Committee appointed by
Attlee), were all themes which failed to achieve any
standing in the Parliamentary anatomy. Thus the debate was
conducted on terms which evidently suited the Government.
The absence of themes within the European Economic sphere is
particularly significant, as although it would be expected
that domestic economic implications would be scrutinised,

the Plan was after all about the economy of western Europe and points raised by advocates of British participation often fell within this sphere. Presumably the lack of probing attention to the issue on the part of representative business and trade union groups is related to this gap in the debate: because topics in this sphere did not figure in the anatomy of the issue, these groups were not provoked to become involved in the debate. As MPs frequently take their cues from such representative groups, this provides further explanation of the failure of the European Economic sphere to appear in the Parliamentary anatomy of the issue. Indeed the slogans within the European Political sphere regarding federalism and supranationality were simply easier to adopt than to conduct detailed analysis of the likely impact of such a scheme on the European economy.

In explaining the salience and anatomy of the issue, emphasis has been laid on the predispositions of the leadership of the Labour Government and the Conservative Party. It is though, important not to lose sight of the part played by other agents in the system in contributing, often passively, to this state of affairs. The evidence suggests that with a few exceptions, a national state of mind existed, which after an early post-War sympathy, became apathetic to ideas of British participation in the European economic integration in general, and the Schuman Plan in particular. This was evident among senior civil servants (who paid little attention to the economic implications for Britain, trade unionists, representatives of business, and the majority of Labour and Conservative rank and file membership. With the exception of The Times, the press only became interested in the Plan as it encroached on British Parliamentary debate. Even the European Movement, in contrast to its earlier high profile activities, was all but impotent after the Schuman Plan announcement, due either to concrete objections among some of its members to the Plan, or due to the divisions caused within the Movement by the inter-party conflict.

What were the implications of the anatomy depicted for the policy outcome not to participate in the Schuman Plan? Clearly, there was little initial likelihood of British participation in the Plan, given the attitudes evident in the Cabinet, Whitehall, business organisations and trade unions. The elevation of the issue on the spectrum of salience, at least created the opportunity for it to be debated. However, in British politics when the Government has a working majority in Parliament, the achievement of a policy against the wishes of the Cabinet is rare, and dependent on one of a number of special factors: either the Government must be convinced by forceful persuasion and or pressure from Whitehall, a sectional or promotional interest, or else a sufficient number of its own followers must be so committed to a policy as to defy their whips and abstain or vote against the Government. There appeared to be no general predisposition for any of these groups to act in such ways. This is not very surprising as their perceptions of the issue closely matched its Parliamentary anatomy, which in turn was very much akin to the Government's portrayal of it. This militated against an alternative policy outcome, as debate was largely restricted to two themes which were particularly sensitive to British institutions, groups and MPs, those of sovereignty and the Commonwealth. The anatomy did not extend to include attention to themes which might have shown the Schuman Plan in a more favourable light.

5 P2: Britain and the ECSC

This period begins with the return of the Conservative Party to office in 1951. The plans for the formation of the ECSC were implemented by the Six during P2, but Britain continued to remain apart from these developments. In 1954 the Government negotiated Associate Status with the ECSC which was ratified by the House of Commons in February 1955, at which point P2 ends. The most distinctive feature noted in the analysis of the issue in P2 was its very low salience. It occupied less than 0.1% of all Parliamentary debate in the period. Turning to the issue's anatomy there was a much smaller proportion of statements for or against than in P1, and a rise in the proportion of neutral statements (from 35% to 70%). There was also much less attention paid to party scoring (only a quarter of the share of points it achieved in P1), and a low level of substantiation was recorded in P2 (58%) in contrast to P1 and P4.

In the case of the policy aspects of the issue in this period (summarised in figure 7), there was a clear drop in the proportionate size of the Political aspect, from 70% in P1 to 48%. This was matched by increases in the Economic (from 24% to 39%) and Social (from 6% to 13%) aspects, which in combination exceeded the Political aspect. There was a marked drop in the stature of the Extra European focus (from 29% to 9%) with significant concomitant increases in the British (from 30% to 42%) and European (from 40% to 49%) focuses.

FIGURE 7

SUMMARY OF ASPECT AND FOCUS IN P2

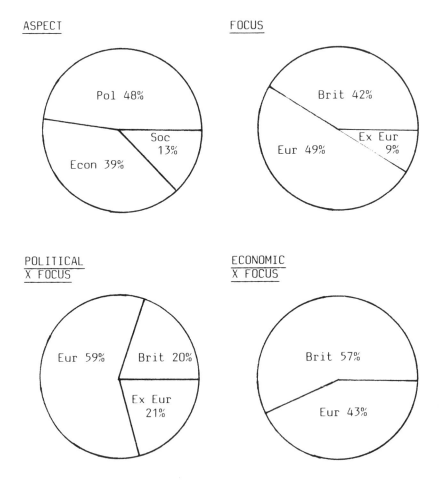

ASPECT

Pol 48%

Soc 13%

Econ 39%

FOCUS

Brit 42%

Ex Eur 9%

Eur 49%

POLITICAL
X FOCUS

Eur 59%

Brit 20%

Ex Eur 21%

ECONOMIC
X FOCUS

Brit 57%

Eur 43%

The Political aspect was dominated by the European focus which was mainly characterised by views on the merits, method of operation and implications of a European supranational authority. The remaining details raised in this sphere were mostly related to whether association with, rather than membership of the ECSC might be preferable. The details within the Extra European focus were more diverse, and due to the low numbers involved, it is not possible to deduce any distinct pattern. The British focus was monopolised by the implications of membership for British sovereignty, notably her ability to continue independent economic planning.

Over half of the details raised within the Economic aspect fell into the British focus. These referred almost exclusively to one subject area: the impact of membership upon the British coal, iron and steel industries. The European Economic sphere was monopolised by perceptions of the operation of free trade and the role of cartels in the ECSC. Unfortunately there were too few cases in the Social aspect to do more than point out the prevalence of British concerns.

In analysing the views and activities of interested groups outside the Parliamentary debate, the following questions will be uppermost. Firstly, why was there such a dramatic fall in the stature of the issue from P1 to P2, accompanied by a distinctly lower level of substantiation in the latter period? Can any significance be attached to the doubling of the proportion of neutral statements from P1 to P2 and the simultaneous fall in party scoring? Further, what explanation can be posed for the fall in status of the Political and rise of the Economic aspects? In addition it is significant that, despite the rise in the Economic aspect, the Extra European Economic sphere disappeared entirely. Why were concerns in the Extra European focus of such little significance and why, when they did occur, were they solely within the Political aspect? Finally, having tried to account for these changes in the salience and anatomy of the issue, some attempt will be made to assess the relevance of the Parliamentary debate for an understanding of the range of views outside Parliament and to the eventual policy outcome. There was, in effect, no change in policy: the Government chose not to participate in the process of economic integration engaged in by the Six during this period.

119

The newly elected Conservative Government saw its major mandate as 'to undo the chains' with which Labour had bound the country and the economy. However, in matters of foreign policy, it adhered to the guidelines followed by Bevin. A ditty of the period sums up the continuity of foreign policy:

> 'The Bevin or the Churchill touch seems both alike to Danes or Dutch; if Socialist or Tory speaks it's all the same to French and Greeks.' (Sked and Cook, 1979, p.122.)

This certainly applied in the case of policy towards the ECSC. In reply to a Parliamentary question asking for a statement of the Government's intentions regarding the Schuman Plan, Anthony Nutting (Under Secretary of State for Foreign Affairs) made direct reference to the policy of the previous Government, indicating that the Washington Declaration of the 14th of September 1951 made between Acheson, Schuman and Morrison would be the Government's policy:

> 'The Government of Great Britain desires to establish the closest possible association with the European Continental Community at all stages.' (Hansard, Vol. 498, col. 32, 24.3.52.)

This avoided the necessity of making an express policy preference, and British policy towards Europe remained unchanged, despite hopes held to that end on the Continent. No attempt was made to join the Six although the Government requested that it be kept informed of developments, and later negotiated Associate status with the ECSC. This required no major commitments of Britain, and, it should be added, was not a cause of contention between the major parties within the Commons.

The low salience of the issue noted in the content analysis is compatible with Sir John Colville's (Churchill's personal secretary) recollection that Churchill did not even talk about his European rhetoric in the first six to nine months of the new Government: Churchill was preoccupied with the Anglo-American alliance and with 'houses, meat and not getting scuppered (by which he meant defence)'. When he came round to addressing European problems, it was in the context of the European Defence Community (Charlton, 1981). (It is perhaps a tribute to Churchill's tactical ability in earlier years that pro Europeans - at home and on the Continent - felt let down by his apparent change of heart.) A further piece of evidence of the Government's attitude to the question is Oliver Lyttelton's (Colonial Secretary from 1951 to 1955) comment that

'I cannot remember a single occasion when the question of Europe was brought before the Cabinet. If it had been, I should have been sceptical, but interested.' (Boothby, 1978, p.222.)

Boothby added somewhat bitterly that David Maxwell-Fyfe, Harold Macmillan and Duncan Sandys, who all held Government posts in this period, and all purported to believe in a European union, did nothing about it. In contrast, Macmillan, in his memoirs, recalled how he (supported by Maxwell-Fyfe, Peter Thorneycroft and Sandys) had wanted to join the ECSC, but that Churchill had opposed them. In any event, Macmillan considered that it was

'too late for us to reverse the Labour Government's decision not to enter into the ECSC'. (Macmillan, 1971, p.65.)

As Foreign Secretary, the most senior Cabinet member after the Prime Minister and Churchill's heir-apparent, Eden's views were central to the Government's European policy. Shortly after taking office he stated in early 1952

'that the United Kingdom could not join a federation on the continent of Europe: this is something which we know in our bones we cannot do.' (The Times, 12.2.52.)

This is interesting, not only because he equated the European developments with a federation, but also for Eden's belief that there was something integral to the UK which prevented her from fully participating with other west European countries.

Evelyn Shuckburgh (Eden's private secretary at the time) commented that Eden was 'aping' Churchill, in attempting to appear the representative of a country with a world role. Christopher Soames (Churchill's private secretary) thought that Eden was a restraining influence on Churchill regarding European matters. This view is backed up by Nutting who claimed that Churchill had confided in him that his own European stance was born out of a desire not to embarrass Eden. Thorneycroft also saw Eden's priority as being the special relationship with America. (Charlton, 1981).

Whichever of the two was ultimately responsible for Britain's European policy is less important than the fact that they were both against any change from the pattern established under Labour, and that other Cabinet members accepted this policy.

In summary, the Cabinet evaluated the question of a British role in European economic integration as a matter of very low profile. In as much as they discussed the issue at all, the emphases were on Britain's inability to join a federation, and that in any case, it was too late to join. Clearly, this being so, it would not have been in the Government's interests for the issue to acquire high salience in Parliamentary or Conservative Party circles, nor for a significantly different anatomy of the issue to prevail, which might arouse a review of British policy.

In keeping with the interests of the Party leadership, no emphasis was placed upon the ECSC, or the more general matter of European unification, at any Conservative Party Conference in this period. Foreign policy remained firmly based upon the three circles policy, with the European circle usually treated as the least important of the three. Emphasis was more usually placed upon Britain's role at the centre of the Commonwealth and Empire. In summing up the foreign policy debate at the 1954 Conference, Eden said that the 'principles of foreign policy do not change'. This aptly summarised the approach of the Party towards European economic integration.

One of the few relevant Conservative publications on the European issue appeared in 1953, produced by the Conservative Political Centre. Such a publication does not constitute official policy, but is produced in order to provide background information and a survey of the main points of discussion. It argued that when Labour was in office the situation (regarding Britain's membership of the ECSC) was still 'fluid' enough for Britain to play a part in the talks following the Schuman Plan. However, it quoted Churchill as saying that 'a hard and fast concrete federal constitution for Europe is not within the scope of practical affairs.' (Branston, 1953.) It argued that the ECSC was federal and as such Britain could never join. (Whilst this might be considered a vindication of Government policy, it does imply that Churchill had misjudged the situation in 1950.) The pamphlet concluded by emphasising the value and pre-eminence of Britain's Commonwealth and NATO connections: the recurring themes of Britain's wider commitments.

Even the commitment displayed in P1 by Robert Boothby towards British participation in European economic integration appeared to have become diluted in the early years of P2. Writing on the 'Economic Policy of the Conservative Party', he concluded that one of the major problems of the world economy was the inadequacy of dollar and gold reserves in the non-dollar areas of the free world. He suggested a deflation of non-dollar currencies, and the building of a single economic unit of the sterling area and western Europe with policies of trade discrimination and international planning of investment, production and trade, in order to compete on more equal terms with the USA. Having made these proposals, he did not mention negotiating British membership of the ECSC as a step towards these goals.

In Parliament the Government treated the question of full participation of Britain in the ECSC as totally inapplicable. For instance, Duncan Sandys (Minister of Housing and Local Government), introducing the motion to Parliament to ratify the Agreement made for the Association of Britain with the ECSC, asserted that it was out of the question for Britain to have joined the ECSC in 1950 given the accompanying loss of sovereignty required. (This was a considerable volte face, given Sandys' efforts in 1950 at urging full British participation in the Schuman Plan.) He continued by emphasising the absence of any political strings attached to the Association package:

'We are not committed to anything beyond exchange of information and consultation.' (Hansard, Vol. 537, col. 888, 1955).

Anthony Nutting (Minister of State at the Foreign Office), summing up for the Government, stated that the Conservatives had never advocated the surrender of sovereignty, and by this agreement Britain gained association yet retained her freedom. Association, he argued, was required to avoid certain dangers of economic competition between Britain and Europe. This view of the issue was not challenged, though how association would achieve this end was not really explained.

The level of importance which the Government appeared to attach to the question of greater economic integration mirrored the stature of the issue noted in the content analysis. It should be mentioned that the Government always exercises considerable influence over the business of the House of Commons, and thus the issue's salience is to some extent a direct product of the Government's own priorities. Having said that, there is evidence that the Government's evaluation of the merits of this issue was either fairly infectious or else matched existing attitudes of others in the House of Commons. Government contributions accounted for only one fifth of the points of detail which occurred in the content analysis. It should also be noted that in these debates, Government spokesmen gave somewhat disproportionate attention to the Political aspect. Not a single Government statement showed any favour towards the ECSC, and three quarters were neutral. The distribution of details among the three focuses was broadly similar to that recorded overall. Thus it can be concluded that whilst there were those who might have desired that the issue be accorded a higher status, they were unable to (given the Parliamentary timetabling practices), or not sufficiently motivated to promote it to this end. Secondly, those who viewed the anatomy of the issue in a different light also failed to achieve impact on the overall anatomy of the issue as exhibited in the House of Commons.

In both Government and Party circles, the question of British membership of the ECSC was of low priority for Conservatives. This evaluation was clearly reflected in relevant House of Commons debate. Also, the depiction of the issue by the Conservative leadership in Cabinet and in the Party was consistent with the overall P2 anatomy derived from the content analysis. The developments of the ECSC were consistently given the blanket description 'federal', irrespective of its actual characteristics. This theme was given considerable emphasis in the Commons, as was that of Britain's wider international ties – another objection to ECSC membership raised by Conservatives.

The extent to which the Government did react to the newly formed ECSC was to establish a permanent delegation at Brussels and later to negotiate Associate status. These moves symbolised the relegation of the issue from the realm of the politically controversial, to that of the routine business of Government. A style of relating to the ECSC was established which enabled the Government to maintain contact with it at an official level. It was assumed that this would keep Britain in touch, without making 'unacceptable' political or economic demands of her.

WHITEHALL

In his radio series The Price of Victory, Michael Charlton

(1981) interviewed several individuals who were strategically placed during P2, in order to inquire into the nature of official British opinions towards Europe. The overwhelming impression these interviews gave was of staunch Foreign Office opposition to the Schuman Plan: a viewpoint which persisted from P1 to P2.

Peter Thorneycroft (President of the Board of Trade) stated quite simply that in his experience the Foreign Office was against the Schuman Plan. He considered that the Foreign Office was preoccupied with problems of Britain maintaining the balance of power and preventing the division of Europe. It was perceived that British participation in the Plan would flatly contradict her externally based European role. Thorneycroft put it that the Foreign Office was not just cautious towards British participation in the Plan, but hostile.

Christopher Soames, concurred with this view, stating that the Foreign Office had a restraining hand on Churchill. Evelyn Shuckburgh (Eden's Private Secretary) went further, saying that the Foreign Office considered Churchill's pro European views as 'romantic.'

Whilst it is not possible to say much on the Whitehall depiction of the issue's anatomy, other than that British participation would not be compatible with her traditional role, one clear point does emerge; the issue had a very low standing within the work of the British higher civil service, and this derived from Foreign Office hostility to the Schuman Plan and the ECSC.

THE LABOUR PARTY

The Labour Party, like the Conservative Government, did not give much attention to the possibility of full British participation in the ECSC during P2. The issue was not mentioned at the 1952 Party Conference. A resolution proposed by Attlee at the 1953 Conference mirrored Government policy on European cooperation: priority was given to the use of the Council of Europe, the OEEC and other inter-governmental arrangements, and a preference expressed for 'association only' with any supranational authority that did come into being. (Labour Party Conference, 1953, p.150.)

It is worth noting that among the 1953 Conference documents was a resolution which had been passed by the Socialist

International on the subject of Socialist cooperation in Europe. It spoke of supervision by European Parliamentary representatives over governmental cooperation, stated that certain features of the ECSC were not fully satisfactory, and proposed that

> 'Efforts should be made to promote more complete planning, more effective control over prices and the extension of the Community's competence in the social field. Progressive expansion of the common market of the ECSC is necessary in order to bring about complete economic integration.' (Labour Party Conference, 1953, p.212.)

Despite the attendance of British delegates at the International and the appearance of these motions in Party documents, such sentiments did not influence the thinking of the British Labour Party. These notions were unacceptable and thus did not even appear to threaten the prevailing views on the matter.

The 1954 foreign policy debate saw no mention of European economic integration: the question of German rearmament was foremost. Also, a policy document 'From Colonies to Commonwealth' was endorsed (Labour Party Conference, 1954, p.199.) This expressed optimism that a Commonwealth of free and equal peoples would evolve, implying that the Commonwealth would strengthen as a political and economic force: the question of fuller involvement in Europe was not really posed as a viable option. The Labour Party in Opposition were prepared to concur with the Government on this issue (unlike the Conservative Party when they were in Opposition in Pl). This was evident in the debate on Britain's Associate status with the ECSC, when no motion was tabled by the Opposition criticising the Government's handling of the matter.

The one European issue to which the Party did give attention was that of German rearmament, which became one of the most controversial issues for the Party since the War. The main ingredients of the debate were the possibility of further world polarisation, solidarity with the German Social Democratic Party, the dangers of rearming a capitalist power and the response to American pressure on the matter. Thus the debate was couched in fairly traditional Labour foreign policy language: the relevance of British ECSC membership to the problem of German rearmament was not mentioned.

126

In Parliament, most Labour speeches indicated contentment with Government ECSC policies. Indeed, opportunities were also taken to provide justification for the previous Labour Government's policy on the Schuman Plan, in the light of European developments. Only one or two Labour MPs dissented from this view. John Hynd asserted that Britain should accept full membership of the ECSC, rather than take up only an Associate status. Similarly, Harry Hynd noted the irony that some members of the Opposition were defending aspects of the Government's policy against certain Conservative critics, (notably H. Legge Bourke), and he regretted that Britain had not accepted full membership of the ECSC, describing the association as 'very slight'. Hynd characterised Britain's attitude as basically selfish and hypocritical: certainly not a prevalent view within the Labour Party or outside it, and concluded by

'regretting that we are not more closely associated with what I regard as an important body, with which it will be essential for us to associate more closely in the future if we are not to suffer economically by attempting to compete against the combined coal and steel industries of those six countries.'

Two articles published in the Political Quarterly during this period by prominent members of the Labour Party give some impression of views towards Europe. Ernest Davies MP (Under Secretary of State for Foreign Affairs 1950-51), discussing Labour's foreign policy, stated that

'political federalism has been rejected by the Labour Party for understandable reasons. As the main partner of the Commonwealth, and as the centre of the sterling area, Britain as yet cannot surrender that measure of sovereignty entailed. With so few completely sharing the socialist ideology, no Labour Government could surrender its sovereignty to an organisation which might be dominated by elements differing from it politically and socially.' (Davies, 1952, p.131.)

He argued that a European community would be too small an arena for Britain and that in any case, western Europe – even with the United Kingdom – would not be a viable unit, whereas an Atlantic pact would be. The fact that the possibility of British participation in the European economic integration process was discussed in such an article, indicates that the issue was not totally moribund: it enjoyed no high level public salience, but was referred to in this forum of informed discussion. Even so, a change in British policy in this field was depicted by Davies as a non alternative.

In an article on the economic aims of the Labour Party, Hugh Gaitskell MP (1953) (Chancellor of the Exchequer 1950-51), stated that the economic ends and means of a future Labour Government rested on its ability to control the British economy in order for example to prevent inflation and avoid a balance of payments deficit, while at the same time maintaining full employment. There was no suggestion, however, that these plans might be compatible with the pooling of resources on a European basis and their control by a central authority.

Was Labour's ECSC policy an example of responsibility and consistency on the part of an Opposition party? It is unlikely that this constitutes a full explanation. Broader factors unrelated to the merits of the European question should be borne in mind. The style of Labour's Opposition until the 1955 election was dictated by Attlee, and 'the posture of the leadership was essentially defensive' (Bogdanor, 1970). It was generally assumed that the Party would be returned to office at the next election anyway, hence it was not considered necessary to exploit issues with which to castigate the Government.

In summary then, the Labour Party had no axe to grind with the Government's policy towards the economic developments in Europe. This was probably a crucial contributory factor in accounting for the low stature of the issue in this period. Without inter-party controversy on the issue, Britain's relationship to European economic unification was not elevated from the realm of routine politics. In common with the Government, the Labour Party used the term 'federalism' to describe developments on the continent, and the Commonwealth objection was also raised. The overall Labour view was encapsulated in a speech by Patrick Gordon-Walker MP, a delegate of the Labour Party at the Assembly of the Council of Europe:

> 'Even if Britain were not a member of the Commonwealth, she would still have to retain essential autonomies. The people of Britain would never allow any British Government to surrender the powers necessary to preserve full employment there. Britain, further, must retain the independence of a power bounded by the sea.' (The Times, 30.11.51.)

This was essentially a British view of the issue, rather

than a distinctly Labour one.

THE LIBERAL PARTY

In contrast to the low salience of the issue derived from
the content analysis of Parliamentary debate, the low
salience of the issue within the work of Government and
Whitehall, and within the Conservative and Labour Parties;
the salience of the European question in the Liberal Party
continued to be high in P2. It remained a topic of debate
at Liberal Assemblies and at the Council of the Party, and
individual MPs sporadically raised the issue within the
House of Commons.

Liberal Party policy towards Europe is well illustrated by
reference to motions passed at Annual Assemblies and the
General Council during this period. The tenor of these
resolutions was consistently pro European. The 1952
Assembly believed the unification of Europe to be

'essential to our own prosperity and security, and which
will make but halting progress until Great Britain is
more clearly identified with the movement (towards
European unity)'. (Liberal Party, p.4.)

This reference to British participation being essential to
her prosperity and security is consistent with the Liberal
portrayal of the issue in P1, and in P2 it was similarly
unrepresentative of wider views. In 1953, the Liberals
called on the Government

'to support the measures being taken to unify Western
Europe by the intimate association of the United Kingdom
with the various organs of administration now being set
up, a policy which in no way endangers its special
relationship with the countries of the Commonwealth.'
(Liberal Party, p.4.)

There is a certain ambiguity over the term 'intimate
association', which was reflected in the debate, but in the
following year the Assembly was more specific when it urged

'the Government, particularly in view of France's fears,
to make formal entry as a full member, not only of the
EDC, but also into the Coal and Steel Community and the
other organs of Western Europe in being.' (Liberal Party,
p.4.)

129

As mentioned, Liberals occasionally expressed their criticism of Government policy towards the European question in Parliament. For example, Clement Davies (the leader of the Liberal Party) asked the Government, prior to the launching of the ECSC, its attitude to the Schuman Plan, expressing his own preference for close association if not membership. Davies later described the Agreement for British Associate status with the ECSC as 'only a modest step', and expressed the need for Britain to go much further.

It is quite clear then that the Liberal Party saw the question of Britain's participation in the economic integration of Europe as a much more crucial one than did either of the main parties. Liberals saw the consequences of non participation as serious both for the country and for Europe. Their reasons were based on political hopes of increased stability and peace, and on economic prosperity and security for Britain. These themes appeared to have had little impact on the overall anatomy as noted in the content analysis, which illustrated a much greater emphasis on the problems of governing European bodies and the economic disadvantages for the British coal, iron and steel industries. Thus the overall stature and anatomy of the issue bore no real resemblance to the value and perspectives attached to it by the Liberal Party.

BUSINESS

The European issue in this period received a similar degree of attention from British business organisations as it did from most of the other groups discussed. The various relevant committees of the Federation of British Industry showed fairly scant regard for the ECSC. The Economic Policy Committee minutes of the FBI indicate that the matter was not discussed at all during the time of the ECSC's inception in 1952. The Overseas Trade Policy, whilst making several allusions to the need for liberalisation of trade in Europe, made no reference to the creation and role of the ECSC until 1953. Even this only occurred as a result of a meeting between Dutch and British industrialists, at which a Dutch delegate argued that different industries ought to adopt a fully European perspective. He advocated increased regulation of production and prices, and also added that economic cooperation implied the retention of each country's national sovereignty. The response of a British representative, Sir Archibald Forbes, is illustrative of prevailing attitudes in British industry. He said that

British industrialists had not studied the problem with the intensity that their colleagues in Europe had done, and thus that they were not in a position to express any definitive views.

Also indicative of FBI attitudes was when a member of the Overseas Policy Committee asked whether the forthcoming visit of Jean Monnet in connection with the ECSC was a matter of policy to be considered by the Committee. After discussion it was agreed that it was not, and it was decided to leave the matter to the Chairman and the Overseas Director. They would keep in touch with developments and call the Committee together if it appeared that this would serve a useful purpose (FBI, Overseas Trade Committee, 22.9.53.) The Committee was not recalled on this matter.

As in the case of British labour organisations (below), the FBI did encounter questions raised by European integration in connection with their respective European organisation, the Council of European Industrial Federations (CEIF). The CEIF's report for the period 1950-1954 included a copy of the Treaty of the ECSC. The English version was described as unchecked, for it was noted that there was no authorised English translation of the Treaty available.

Apart from a note in the minutes of the Overseas Committee of the Association of British Chambers of Commerce to report that the Schuman Plan had been implemented in the form of the ECSC, the ABCC ignored the European developments during P2.

Thus European economic integration was deemed as irrelevant by these organisations representing British business, and accordingly no more can be said about their depiction of the anatomy of the issue.

TRADE UNIONS

The consideration by trade unions of the questions raised by the formation of the ECSC during this period was scanty, and where it did occur, was restricted to the issue of association with, rather than participation in, the ECSC. At the Trade Union Congresses of 1952 and 1953, the question was not raised. The only mention of the ECSC at the 1954 Congress was in a report of the Trade Union Committee of the ECSC which discussed the future of work within the Community. In the same year the TUC Economic Committee produced a paper following speculation that Britain might gain associate status with the ECSC. It outlined the

Government's main concerns: the protection of British industries, the ability to conduct national planning, and the attitudes of European trade unions. The paper recommended that the TUC be kept in touch with developments, but there was no attempt to formulate specific TUC policy on the matter.

It is clear from the National Union of Mineworkers' records that the ECSC became an object of routine scrutiny, given the obvious sectoral interest. Soon after the creation of the ECSC, it was suggested at the Coal Industry National Consultative Council (National Coal Board and relevant unions) that the NUM should be represented on the official delegation of British observers at Strasbourg. When the nomination of its delegates was announced, the NUM emphasised the need to see that the interests of both sides of the industry were safeguarded, though it was thought that their interests would be identical and that the two delegations would work in consultation (NUM, NEC, 9.9.52.)

Whilst delegates from both sides of the industry reported that British exports to the Six ECSC countries between 1948 and 1952 had increased by 70%, there was soon some disquiet concerning the effect of the new Community on the British industry. At the NUM's 1953 Annual Conference, a South Wales delegate proposed a motion 'to enable all countries to get a fair share of the coal market', observing that there was uncertainty about future British coal exports to the Six and as changes in European coal markets were undoubtedly taking place, a new approach to the export of British coal was required. Also, M.W.E. Jones, an NUM Vice President and delegate to the ECSC, stated that after five years the coal production of the ECSC was expected to rise by 30 million tons per year. He too was worried about the possibility of unfair competition as British miners were the only ones who worked a five day week, and enjoyed the highest pay and best conditions. Despite these worries there is no evidence that the possibility of ECSC membership was considered as a solution to this problem.

Throughout the period the NUM was able to send observers to Strasbourg and to special ECSC conferences, and this was probably responsible for the moderate salience the ECSC topic enjoyed within the union. This access to the ECSC though, had no marked effect on the union's policy position or depiction of the isse: membership of the Community was never seen as a possible policy alternative.

The Iron and Steel Trades Confederation also had a sectoral

interest in the work and progress of the ECSC, and was represented on the British delegation to Strasbourg in 1952. However, the subject of the ECSC did not trouble the Executive Council at all from then until a meeting in February 1954. At that meeting the General Secretary provided a report on the progress made by the Six. He concluded that nothing had transpired which would enable Britain to partipate as a direct partner in the ECSC, but he considered there was ample scope for consultation in respect of such matters as investment policy and prices. This view went unquestioned. (ISTC, Executive Council Meeting, 18.2.54.) The ISTC continued to send delegates to meetings of the Trade Union Committee of the ECSC, but the issue of full membership was never raised as one for consideration at a policy-making level.

The ISTC journal did run a leading article on the transformation of the Schuman Plan into the ECSC. It stated that there were good reasons for Britain remaining outside the Community, and repeated the objection to supranationality. The article did continue to express the hope that Britain might be able to cooperate and associate with the scheme (Man and Metal, Vol. XXIX, no.1, September 1952). However there were no further mentions of the ECSC in the journal throughout the rest of this period.

In summary, the idea of British membership of the ECSC did not appear to be posed as a viable policy option in British trade unions. Even those unions who operated in the coal and iron and steel sectors dealt with the ECSC only on a level of bureaucratic routines.

PROMOTIONAL GROUPS

The activity of promotional groups regarding the European issue during this period was extremely low. Indeed, for several years there was even a decline in the activity of the UK Council of the European Movement, which had previously constituted the most prominent of the groups campaigning for greater British involvement in European economic integration. As in P1, there existed no organisation whose aims were specifically to campaign against Britain playing a full role in the ECSC.

In early 1952, the European Movement published a pamphlet on the economic aspects of European integration. It began by outlining the main elements of the west European international economy, and concluded that international economy, and concluded that

> 'One must start by uniting and integrating Western Europe
> ... The figures show that Western Europe contains all the
> essential strength in the economic field. It is
> unnecessary to stress its work on behalf of civilisation
> generally ... The integration of Europe is not a utopian
> dream ... all responsible men and women are invited to
> devote their energy to the primary task which history
> requires of them: to remake Europe.' (European Movement,
> 1952, p.26.)

This was rather an isolated expression of enthusiasm. In
contrast, a luncheon put on by the Movement was addressed by
Lord Layton, (a founder member of the Council of the
European Movement), who suggested that the Movement's first
task was to urge whichever Government held power in Britain,
actively to support the Council of Europe. He made no
specific mention of the ECSC. However, some supporters of a
greater British role in Europe were indignant at the
Conservative Party's change of heart. The secretary of the
Federal Trust wrote to The Times shortly after the return to
power of the Conservatives, advocating the creation of a
supranational authority in Europe, and criticising Britain's
non entry into the ECSC. His major reason for holding these
views was that such an authority would provide a safeguard
for human rights (The Times, 29.12.51.)

No meetings of the European Movement took place between
March 1952 and July 1954, though one activist, Major Edward
Beddington Behrens, wrote a substantial letter to The Times
(2.3.53), referring to the fact that the Six were becoming
increasingly impressed with the idea of creating a single
market, and arguing that Britain had put forward no
constructive alternative, so she should not be surprised at
such a trend. He suggested that by adopting such a policy,
the Six would be free from GATT obligations and protected by
a tariff wall against British imports. Britain would be
tied and handicapped in a most important market of some 150
million people on our immediate doorstep. Beddington
Behrens argued that in the face of these facts, Britain
should lead Europe, or else she would run the risk of high
unemployment in some of her key exporting industries. It is
interesting to note that, later in the same year, letters to
The Times from two other prominent members of the European
Movement did not suggest the gravity of the situation
conveyed by Beddington Behrens, but gave emphasis to the
question of British association with the Six. It is
possible that these members considered this to be a

sufficient step for Britain to take. Alternatively, they may have concluded that this was the only realiseable goal in view of the weight of British opinion.

The European Movement did not awaken from its dormant state until July 1954. It is possible that in the intervening years all initiative had been sapped by the fierce division of the major political parties in Pl and the lack of interest shown in European economic collaboration by the new Government. The first meeting of the newly formed Movement was attended by representatives of the European League for Economic Cooperation, the Federal Union, the United European Movement and several members of the Parliamentary Labour Party. Beddington Behrens, who was elected the Chairman, stated that he thought European federalism was no longer a realistic goal, and that the opinions of the Movement should change accordingly. General discussion ensued on what the aims of the Movement should be, though this was rather inconclusive. It was however decided at the next meeting that the UK Council of the Movement should not be a 'policy lobbying body', but should attempt to present an all party point of view for Britain at the conferences of the European Movement. (European Movement, Council Minutes, 21.1.54.)

Thus the decline in stature of the issue noted from Pl to P2 even permeated the very organisation which set most store by a greater European role for Britain. In addition, the aims of the Movement appeared to shift during these years. Some of the sentiments expressed in Beddington Behrens' letter to The Times, notably the potential loss of an export market and the consequent impact upon employment, did not appear to impinge upon the issue's anatomy. However, the Movement's developing preference for association was more compatible with the overall anatomy, and thus less controversial. The conscious decision made to assume a predominantly educational role contrasts vividly with Churchill's delegation of 1947, which urged the Labour Cabinet to take a more positive approach to European economic cooperation.

As the salience and anatomy of the issue changed from Pl to P2 in such a way as to further militate against a greater British role in European economic integration, the activity and role of the Movement also changed. It is not suggested that a mechanistic relationship existed here. Rather, it appears that the Movement viewed their cause as a doomed or an inappropriate one, and were thus discouraged from assuming the role of a voice in the wilderness.

Press attention to the question of Britain's role in
European economic integration proved to be fairly
commensurate with the findings for salience and anatomy
within the content analysis. One possible exception to this
generalisation was that of The Times, which did attribute
greater importance to the European developments than its
competitors, even though British participation was not
proposed as a policy alternative.

There was virtually no coverage of the ECSC developments
among the popular dailies during the period after the 1951
General Election. Three leaders in The Times did address
the issue, adopting a view very similar to that held by the
Government. It was asserted that Britain would never be
able to join the ECSC as a member: the three pillars theory
of Britain's international policy – the USA, the
Commonwealth and Europe – was reiterated (The Times,
19.11.51). Ten days later, a leader asserted that Britain
had never led the Europeans to believe she would be any more
involved in European cooperation than at an inter-
governmental level, and that Europe would have to federate
without Britain (The Times, 29.11.51.) A third leader spelt
out that Britain could go no further than association and
the establishment of a permanent delegation to the high
authority. (The Times, 19.12.51.)

With these exceptions, it was defence issues which
dominated the European news and comment columns in the
ensuing years.

A leader in The Times in 1954 on the possibility of British
association with the ECSC expressed the need for any
agreement made to be consistent with Britain's development
in the world at large. When association was finally agreed,
it was seen as a political, symbolic move and not an
economic one as it provided only for consultation and
discussion: no undertakings were required of Britain
(The Times, 21.12.54.) Thus, The Times' perceptions of the
issue were fairly compatible with those which comprised the
overall anatomy of the issue. The European developments
were described as 'federal' and Britain's wider commitments,
notably to the Commonwealth, were found to be significant
objections to full participation.

The choice of other elite papers and the popular dailies
not to discuss the formation of the ECSC and the process of
the integration of the Six is possibly more significant than

the integration of the Six is possibly more significant than what one paper with a narrow readership (even though a significant proportion of those were close to the policy-making process) did say about it. The conclusion to be drawn is simply that the developments among the Six were not seen, by the journalists and editors, as relevant to the British political and economic system. In consequence, the readers who relied on any newspaper but The Times for news and comment may have been ignorant of the events in the ECSC. The readers of The Times were provided with a depiction of the ECSC which emphasised its inappropriateness for Britain.

PUBLIC OPINION

There is no evidence available of any public opinion polls taken during this period concerning attitudes towards either the ECSC or the proposed common market. This itself is considered indicative of an estimation on the part of the pollsters and those who commission opinion polls, that the question of British participation in the process of European economic integration was of little interest to the British public. This interpretation is certainly in line with the stature of the issue suggested by the content analysis. If those in a position to conduct or publish such polls did not do so for a particular issue, it is reasonable to conclude that they did not attach any importance to it.

DISCUSSION

The most dramatic contrast between the issue of European economic integration in P2 with that in P1, is its drop in salience. The Government showed little interest in the issue and thus made no attempt to introduce it to the House of Commons. Whilst in P1, the Opposition were instrumental in elevating the issue to a moderate level of salience (albeit short-lived), these circumstances were not repeated in P2. The Labour Party was content to concur with the Government's policy in this matter. This level of salience was probably related to the low level of partisanship evident in the content analysis of the relevant debate. The additional feature of the high proportion of neutral statements in connection with the low level of substantiation, suggests that the issue was not debated with passion or penetration. A British, rather than a party view seemed to prevail; one which deemed British participation

in the process of economic integration among the Six as an
irrelevant question. This attitude was underpinned by
Whitehall, business and trade union circles, press coverage,
and the absence of pressure group activity and public
opinion surveys. The only occasions when the issue was
raised in these circles, was within the context of British
Association with the ECSC - a substantively different
question - or by virtue of the maintenance of routine
bureaucratic relations with the Six.

What then, can account for the policy aspects of the issue
in P2, and the changes it had undergone since P1? The most
distinct feature here was the drop in the proportionate
status of the Political aspect, and an increase in that of
the Economic. It should be noted that the Political aspect
still accounted for more of the details than the Economic.
The European Political sphere continued to be of importance,
with special reference to the federal and supranational
implications of the ECSC. This European Political emphasis
matched that found among depictions of the issue outside
Parliament by Cabinet members, and by leading members of the
Labour Party.

However, other major organisations (e.g. FBI, TUC, NUM,
ISTC) who did refer to the ECSC in the course of their
business, did not allude to political themes. Thus the drop
in proportionate importance of the Political aspect in the
Parliamentary anatomy of the issue was matched by the
disappearance of references to this aspect among business
and trade union organisations whose professional interest in
the workings and impact of the ECSC tended to give emphasis
to economic matters. As noted, the Economic aspect enjoyed
greater status in P2 than in P1. It does not directly
follow from this that the change in the anatomy was solely a
product of the preferences of these organisations. The very
fact that the policy option of participating in the ECSC was
not advocated by either Government or Opposition meant that
the issue was not one of central political contention, and
economic implications thus enjoyed greater proportionate
status. In P1, the issue was politically contentious, in
the inter-party sense. Political perceptions of the Schuman
Plan (e.g. federal) and its implications for Britain (e.g.
loss of sovereignty) were easier objections for the
opponents of participation to wield than were economic
perceptions. The former were simply more potent in public
discourse, in Parliament and the press. Thus, advocates of
entry compounded this emphasis in P1 by attempting to refute
these perceptions. In P2, as the issue had no party
political currency, a somewhat more even balance of the

Political and Economic aspects prevailed, albeit of a very muted issue. Similarly, raising the theme of the Commonwealth in P1 (both within the Extra European Political and the Extra European Economic spheres), had proved to be an effective debating tactic on the part of opponents of British participation in the Schuman Plan, and this was reflected in the Parliamentary anatomy of the issue. However, in P2 the proportionate stature of details relating to the Commonwealth had dropped markedly. Again, it is probable that this was related to the absence of an overt threat of participation in the economic integration of the Six.

Once again the views on the issue of the Liberal Party stood apart from those which prevailed overall. It is well known that the Liberals have had little effect on the salience or outcome of most post-War issues. Comparison of the Parliamentary anatomy of the issue and perceptions of it by the Liberal Party shows that the latter also had no real impact upon the anatomy of the European question: the Liberals perceived it in a different way, and failed to impress this perception upon other groups or MPs. The contribution of British participation in the ECSC towards increased European stability and peace, and to economic security and prosperity for Britain were themes rarely considered outside the Liberal Party, either in P1 when the issue was one of contention between the two major parties, or in P2 when it was a more muted issue. Whereas in P1, due to the part played by the Conservative Party in Parliament, the issue achieved a measure of the salience attributed to it by the Liberals, this was not the case in P2. The Liberals were not only without a powerful ally in Parliament, but also the press ignored their view of the issue.

The European Movement did virtually nothing to advance the cause of European economic integration (other than the individual efforts of those writing to The Times), due largely to its own state of disorganisation and inertia. Even when the Movement was relaunched in 1954 its outlook on the issue was not radically different from that which prevailed overall. In contrast to earlier demands for a united and federal Europe, a move towards British membership of the ECSC was not advocated.

Thus in summary, the issue in P2 was muted due to the lack of a strategically placed group to espouse and promote it. As the issue was not one of contention between the two major parties, it was not dominated by party scoring. This position, out of the party political limelight, was instrumental in the reduction in the status of the Political aspect of the issue overall in P2. The routine relationship of information exchange and later Association with the ECSC, and the withdrawal of the possibility of full British membership, also contributed to the reduction in the standing of the Political aspect. The depictions of the issue by the Liberal Party and a handful of other backbench MPs who did advocate British ECSC membership did not figure significantly in the Parliamentary anatomy of the issue.

6 P3: Britain and the formation of the EEC

This period begins after the House of Commons approval of the Treaty granting Britain Associate membership of the ECSC in February 1955. The first important development of P3 was the Messina Conference at which the ECSC members discussed ways of achieving a greater degree of economic integration. (Britain was invited to send a Minister to this conference but declined). The Spaak Committee (to which Britain did send an observer) was established in the wake of the Messina Conference, and it drew up the guidelines for the establishment of the EEC, as embodied in the Treaty of Rome, 1957. At the same time, Britain was making considerable efforts to create a broader and more loosely organised west European trading system; the free trade area, but this initiative failed in 1958, and EFTA was formed by seven non EEC countries in the following year. This provided for the reduction of tariffs on certain industrial goods moving among member countries. EFTA differed from the EEC in that it did not possess its own institutions, and had no intentions of economic integration.

No content analysis was conducted on Parliamentary debate of the European question in this period, as it only occupied thirteen Hansard columns. These occurred in an adjournment debate moved by Geoffrey Rippon, MP, a Conservative backbencher, on the 5th of July 1956. Content analysis of such a small amount of debate would clearly not produce reliable indicators of the anatomy of the issue.

In the debate on a motion put by another Conservative
backbencher, Julian Ridsdale, urging the 'need for a close
association of (the EEC) with other countries who are
members of the OEEC', the emphasis was entirely on the
nature of economic cooperation within the OEEC, rather than
on Britain's possible participation in the EEC. (Hansard,
Vol. 585, Col. 711, 28.3.58).

Whilst it is not possible to make any comment as the
issue's anatomy in P3, one point stands out clearly, that
the issue was of extremely low salience. This is further
illustrated by the comment by John Edwards MP (Labour) that,
even in November 1956, he was unable to obtain an English
translation of the Messina Resolution in which the ECSC
countries stated their intention of achieving further
economic integration. (Hansard, Vol. 561, Col. 146,
26.11.56.)

The purpose of the rest of this chapter is to account for
this extremely low level of salience. Whilst no
Parliamentary findings for anatomy are available, the
various depictions of the issue by interested parties will
be analysed where possible, as these may throw light on the
issue's low level of salience.

THE CONSERVATIVE GOVERNMENT

The aims of the Conservative Government during this period
clearly did not include full British participation in
European economic integration. The accession of Eden to the
premiership on Churchill's retirement in April 1955 did not
precipitate any broad policy change. The attitude of the
Government leadership to the Messina talks was well
illustrated by Britain's delegate, Robert Bretherton from
the Board of Trade:

    'I don't think the Cabinet took much notice of it (the
    Messina Conference) altogether.' (Charlton, 9.3.81.)

The Government did produce a White Paper in July 1955
following the Messina Resolution, but this only consisted of
the correspondence between European representatives and
Harold Macmillan (Secretary of State for Foreign Affairs).
An official invitation was made for Britain to take part in
the Spaak Committee. Macmillan gave his reply on the very
next day, indicating that Her Majesty's Government

    'will be happy to examine without prior commitments and

on their merits, the many problems which are likely to emerge from the studies, and in doing so, will be guided by the hope of reaching solutions which are in the best interests of all parties concerned'. (Cmnd. 9525, Western Europe, 1955.)

This was ironic because the Government's examination was certainly cursory and based on 'prior commitments', viz. the maintenance of broad policy preferences incompatible with the objectives inherent in the proposals of the Six. The Government continued to give the issue a low profile by failing to send a senior Minister to the Messina conference. It is further indicative of the British attitude that the civil servant who was selected to attend the conference was from the Board of Trade, and not from the Foreign Office or even the Treasury. The British Government was emphatic that he was a 'representative' and not a 'delegate', due to Britain's 'non commitment' to the Messina Resolution. Thus he had no mandate from the British Government to pursue a particular predetermined policy. Although Bretherton was later joined by a Foreign Office official, John Coulson, British participation in the Committee's proceedings was minimal. Spaak tellingly described Bretherton as 'discret et sceptique'. (Mowatt, 1973, p.133.) A final indication of the importance attached by the Conservative leadership to the issue, is that European economic integration was not mentioned in the 1955 Conservative Party General Election manifesto.

Turning to the depiction of the anatomy by the Government, Macmillan recalled that the invitation to take part in the Messina Conference was fully discussed in Cabinet, who were agreed in not wanting to see the OEEC duplicated and in being unwilling to make prior commitment to the principles of Messina, (Macmillan, 1971, p.68), confirmed in his correspondence with M. Bloch (above). It would surely be surprising if the British Government really perceived the plans of the Six to duplicate the OEEC, as the latter was expressly opposed to any measure of supranationality, integration of economies, or common external tariffs. The Government was making a statement of preference, couched in terms of loyalty to an existing organisation, thus diverting attention from the real questions posed. Macmillan went on to mention that there were "special difficulties for this country in any proposal for a European Common Market." These were not outlined in the correspondence, nor aired domestically.

Bretherton's main contribution to the work of the Spaak

Committee was to outline Britain's apprehensions both about the Messina Resolution and the imminent measures of further economic integration in western Europe, regarding her Commonwealth commitments and preference for an OEEC type framework for economic dialogue and cooperation. Subsequently, no further British representation was invited to meetings of the Spaak Committee. The British Government appeared to have been slow to appreciate the significance of the Messina Resolution and unprepared for the consequent developments towards the EEC. It is arguable that this was in some measure due to its non-involvement in the ECSC, and lack of experience in its operation and achievements. It remains difficult to avoid the conclusion that the Government was simply not interested in any departure either from the traditional mode of inter-governmental cooperation or from the Conservative anti-planning ethos. It was therefore both simple and politic to depict the 'Monnet approach' as inapplicable and undesirable for Britain.

During the period of the free trade area talks the British Government did express some willingness to use the Treaty of Rome as a 'guideline in some instances'. Such attempts at compromise were to no avail as the concomitant British proposals continued specifically to omit agriculture, harmonisation of social and economic policies, and common external tariffs.

Given this predisposition, how did the Government leadership handle the issue in Parliament and in the Conservative Party? The Government did not introduce discussion of the Messina proposals to Parliament and it was left to Robert Boothby to raise the Common Market proposals in the House of Commons in June 1956, asking Harold Macmillan (now Chancellor of the Exchequer), whether he would join the negotiations entered into by the Six, given the reciprocal benefits of participation. Macmillan replied that the Government was giving the matter the most careful consideration, adding that it was a difficult question and that the Commonwealth countries would be given a chance to express their views. (Hansard, Vol.555, Col.1667, 5.7.56.)

In the adjournment debate alluded to above, Geoffrey Rippon raised the question of the Messina talks a year earlier, and that he was still unsure as to what Britain's response had been, and if she had ceased full participation at the talks. He stated with obvious indignation that over a year ago the Government must have formed some view on the general principle, and asked when the House would hear a statement on this vitally important matter. Rippon concluded by

144

warning of the danger of Britain becoming economically isolated from the rest of Europe. Robert Boothby and John Biggs Davison (both Conservative backbenchers) also made remarks advocating a more positive attitude towards Europe.

Sir Edward Boyle (Economic Secretary to the Treasury), commented somewhat evasively that he could not make a Government policy statement on such a major matter but stated that whilst the Government had withdrawn its observer at the talks, it had maintained close contact with the proceedings through the OEEC. Boyle also mentioned Britain's world wide trade commitments and the possibility that the Common Market talks might yet fail. He stated that

'There is no question at all of the Government having closed their mind on the subject. I am not putting up, as it were, a smoke screen to conceal the fact that the Government have made up their mind in a negative direction ... we do not want to associate ourselves too closely at this stage and then to be open later to a charge of bad faith. We must, first, make the basic political decision ... I know that I am absolutely safe in saying that there is no subject which will more attract the attention of the Government during the months ahead than this. We fully realise that there is a major policy decision to be made here. We are completely open-minded and will be guided solely by what we conceive to be the proper harmony of the interests of the Commonwealth, the interests of Europe and of the free world as a whole.' (<u>Hansard</u>, Vol. 555, Col. 679, 5.7.56.)

Commenting upon these remarks, Miriam Camps observed that

'Although Sir Edward Boyle's statement might be read to imply that consideration was being given not only to links between the United Kingdom and the Six, but to British participation in the Common Market, it seems clear enough from other statements that the British did not, at this early stage, seriously consider the major break with past traditions that participation in a full customs union would have implied. Rather, it appears that they were then considering either full membership in a 'common market' based on a free trade area and excluding agriculture, if, in the end, the Six failed in the attempt to form their own common market and were prepared to go ahead with the British on this basis; or, if the Six succeeded, as by this time seemed more probable, a free trade area link between themselves and

145

the customs unions of the Six.' (Camps, 1964, p.96.)

A debate did take place in the House of Commons during November 1956 on Britain's European trade policy. This was mainly concerned with ideas consitent with the free trade area proposals, though in his opening remarks, Macmillan (Chancellor of the Exchequer), did allude to the development among the Six:

'If the UK were to join such a Customs Union, the UK tariff would be swept aside and would be replaced by this single tariff. Judged only by the most limited UK interests, such an arrangement would be wholly disadvantageous. We could not expect the countries of the Commonwealth to give preferential treatment to our exports to them, if we had to charge them full duty on their exports to us. Apart from that, our interests and responsibilities are much wider ... So this objection, even if there were no other, would be quite fatal to any proposal that the UK should seek to take part in a European Common Market by joining a Customs Union.' (Hansard, Vol. 561, Col. 35, 26.11.56.)

The issue did not receive much attention at Conservative Party Conferences. In 1955, Eden, in his leader's closing address, gave rather distant support for growing western unity - presumably a reference to the Messina developments - but he gave major attention to the American and Commonwealth spheres of British foreign policy. At the 1956 Conference the Colonial Secretary, A. Lennox-Boyd, asserted that

'Some European countries are seriously considering a Customs Union. We can do three things: remain outside, losing rich makrkets and sources of investment; go in, in which case we would lose our imperial preference system; or we can have some association with it which would give us the best of both worlds. (Conservative Party Conference Report, 1956, p.44).

There was no other mention of European economic integration, and the main foreign policy motion (other than that on Suez) debated and unanimously passed at this Conference left little doubt as to the main international concern of the Party:

'This Conference welcomes the substantial progress made in (the) granting of new constitutions to the Colonial Territories and pledges its fullest support to the continuation of this policy, believing that the

146

increasing volume of inter-imperial trade resulting from an expanding Commonwealth, will assist in solving its economic difficulties. (Conservative Party Conference Report, 1956, p.37.)

The 1957 Conference included a debate on the proposed free trade area in Europe, but no mention was made of the possibility of EEC membership, and emphasis was upon whether more attempt could be made to stimulate Commonwealth trade. The main foreign policy debate at the 1958 Conference was on the challenge of communism and the part to be played by the Anglo-American partnership and the Commonwealth in combating this threat: the possibility of British membership of the EEC as a means to this end was not raised.

Thus during P3, the depiction of the issue by the Cabinet, that British participation in European economic integration was really irrelevant to Britain's needs and commitments, also prevailed in Parliament and within the Conservative Party. The isolated challenges to this view, notably by Boothby and Rippon, were ineffective and not subsequently pressed.

WHITEHALL

The evidence available suggests that Whitehall's perception of developments among the Six as irrelevant for Britain, which had been evident in P2 persisted into P3. This view is confirmed by the report of a French official phoning London to invite a British minister to attend the Messina talks, being told by his British counterpart that

'Messina was really a devilishly awkward place to expect a minister to go.' (Beloff, 1963, p.71.)

Bretherton, the British representative at the talks, recalled that he did not appreciate the political dimensions of the proposals until he arrived at the Conference, which suggests that he had been inadequately briefed, and that Whitehall was out of touch - presumably due to a general antipathy towards the European developments.

R.A. Butler (who had replaced Macmillan as Chancellor of the Exchequer in 1957), whilst admitting that the Government didn't take the Messina talks very seriously, added that he was never advised by anyone to do anything else: this included the Foreign Office and the Treasury. Such a view was confirmed by Lieber:

'most officials held the view that this was merely another elaborate paper scheme of the Continentals, and nearly certain to fail.'

He added in a footnote that

'This skepticism, often privately expressed in earthy language was widespread among civil servants and others who dealt with European matters.' (Lieber, 1970, p.25.)

The low value placed upon the European question by ministers owes something at least, to the attitudes among their senior advisers. It is likely that Whitehall opinions towards the activities of the Six, which had emerged in response to the Paris Conference, and the Schuman Plan, were so firmly established as to be unchallenged during the mid to late 1950s. European economic integration was considered irrelevant to Britain's role and her needs.

As the negotiations for the free trade area, and later for EFTA developed, various Whitehall departments became deeply involved, either in direct negotiation with European governments or with British sectional interests, notably the FBI, the TUC and the NFU over likely acceptable terms of agreement. The option of EEC membership was dwarfed by these other European activities.

THE LABOUR PARTY

As in P2, the Labour Party did not oppose the Conservative Government's policy on European economic integration. The only significant criticism of the free trade area initiative was that the Government had not produced a White Paper on the subject in advance of the debate as had been intended: not a serious objection as the issue was not at a legislative stage. The main contributions of Labour members to the Commons debate on the Government's free trade initiative, concerned Commonwealth trade, protection of British agriculture, the maintenance of full employment and the balance of payments prospects. No preference was expressed for participation in the Six's drive for a common market, and no Parliamentary division was forced.

The issue did not enjoy great stature within Party debate either. It was not aired at the 1955 Conference though it was reported in 1956 that the Party had been invited to send a delegate to the Conference of the European Socialist parties on the problems of the ECSC, and the relaunching of Europe. L.J. Edwards, MP, was sent and his report was considered by the Party's subcommittee on European Cooperation. There was no attention to the Messina developments or the Treaty of Rome, and discussion was almost entirely confined to the Euratom proposals.

References to contemporary European developments in further Conferences were cursory. In 1957, during her Chairman's address, Miss Margaret Herbison, MP, mentioned the Government's free trade area initiative, to which the Labour Party was giving cautious welcome

'for the risks of staying completely outside, are greater than those of going in.' (Labour Party Conference Report, 1957, p.73.)

There was no mention however of the policy alternative of seeking EEC membership. Thus the issue became neither one of contention within the Party, nor one used by the Party as a means of attacking the Government.

THE LIBERAL PARTY

The Liberal Party, as in P2, differed from other organisations in the British political system in their attitudes towards European economic integration. After the Messina Conference and while the Spaak Committee was sitting, the 1956 Liberal Party Assembly stated that

'the economic integration of Western Europe and particularly the establishment of a common market, should receive the active participation of Britain as essential both to the peaceful future of Europe, and the economic prosperity of our own country.' (Liberal Party, undated, p.4.)

The theme noted earlier of the contribution that a British role in European economic integration would make to her own economic prosperity, coupled with European peace: a portrayal of the nascent EEC not widely held in British politics. Even for the Liberal Party however, the Commonwealth remained an important sphere and was coupled with the European dimension in a resolution of the Liberal Council which looked forward to 'better political and economic integration of European and Commonwealth institutions.' Unlike the leadership of the Conservative and Labour Parties, the Council of the Liberal Party formally acknowledged the work of the Spaak Committee:

> 'the Liberal Party Council warmly welcomes the initiative
> of the six Messina powers in formulating proposals for
> the economic integration of Europe and the decision of HM
> Government to be associated with the Common Market by
> participating in the projected Free Trade Area.
> Recalling the Liberal Party's consistent advocacy of a
> closer political union in Europe, the Council declares
> that the implementation of these plans would be a
> significant advance towards a united Europe..' (Liberal
> Party, undated, p.4.)

Thus the Government's approach of subsuming the question of
EEC membership under the issue of the free trade area, was
temporarily duplicated by the Liberal Party view on the
matter, as was also evident at the 1957 Assembly, which
called upon the Government to take a positive lead in the
negotiations of the free trade area, but said nothing of
membership of the EEC.

In Parliament, the Liberal Party made little impact on the
standing of the issue. At the time of the Common Market
negotiations, Arthur Holt MP asked the Chancellor of the
Exchequer to make a statement on the Government's position
regarding the Common Market, adding that the Government had
had plenty of time to consider the question, and that he
considered it disastrous for Europe to move ahead leaving
Britain isolated. He reiterated this theme, arguing that
small economic entities had little future, whilst at the
same time there was a need for a united Europe to play a
large part in the world (Hansard, Vol.555, Col. 1682,
5.7.56.) Both these sentiments achieved little standing in
wider debate of the European question.

During the period of the formation of the EEC, the Liberal
Party differed in its depiction of the importance and the
nature of the European issue from other British political
actors. Its position did change in the later years of P3,
when it adopted the viewpoint which prevailed in most other
quarters of the British political system, of the
desirability of a European free trade area. Thus the policy
option of EEC membership was dropped even by the Liberals
towards the end of this period.

BUSINESS AND TRADE UNIONS

During P3, whilst British business organisations did become

centrally involved in the negotiations towards the free trade area and EFTA, there was virtually no consideration at all of EEC membership. In October 1956, the ABCC Overseas Committee (3.10.56) received a letter from the President of the Board of Trade, which asked for views on the form of possible 'association' with the European Common Market. However, the Committee discussed the matter on the general basis of a common free trade area, rather than considering membership of the Common Market per se. Turning to the FBI, there was no specific attention to the question of British membership of the emerging EEC. As outlined in Chapter 2, the FBI, in conjunction with other non EEC west European industrial federations, was instrumental in launching EFTA.

This was also the case for British trade unions. Those unions which in P2 had established routine relations with the ECSC maintained these. The TUC, whilst also involved in discussions with the Government (notably through the Board of Trade) on the free trade area and EFTA proposals, did not appear to address the question of participation within the EEC either at General Council or Congress level.

PROMOTIONAL GROUPS

It was noted that during P2, the European Movement (UK Council) went through a period of little formal activity, but that towards the end of the period, the organisation was reconstituted, if with rather different aims. These were generally less favourable to the activities of the Six than had been the case in P2, and more supportive of the policy of the British Government. Such a state of affairs persisted in P3.

The Movement did hold a series of meetings in the form of brains trusts during 1955 and 1956 though these met with a fluctuating response: more successful in London than in the provinces. The Council adopted a non-committal stance on the Messina Plan, and no campaigning activity was embarked upon, as was the case in the late 1940s. The minutes indicate that the Movement did provide a small education function by organising meetings on the subject of the Messina Conference in the House of Commons and the House of Lords (though there is no indication as to how these went.) In summary, the Movement and its constituent organisations engaged in no effort to campaign for any position at variance with Government policy, and supported the free trade area and EFTA initiatives. In common with P1 and P2, no organisation was formed to oppose British participation

in the EEC, suggesting that the question of British EEC
membership was not considered a likely alternative by those
who might otherwise have organised and campaigned against
it, as they did in P4.

THE PRESS

The developments which led to the formation of the Common
Market did not figure very highly in the British press. The
Daily Telegraph (22.6.55) reported in an editorial on the
call from Beyen for further European integration; however
it also reminded its readers that Britain's role was one of
'permanent mediator, guardian and counsellor for the Western
European Union.' Presumably this was to be taken to mean
that Britain was not to become fully enmeshed into the
activities pursued by the Six. In any event, the issue did
not recur in the Daily Telegraph during 1955. The paper was
preoccupied with the issues of German unification, Suez,
Burgess and Maclean, and Cyprus. The Daily Express and the
Daily Herald gave no space whatsoever to the events
preceding further economic integration among the ECSC
countries during the summer of 1955.

A front page article in the Daily Telegraph (14.3.56)
entitled 'Six Nation Atom and Tariff Pool Planned'. The
discussion which followed gave no mention of a British angle
on the proposals. The emphases of the Daily Telegraph
during this period had been upon the Middle East, Cyprus,
East/West relations and the imminent marriage of Grace
Kelly. Another editorial on the proposed further
integration of the Six gave greater emphasis to Euratom and
considered that Britain could afford to be non-committal on
economic union, though the implications of Euratom may
require a future change of British attitudes. On the same
day that a front page article appeared reporting the
'Franco-German Plea to Britain' to play a more active role
in the building up of Europe, more space was devoted to the
problems encountered in landing the plane carrying M. Monnet
on a ministerial visit to Britain to discuss this very plea!
(Daily Telegraph, 1.10.56.) Towards the end of the year,
considerably greater coverage was given to the British
proposals for a European free trade area than had been
accorded to the proceedings on the continent. The news that
the Common Market and Euratom treaties were to be signed
appeared in a two column inch report in one of the back
pages of the Daily Telegraph (10.12.56.) It did not feature
at all in the pages of the Daily Express and the
Daily Herald.

Once again, The Times did differ somewhat in the coverage given to European economic integration. An editorial of June 1956 made clear the importance of the proposed treaties among the Six, both for Europe generally and Britain in particular, and reported that although many in Britain thought the project would founder, and there were others who hoped it might, there was a growing volume of opinion who thought otherwise. This was not elaborated upon. It was added that whilst many established interests would be shaken by the cold wind of competition, there were attractions of a wider free trade area in which Britain might participate (The Times, 22.6.56.)

This survey of the treatment given by the mainstream British press to the European economic developments suggests, as in P2, a considerable degree of cohesion of views with the findings of the overall anatomy of the issue. Popular dailies, and to a lesser extent the 'more serious press', assigned the issue a very low news status. Where the subject did occur it was implicitly assumed that it had little relevance for Britain. A degree of ethnocentricity was revealed in the sudden attention given to the more general question of a free trade area following the British proposals on the subject. The suggestion in an editorial of The Times that there was growing opinion favouring British participation in talks for the formation of a common market, is not however validated by our other findings.

PUBLIC OPINION

The absence of political controversy over, and press coverage of, this issue would suggest that in P3 the public would have been generally ignorant of its implications. Such a view is confirmed by Robert Matthew MP, who complained that

'In spite of your important leading articles on the subject, remarkably little public interest in the country at large has been focussed on the vital question of the establishment of a common market in western Europe, at present under discussion.' (The Times, 13.7.56.)

The one public opinion poll finding during this period suggested not only that the majority of respondents had never heard of the EEC, but a large proportion of those who had, believed that Britain was a member.

DISCUSSION

The findings of the virtual absence of Parliamentary debate
on the issue of European economic integration in P3 was
closely matched by low levels of attention paid to it by
other strategically placed organisations and groups in the
political system. This is in marked contrast to the
salience which the issue achieved in the countries of the
Six. Whilst the events among the participating countries
were certainly far reaching, there was no communication of
this to the British political system. None of the
organisations capable of raising the salience of the issue
were interested in doing so.

The Conservative Government and Whitehall were agreed as to
the main objectives of British European policy, which
consisted of trying to avoid a division of western Europe
and the promotion of the free trade area ideas, with certain
safeguards for British agriculture and Commonwealth
products. Membership of the EEC was assumed to be out of
the question. The efforts of Boothby and Rippon to question
Government policy did not turn into campaigns. The Labour
Party leadership had no interest in adopting the European
issue, and again there was no group within the Party who did
so. The respective business and labour organisations,
whilst maintaining routine contacts with the ECSC, the EEC,
and their individual counterparts in the countries of the
Six, showed no inclination to give consideration to the
possibility of British membership of the EEC. For the most
part the British press ignored not only the question of
British EEC membership, but even the practical developments
among the Six towards economic integration. Thus the
salience attributed to the issue by these groups was low.
As far as it was depicted, the issue was characterised as
irrelevant for Britain.

The Liberal Party and the European Movement were both
observed in P2, to attribute the issue with a higher status
than any other groups discussed above. In P3, the Liberal
Party was incapable of promoting the issue effectively, and
the European Movement incapable, and possibly unwilling, to
do so. Indeed both organisations chose to support the
Government's free trade area and EFTA policies and set aside
their previously preferred option of participation within
the integration of the Six.

These factors all combined to render the European question
a muted issue during P3.

7 P4: The EEC arrives in British politics

It will be recalled that the European question in P4 differed markedly in terms of its Parliamentary salience and anatomy from the findings noted in Pl and P2. With regard to the issue's overall Parliamentary salience, it attracted a substantially greater amount of attention, accounting for almost 1.5% of all statements made in the House of Commons debate; twice the proportionate significance of the issue during Pl, and over twenty times that in P2.

Turning to the issue's anatomy, in common with P2, there was a very high proportion of neutral statements in P4, but in contrast to P2, the statements for exceeded those against. A significantly higher level of substantiation of statments occurred in P4 than in Pl or P2. Considerable differences were also noted for aspect and geographical focus when P4 was contrasted with Pl and P2. For the first time the Economic aspect exceeded the Political, accounting for almost half of all statements made. Though the Political aspect also exceeded the 40% mark it achieved its lowest standing throughout in this period. P4 was also the only period when the European focus did not dominate: it was exceeded in this instance by the Extra European. However, in this period there was a much more even distribution of points of detail among the three focuses, with less than 8% dividing the British and Extra European focuses. A summary of aspect and focus in P4 is provided in figure 8.

Within the most significant aspect, the Economic, the Extra European focus attracted the most attention: Commonwealth considerations far outweighed all others. Over 60% of the details falling within this category were concerned with the specific commercial features of individual countries, and more than half of these were related to Australia, Canada and New Zealand. Other prominent themes were the trading obligations owed by Britain to the Commonwealth, and the six of the export markets enjoyed by Britain in these countries.

The European Economic sphere consisted largely of varying views of the overall economic experience of the Six, particularly regarding the nature of the benefits derived from their economic collaboration; the export markets available, the operation of free trade, and economic planning in the EEC. Details related to the more specific topic of agriculture exceeded all of these comparatively broad subjects. The proposed common agricultural policy, budget contributions, the efficiency of French farming and the agricultural terms of membership, were all notable subjects of Parliamentary discussion. In addition, there were a number of references to the economic implications for the relationship of Britain and the Six to EFTA.

The British Economic sphere was similarly largely occupied by the question of agriculture, though in this case, more specifically with the effects of entry upon the British agricultural support system. Other features of this sphere were the implications for Britain's balance of payments and the extent to which Britain could survive and prosper alone.

In the case of the Political aspect during this period, Extra European matters were again of great significance, accounting for 42% of the details, followed by European 38% and British 19%. About 40% of the Extra European details were taken up with Commonwealth concerns; Britain's Commonwealth role and the views of the Commonwealth countries on the question. In addition, questions of a more general nature were discussed, particularly related to the principles of federation and sovereignty. Views of Britain's world role accounted for just over 10% of this sphere.

The European focus gave more specific attention to the implications of membership regarding the operation of a

FIGURE 8

SUMMARY OF ASPECT AND FOCUS P4

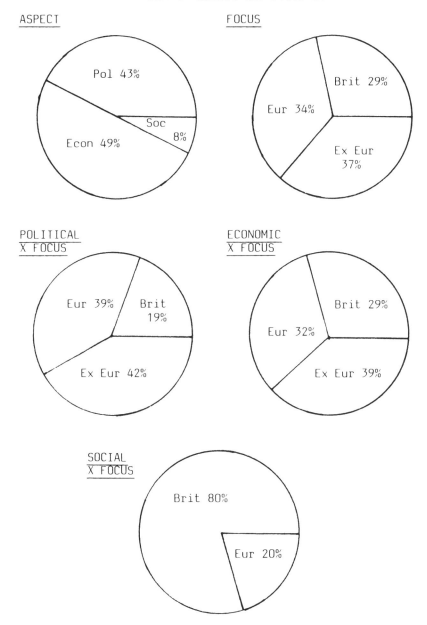

ASPECT

Pol 43%

Soc 8%

Econ 49%

FOCUS

Brit 29%

Eur 34%

Ex Eur 37%

POLITICAL X FOCUS

Eur 39%

Brit 19%

Ex Eur 42%

ECONOMIC X FOCUS

Brit 29%

Eur 32%

Ex Eur 39%

SOCIAL X FOCUS

Brit 80%

Eur 20%

supranational authority. Views were also expressed on the long-term prospects for European political integration. As noted, the British focus accounted for under 20% of the Political aspect. Here specific attention was given to British sovereignty and Britain's traditional role of isolation from restrictive European developments.

The Social aspect was once again proportionately small, accounting for only 8% of the total points of detail. However, in this period the number of relevant references is sufficiently large to enable further analysis. The points of detail were almost exclusively within the British focus, on the subjects of food prices, wages and living standards and the effects of entry upon employment prospects in Britain.

Finally, despite the prominence which the issue achieved, in P4, the level of party scoring was small, particularly compared to P1. It accounted for about 7% of the total number of details. As one might expect, given that the negotiations directly involved Britain in this period, the component of the state and nature of the negotiations was of increased prominence, embracing 14.9% of all points of detail, compared to 9.1% and 7.9% in P1 and P2 respectively.

Certain significant changes in the anatomy of the issue were also evident within P4. Three sub periods have been distinguished. P4a lasted from the beginning of 1961 until the announcement of Macmillan of the Government's intention to explore the possibilities of EEC membership in July 1961. P4b lasted from that announcement until August 1962, from which point the Government, according to Lieber, attempted to further politicise the question of Britain's application for EEC membership. P4c lasted from then until the breakdown of talks in January 1963. In each sub period there was sufficient debate by the House of Commons (around 280 Hansard columns for each of these) to enable extensive analysis.

The most notable feature in contrasting these sub periods is the demise of the Political aspect from P4a to P4c, and the corresponding rise of the Economic aspect (figure 9). There was little in the way of significant shifts in overall focus, with the British consistently achieving the lowest stature (figure 10). Within the Economic aspect there was a particularly pronounced shift in the status of the Extra European focus, from 31% in P4a to 43% in P4b and P4c respectively. This was primarily composed of an increase in attention on economic implications of British EEC membership

FIGURE 9

POLICY ASPECT P4a - P4c

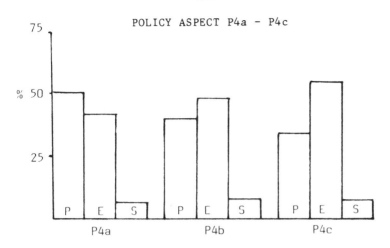

FIGURE 10

GEOGRAPHICAL FOCUS P4a - P4c

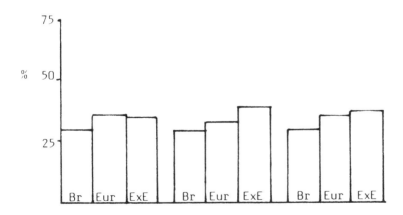

for various Commonwealth countries. Also there was a clear decline in the status of the British Economic sphere from a 36% of the details in P4a to 27% and 25% in P4b and P4c. This decline of emphasis on Britain was however compensated for in the Political aspect in which the British focus rose from a 20% standing in P4a and P4b to 28% in P4c. Here there was greater emphasis upon the theme of Parliamentary sovereignty. The remaining spheres appeared fairly stable from P4a to P4c.

Three other trends should be pointed out. First, although party scoring for the whole of P4 was seen to be low in comparison with P1, it did increase from 5.2% and 4.0% in P4a and P4b to 8% in P4c. Also the proportion of details devoted to the state and nature of the negotiations rose from 14.2% and 13.2% in P4a and P4b to 18% in P4c. Finally there was a marked trend of an increase in neutral statements from P4a (51%) to P4b (59%) and P4c (73%) indicating a greater reluctance to be committed either for or against the policy option.

In analysing the views and activities of those outside Parliament during P4, attention will be given to answering questions on two levels. First and most importantly, an attempt will be made to explain the overall Parliamentary salience and anatomy of the issue noted in P4, particularly when contrasted with those of P1 and P2. In addition analysis will aim to throw light on the differences which emerged among the three sub-periods P4a, P4b and P4c.

It has become clear that the stature and anatomy of the issue in P4 differed dramatically from that in P1, P2 and P3 (stature only). Why was it that Parliament devoted so much attention to this question in P4? Further, given this increase in salience, it would seem strange that there should be a comparatively low level of party scoring and that such a high proportion of statements should be neutral. Can these features be explained? Why also was there a discernible increase in the proportion of statements substantiated?

The rise in the proportion of the Economic aspect from P1 to P4 at the expense of the Political has been pointed out, but what gave rise to this change? Equally, whilst there was an increase in the Economic aspect, the British focus within this was markedly smaller in P4 than in P1 and P2. The emphasis which Commonwealth and agricultural considerations received, especially in contrast to other economic arguments is worthy of further scrutiny: no other subject received nearly as much attention as either of these matters. Having said that, there was generally a more even spread of details among the aspects than in P1 which was so heavily dominated by Political considerations. In examining the sub periods of P4, it became clear that differences, often substantial, existed among them. What accounts for the trend of a steady increase in neutral statements from P4a to P4c, and a particular drop in those against? Equally, what explains the trends of the decreasing status of the Political aspect and the increasing status of the Economic aspect? Alongside this overall trend it should be noted that within the Economic aspect there was a considerable fall in the stature of the British focus, matched mainly by an increase in the Extra European. This indeed was the case overall, and both of these trends will be considered in analysis of wider views and activities. In addition, the rise from P4a to P4c of the party scoring component warrants examination.

THE CONSERVATIVE GOVERNMENT

An analysis of the contribution of the Government ministers towards the stature and anatomy of the issue in P4 would not be complete without some account of the events which foreshadowed the announcement by Macmillan in July 1961 of the Government's intention to explore the possibilities of EEC membership.

As outlined in Chapter 2, the Conservative Government had reconsidered its policy of remaining outside the trend towards European economic unification. Its attempts to establish a Free Trade Area had floundered, and the creation of the European Free Trade Association threatened to divide the Six from the Seven more permanently. However, in the early years of the new decade a remarkable shift took place, some would even say a reversal, of opinion within the Conservative Government towards Europe. In addition this change corresponded with similarly profound policy reappraisals among other groups in the political system.

The extent to which the EEC was intended by some to become a vital plank of Conservative policy was captured by a senior Conservative Party official who reflected that

'Europe was to be our deus ex machina; it was to create a new contemporary argument with insular Socialism; dish the Liberals by stealing their clothes; give us something new after 12-13 years; act as a catalyst of modernisation; give us a new place in the international sun. It was Macmillan's ace, and de Gaulle trumped it.' (quoted in Butler and King, 1965, p.79.)

It should be borne in mind, in examining Conservative views towards the EEC, that the change noted in the mainstream Tory thinking did not occur in a vacuum. Rather, the role played by Macmillan must be recognised as of crucial importance. He displayed an astonishing degree of control over Cabinet and Party thinking on the subject, by virtue of a rather subtle style of leadership. It is likely that had any attempt been made at the outset to provoke a decision of principle within either the Cabinet or Party regarding the EEC as a policy option, it would have been doomed to failure.

Whilst the 1959 Conservative General Election Manifesto made no mention of the European sphere, after their victory, Sir Michael Fraser,

'Macmillan's confidant and the liaison-man between the Conservative Party (who paid him) and the Government ... began thinking that it would be to the Party's advantage to shift public attention before the next elections, toward the fresher and more progressive cause of union with Europe.' (Beloff, 1973, p. 172).

However, Macmillan did not establish a political crusade on the matter, aware that a public failure to persuade his Government and Party to adopt his views, would seriously undermine his position as leader. It was likely that he would inject more principled ingredients into the debate when success was assured, and electoral currency thereby to be gained. The reasons for Macmillan's somewhat tentative approach is perhaps best summarised by himself. He recalled that

'I was under some apprehension that the Conservative Party would be deeply split by the decision that we should enter into negotiations with the six European countries.' (Macmillan, 1973, p.31.)

The Cabinet reshuffle of July 1960 brought some of the most European minded members of the Government into relevant posts. Duncan Sandys became Minister of Commonwealth Relations, and Christopher Soames the Minister of Agriculture, Fisheries and Food. These appointments were presumably made in an attempt to dispel opposition to EEC entry in two likely sensitive areas. In addition, Edward

Heath was moved from the Ministry of Labour to the post of Lord Privy Seal to act as Foreign Office spokesman in the House of Commons and Britain's chief European negotiator. Macmillan's skill in deploying his troops was further illustrated when in due course he appointed Rab Butler - a potential critic of the emerging EEC policy - as head of the ministerial committee responsible for the opening negotiations.

Macmillan's shrewdness in re-arranging his ministers was symptomatic of his ability to dominate the Cabinet. Siedentop (1970) argued that Macmillan had a strong preference for oblique policies, and this was certainly evident in the present case, as he delayed presenting the question of EEC membership as an item for Cabinet discussion. Instead, he controlled the situation and averted collective opposition, by broaching the subject informally with individuals or small groups of Cabinet members. By July 1961 there remained only three significant potential opponents of Macmillan's new direction. Viscount Hailsham (Quintin Hogg), who then held the post of Lord President of the Council, had doubts over the question of supranationality. Reginald Maudling, President of the Board of Trade, would have preferred to persevere with the free trade area negotiations, and the Deputy Prime Minister and Home Secretary, Rab Butler, was somewhat reluctant to abandon any controls over the British economy. However, these doubts were dispelled or remained latent.

'The Prime Minister had carefully arranged to announce his decision on the last day of July (1961) as everyone was leaving London for the August Bank Holiday - the moment least conducive to the organisation of conspiracies. The preparatory work on the various ranks of the Party, the Cabinet, the 1922 Committee, the key advisers at the Central Office was faultless. Few other politicians in British history could have executed such a feat: Macmillan was about to go back on much of what he had said and done in ten years of office, including five years in Downing Street, without losing the smallest Parliamentary Secretary or Junior Whip along the way'. (Beloff, 1963, p.10.)

The planning by Macmillan had even extended to discreet ministerial discussions with the EFTA group and individual Commonwealth countries, over Britain's relations with the EEC before the Parliamentary announcement was made. This averted mobilisation of opposition, which might have been sympathetically received in Britain. In fact, with growing

Commonwealth suspicion as to Macmillan's intentions, there had been some calls for a Commonwealth Prime Ministers' Conference - an unwelcome escalation of the issue for Macmillan - and members of the Conservative Party might well have rallied around the Commonwealth cause in large numbers. Macmillan's tactic of sending ministers to individual countries effectively defused such a danger, in the short-term at least.

The discreet manner in which the Prime Minister prepared for the policy change does not detract from the importance attached to it by Macmillan, or in due course by his Cabinet colleagues. Indeed this could be said to <u>reflect</u> the importance attached to it. Given the obvious importance attached to the issue within Cabinet, what level of salience was attributed to it by the Government leadership outside the confines of Cabinet discussion? When the issue did emerge onto the public forum, the Prime Minister and Cabinet accorded it commensurate status. This was reflected by the fact that it was the Prime Minister who delivered the July announcement to the House of Commons on the initial policy shift, and he also introduced the first Government motion on the EEC in August 1961. Other Government motions on this issue during P4 were introduced to the House of Commons by senior Cabinet spokesmen: two by Edward Heath and one by Rab Butler. Also nine White Papers were published during 1961 and 1962 on the subject, one on Commonwealth consultations, one on the text of an initial Government statement and the rest were all reports on the state of negotiations by the Lord Privy Seal (Edward Heath). The comparatively high salience of the issue derived from the content analysis of Parliamentary debate in P4, matches that attributed to it by the Prime Minister and Cabinet.

The question of EEC membership also figures prominently at the Conservative Party Annual Conferences of 1961 and 1962 with full scale debates on the matter in each year; a reflection of the Government's preferences. The leadership were conspicuous during these debates: in the former, Heath and Sandys gave key addresses and in the latter, Heath and Butler. Sandys placed the issue in sharp relief by suggesting that a Conference vote critical of British entry would be interpreted as a vote of censure on the Government. As a further indication of the importance attached to the issue by the Cabinet within the Party context, Butler opened his remarks in the following year's debate by saying that

'There is no issue in peacetime so vital as this one to our future in this country or to the future of millions

164

all over the world.' (Conservative Party Conference Report, 1962, p. 51).

At the 1961 Conference the Prime Minister devoted about one fifth of his closing address to Britain's relations with the EEC, and in 1962, the question totally dominated his speech.

Illustrative of the importance of the issue within the Party organisation is the fact that during the summer of 1961, six regional briefing sessions were held for key Party workers. About 800 attended the London and Home Counties session alone. The Conservative Party Central Office, in marked contrast to the previous three periods, published a large number of booklets and information sheets on the question during P4: over sixty such publications devoted to the European question appeared. (see Hennessy, 1973.) Among the variety of pamphlets on this theme, five appeared under the authorship of Macmillan and three under that of Douglas-Home. Collectively these indicators suggest that, in contrast even to P1, the Conservative Party, during P4, devoted a very high level of attention to the European issue, corresponding to its salience within the content analysis of Parliamentary debate.

Turning to the question of the anatomy of the issue in P4, it is interesting first to examine the Parliamentary statements of Government front bench spokesmen who accounted for just under 18% of the total statements in P4. As over four fifths of the debate thus came from non Government members, there was considerable scope for significant differences between the overall anatomy of the issue, and the portrayal of it by Government spokesmen.

Given the overall policy objectives of the Government it comes as no surprise that only 2% of its front-bench statements raised objections to British membership of the EEC. More surprising perhaps, is that only 31% of these statements expressed positive advantages of British membership and the remaining 68% fell into the neutral policy preference category. This was probably a design to escape criticism for not respecting British and Commonwealth interests, as the terms of British accession were as important to sections of the Conservative Party as to the Labour Party for whom safeguards became all important. As negotiations proceeded it was increasingly important for the Government to be seen to be vigilant for British and Commonwealth interests as well as for securing EEC membership.

The distribution of points of detail among the three
aspects raised by Government spokesmen was markedly similar
to that overall (43.3% Political, 50.3% Economic and 6.3%
Social). Unlike the Labour Government in P1 which sought to
give emphasis to arguments consistent with its own policy,
the Macmillan Government adopted a broader approach by
anticipating and embracing the likely points of criticism.
Macmillan's introduction of the Government's EEC initiative
to the House of Commons was undramatic, though his
discussion of the arguments was wide ranging:

'We have now reached the state where we cannot make
further progress without entering into official
negotiations ... the majority of the House and Country
will feel that they cannot fairly judge whether it is
possible for Britain to join the EEC until they have a
clearer picture before them of the conditions.'

He mentioned both the political and economic
considerations, praised the value of the Commonwealth to the
UK and

'did not think that Britain's contribution to the
Commonwealth will be reduced if Europe unites. On the
contrary, I think its value will be enhanced.'

He mentioned that EFTA countries were

'all agreed that they should work closely together
throughout any negotiations.' (Hansard, Vol. 645, cols.
928-931, 31.7.61.)

In the ensuing debate the Prime Minister denied federal
implications of membership and repeated his commitment to
the Commonwealth, thus presenting the issue as a fairly non
contentious one. Only Anthony Fell from the Conservative
benches attacked his leader's speech, though up to one
hundred Conservatives were doubtful. (Lieber, 1970, p.205.)
Presumably Macmillan had convinced the rest of his ability
to handle the issue in the best interests of all, and he had
addressed potential points of criticism rather than avoid
them.

Turning to the Government's depiction of the issue with the
Party, Edward Heath, speaking at the 1961 Party Conference,
stated that the issue was greater than one of tariffs, trade
and commercial policies, and he continued to outline
political and economic advantages of British membership, in
the form of European peace and defence against communism,

and the size of export markets. He was at pains to stress that Britain sought special arrangements for Commonwealth agricultural produce. Duncan Sandys, winding up the debate, stated that the economic advantages of entry were well known, and he directly confronted the criticisms of Government policy regarding the Commonwealth and British sovereignty, arguing that the former would not be threatened, and that Britain had already given up some sovereignty by joining NATO.

During a similar debate at the following year's Conference, Butler and Heath, argued at length in support of the Government's EEC policy. The range of topics they raised matched that noted within the overall anatomy; including substantiated discussion of the contribution of membership to European political stability, the costs of British political isolation, and the themes of sovereignty and national identity. Turning to economic factors, they dealt with the impact of membership upon the Commonwealth with reference to individual countries and their export commodities, Britain's changing trade patterns, the British and EEC agriculture and the effect of British membership upon consumer prices.

What then can be concluded from these portrayals of the issue by Government spokesmen in their relations with the Conservative Party? They were generally prepared, or felt obliged, to discuss in detail a wide range of factors associated with the issue. That, however, such disproportionate attention was given to dealing with subjects associated with criticisms of entry, does suggest a somewhat defensive approach, and further guaranteed the importance of such themes as the Commonwealth, agriculture and federalism within debate, at the expense of others (e.g. economic benefits of access to EEC markets, political advantages of a united Europe), which the Government might have preferred to highlight.

Examination of other speeches made during the Conference debates reveals that these themes also preoccupied Party members outside Government who made, if anything, greater emphasis upon the Commonwealth, sovereignty and to a lesser extent on agriculture. This feature was related to the efforts of those opposed to entry who tended to give more weight to political considerations and the Commonwealth factors, whether economic or political. For instance, Sir Derek Walker-Smith, MP, moving an amendment at the 1961 Conference argued that

'We must weigh this momentous matter in the broad scales
of the national interest as a whole, and not of this
generation only, but of generations yet to come. We must
have regard to the past and future of a great people, to
our great national institutions and our unique
Commonwealth connection. We must have regard to
sovereignty and the Commonwealth, for these are the
keynotes – sovereignty, the right to make our own
decisions in our own affairs, and the Commonwealth. We
lost sovereignty under the Treaty of Rome – in tariffs,
in certain financial matters, and in immigration.
Yesterday we were debating immigration on a Motion asking
the Government to take action. Under the Treaty of Rome
we would not be doing that in the future because, so far
as Europe is concerned, the power of sovereign decisions
would pass from our Parliament.'
Conservative Party Conference, 1961 p. 47) 1961, p.47.)

In the same debate Viscount Hinchingbrooke MP appealed to
the traditions of Conservatism:

'The issue of the Common Market is therefore fundamental
to Conservative sensibility. The question is: do we
ally ourselves with our history and all that we have done
to make and maintain this enormous Commonwealth, this
association of six hundred and sixty million souls, a
greater alliance than Russia has ever seen, or do we put
obstacles in its progress at the behest of the United
States of America for the sake of a purely commercial and
ideological connection with a corner of Europe? It is
not the whole of Europe, but a corner of Europe – the
West End of Europe. My own feeling is that the Common
Market will break up, as the European Defence Community
broke up, because the fundamental nationalism of France,
Germany and Italy is still there and because these post-
war ideas of supra-nationalism have not yet been put to
the test of over-production and unemployment.'
(Conservative Party Conference, 1961, p. 56).

Those arguing in favour of British entry often found
themselves having to spend time discussing sovereignty and
the Commonwealth, simply to counter opposition. When they
were able to deal with positive advantages, they
concentrated upon broad economic and political benefits.
David Lane, for example, seconding the main motion at the
1961 Conference, stated that

'Whether or not we enter the Common Market, of course we
must develop to the full our trade with the Commonwealth

and with our EFTA partners. But if we do not enter the Common Market, I do not think that the expansion of Commonwealth and EFTA trade could be enough to compensate us for exclusion from the fast-growing mass market on the Continent. British industry, however efficient, would be in danger of losing ground to its Common Market competitors. If, on the other hand, we go into the Common Market, we can count on three main benefits: on quicker economic growth, on a stronger basis for investment in the Commonwealth, and eventually on a larger market in Europe for exports from the Commonwealth.' (Conservative Party Conference, 1961, p. 47).

Thus, despite the Government's best efforts to defend their policy on its merits, rather than spend all their time deflecting criticisms, the critics of British entry were successful, if not in votes, in tangibly affecting the anatomy of the issue within the Conference forum. It could be argued that the constant airing of concerns about the Commonwealth, sovereignty and agriculture, did actually contribute to the final outcome viz de Gaulle's veto.

This theme was reflected in the subject matter of Conservative Party publications. Of the fifty-five titles listed in James Hennessy's Bibliographical Guide (1973), ten include the word Commonwealth in the title: this is in addition to the fact that others dealt with this component of the issue anyway. Four of the titles included either the words Agriculture or Farmers. Thus, despite the close links between the Conservative Party Central Office and the Party leadership, the latter were not fully able to exploit these positively on this issue: great emphasis was laid on discussing these two major areas of controversy.

There seems to be little doubt that Macmillan's overall motive for taking Britain into the EEC was political. Leo Pliatzky commented that

'I share the view that Macmillan's motivation was primarily political from the outset, and that a crucial factor in his conversion to Europe was the failure of his attempt to gain a niche in history by acting as a bridge between the American and Russian superpowers ..... I had an eye-witness description of the Prime Minister sitting in Number 10 with his foreign policy in ruins around him, and asking himself what he was going to do for a foreign policy now.' (Pliatzky, 1982, p.45.)

In addition, of course, continued electoral success for the Party depended upon continued economic growth and prosperity for the country. However, Macmillan's initial strategy was not to pose the issue as one of principle, for fear of policy failure. This meant that he invited a detailed costs and benefits approach to the issue – so lacking in earlier periods – which itself contributed to the emphasis on terms, notably regarding the Commonwealth, sovereignty and agriculture. This was compounded by the nature of the negotiations which were rooted in the discussion of and bargaining over terms: these would of course have been comparatively superfluous in P1, P2 and P3, when an initial commitment of principle was the only requirement for entry. The emphasis in the White Papers on terms could not ultimately help the Government's cause. Thirdly however, though few in number and comparatively weak in resources, the Conservative opponents of entry were also responsible for contributing towards the emphasis on the Commonwealth, sovereignty and agriculture themes within the Conservative Party at large. The Government were distinctly unsuccessful in enabling points regarding the economic benefits of membership to capture the limelight within the Conservative Party. Within Party publications much emphasis was given to countering objections to entry. Even if this trend was due to anticipated reactions of Tory members (especially from the shires) and voters, rather than to the actual campaign levelled by the few antis within the Party, is of course difficult to specify. The anatomy of the issue noted in the Parliamentary debate, which gave some emphasis to the economic benefits of membership was not entirely reflected within Conservative debate on the issue. In Parliament, the Government could rely on more loyal support and more positive convictions of its backbench supporters, especially in the face of Labour Party criticisms of the policy. Also many Conservative MPs would at least be glad that the Party had some new policy initiative, in the light of the view that:

'many Conservatives felt that the Party had not only alienated the crucial centre element of the electorate, but had somehow lost its way; old traditions and attitudes had been jettisoned without anything positive being put in their place.' (Butler and King, 1965, p.299.)

Macmillan's success in carrying the Party in terms of votes cast both within Parliament and at the Party Conferences is not doubted. Whilst the anatomy of the issue in Parliament reflected a fairly even balance of themes, this was not the case within the Conservative Party and this reflected widely held depictions of the issue which were not conducive to British membership of the EEC.

WHITEHALL

Due to the unavailability of Whitehall records for this period, analysis will rest upon evidence derived from other secondary works, and personal recollections. Most commentators point to the part played by Sir Frank Lee's committee of investigation into the possibilities of EEC membership, in signalling a change in attitude: for example, Sir Leo Pliatzky stated that

'Among people who were close to these events at the time, a good deal of credit for the shift of policy on Europe is given to Sir Frank Lee, who was at that time Permanent Secretary at the Board of Trade and was later to succeed Makins at the Treasury. (Pliatzky, 1982, p.45.)

Lee's inter-departmental committee not only reported to the Cabinet, but according to R.A. Butler, its job was also to bring the Foreign Office and the Treasury round to the idea of EEC membership - the Board of Trade was already sympathetic to the idea. (Charlton, 1981.) Prior to any firm Government decision on the issue, whilst the idea was evidently discussed, Sir Herbert Andrew (Second Secretary at the Board of Trade), reported that few people in Whitehall had a clear view on the matter. (Charlton, 1981.) However, the change in attitudes towards British membership of the EEC was rapid: Nora Beloff quoted a Treasury official as saying that

'in 1959, the very idea caused him (an advocate of EEC membership) to be written off as a long-haired eccentric, in 1960 it was getting to be all right, and by 1961, you were a stick in the mud if you thought otherwise.' (Beloff, 1963, p.89.)

After the Government announcement of its intentions, the issue of the EEC came to figure highly in the work of Whitehall. In contrast to earlier years when the departments' views were formed without the pressures of continuing negotiations, the talks which took place in P4 required the active involvement of Government departments. Not only were several of these departments more or less continuously involved between September 1961 and January 1963, but also this involvement was at the most senior level. The negotiating team was led by Sir Pierson Dixon (British Ambassador in Paris) and Sir Eric Roll (previously a Deputy Secretary at the Ministry of Agriculture, Fisheries and Food). In addition to the negotiating team, the individual departments were occupied in preparing papers for the team and in their relations with respective client groups. In contrast to the free trade area and EFTA talks which had mainly involved the Board of Trade, a wide number of departments became closely involved with the EEC developments. Whilst central responsibility lay with the Board of Trade, the Foreign Office, the Ministry of Agriculture, Fisheries and Food (MAFF), the Commonwealth Relations Office (CRO), the Colonial Office and the Treasury were all considerably involved with the issue. This would all go to suggest that the high level of salience noted for the issue in the House of Commons was fully reflected in the work of the Whitehall departments.

Turning to the anatomy of the issue within the bureaucratic circles, the initial brief given to the Lee committee by Macmillan was to consider a wide range of proposals: (a) that the Six as one unit should join EFTA (b) that the UK should join the EEC on the understanding that the Commonwealth be allowed to retain its share of the UK market of non industrial goods and with special arrangements for agricultural support (c) that the UK be allowed free entry of certain Commonwealth goods to be selected commodity by commodity (d) a scheme similar to the original free trade area proposals, excluding agricultural goods, but like the Common Market by having a common external tariff. (Macmillan, 1972, p.321.) This would suggest an awareness of the problems raised by the commercial and economic terms implicit in any likely agreement. There is some dispute over the main motives for the major recommendation that Britain should enter the EEC as a full member. Nora Beloff suggested that the recommendation was made on the basis of Britain's need for economic competition and to redress the recurrent balance of payments deficits. (Beloff, 1973, p.171.) Miriam Camps however said that the 'reasons for their conclusion were primarily, although not exclusively political. (Camps, 1964, p.281.) She emphasised such themes as European stability, membership of the EEC as the shortest means to a real Atlantic alliance. The economic factors were, Camps reported, the advantages of a large domestic market and the benefits of increased competition. This view is confirmed by Lee in an interview with E. Liggett:

'I had great sympathy with the Foreign Office on their view that the move towards Europe was more political than economic.' (Liggett, 1971, p.165.)

Even if the motives were political, it does not mean that the report did not contain considerable economic discussion: Soames divulged that the report, whilst advocating entry, outlined the problem areas of agricultural policy and Commonwealth relations. (Charlton, 1982.)

The Foreign Office, which had viewed the Messina developments as 'commercial', and therefore of little relevance, had some senior 'Europeans' in the figures of Sir Gladwyn Jebb (British Ambassador to Paris 1954-1960), Sir Evelyn Shuckburgh and Sir Patrick Reilly (both Deputy Under-Secretaries at the Foreign Office), yet the predominant attitude, as described by Sir Derick Hoyer-Millar (Permanent Under Secretary 1957-1961) was that 'Britain's European links' were far less important than 'our relations with the U.S. and the Commonwealth'. (Bruce Gardyne and Lawson, 1976, p.49.)

The Treasury's main concern was, as might be expected, not that of diplomatic relations, but economic, namely the balance of payments implications of the tariff system. Whilst the Treasury eventually recognised the political dimensions to the issue, it had for the most part seen it as an economic question. Pliatzky recalled that

'It was only at a late stage in the negotiations that I heard one of my masters in the Treasury comment that the Common Market had developed from being an economic issue with political aspects to a political issue with economic aspects.' (Pliatzky, 1982, p.45.)

The Ministry of Agriculture's central concern was with the complicated proposals for agriculture within the Community. Indeed as the negotiations proceeded, the MAFF was increasingly acting as a mouthpiece for the NFU: 'the Ministry of Agriculture, under consistent pressure from the National Farmers' Union counselled prudence'. (Beloff, 1963, p.144.)

The different approaches of these three departments illustrate the difficulty in assigning a single view of the issue to Whitehall. As the issue took on greater salience, and as the negotiations became increasingly detailed, each department's view was further influenced by its traditional working sphere and client groups. However, this said, it does remain the case that the issue within Whitehall was lifted out of the purely commercial realm (where it had resided during P3) and took on foreign policy characteristics. This is illustrated by the position of Heath within the Foreign Office and the barrage of high level negotiations with <u>non EEC</u> countries (notably the USA and the Commonwealth) which proceeded, in addition to the EEC talks.

E. Liggett (1971) suggested that the absence of 'a community of interest' on the British side was a consequence of the delaying role played by the MAFF and, to a much lesser extent, by CRO. This role was associated with their preoccupation with agricultural and colonial affairs specifically. It is likely that the emphasis of these departments upon the terms under negotiation, could have contributed further to the emphasis of these themes within the overall anatomy of the issue: a development which cannot have helped the Government's cause.

THE LABOUR PARTY

During the period of the free trade area and the EFTA negotiations, the Labour Party had been in broad agreement with the Government over Britain's relations with Europe, and the issue was not a matter of contention between the parties. During the late 1950s Labour had been preoccupied with internal debate particularly on its policies towards nuclear armaments and on its own constitution. Although defeated on the Clause 4 issue, Gaitskell emerged in the 1960s as the leader of a party which was healing its wounds and developing hopes of electoral success in 1963 or 1964. With the announcement of the Government's intention to explore possibilities of EEC membership, this became a major issue for the Labour Party, not simply because elements of the Party strongly opposed the Government's moves, but also because others equally passionately agreed with it. Intra-party division as well as inter-party differences served to raise the salience of the issue. This however, posed a distinct problem for Gaitskell who,

> 'resolutely opposed any public declaration, thinking it unlikely to become an electoral issue, and fearing that any strong line either way would mean another Labour split'. (Williams, 1979, p.703.)

This tactical approach by the Party leader whilst successful in achieving overall Party policies which were fairly non-committal, did not of course assuage the passion felt by those determinedly for or against, nor reduce the high salience of the issue within Labour Party debate.

One indicator of the question's salience within the Labour Party was that of the time devoted to it at Party Conferences. In 1961 a full debate was conducted upon a resolution moved by John Stonehouse MP, provoking two amendments and a speech by the Party deputy leader, George Brown MP, on behalf of the NEC. Eighteen different speakers contributed to the debate and it occupied about one tenth of the total reported debate at the Conference.

The debate on the EEC in 1962 was the centre piece of the whole Conference, taking up virtually a whole day: about one fifth of the Conference proceedings. The debate was introduced by Gaitskell who presented the NEC's lengthy and detailed statement on the issue, Labour and the Common Market, in a speech which received an "unparalleled ovation", (Labour Party Annual Report, 1962, p.65.) The debate included contributions from thirty three speakers, including the NEC members Gaitskell and Brown, and four amendments were moved on the Conference floor. At the same Conference the Fabian Society arranged a fringe meeting at which Douglas Jay and Roy Jenkins respectively put the case for and against Common Market entry. The room booked was designed to accommodate an audience of between seventy and eighty, but about one hundred and fifty turned up, indicating an interest in the issue beyond even that expected by the organiser. (Jay, 1980, p.282.)

In addition to the 1962 NEC statement, the Labour Party devoted at least eight other short pamphlets to this question (Hennessy, 1972, p.59.) Also one million copies of the speeches by Gaitskell and Brown and the policy statment accepted by the 1962 Conference were published together in a forty page document, which was financed by the Transport and General Workers' Union.

These indicators of a high level of salience of the issue within the Labour Party seem to match that noted in the content analysis of Parliamentary debate. The stature of the issue within the Labour Party was most effectively communicated to the public in two Party Political Broadcasts (May 5th and September 21st 1962) which Gaitskell devoted entirely to the questions raised by British membership of the EEC.

Turning to the anatomy of the issue within the Labour Party forum, the one clear and over-riding theme was that of the emphasis placed upon terms of entry. The five conditions

outlined in the NEC statement of 1962 constituted central
areas of Labour Party debate:

'1.   Strong and binding safeguards for the trade and
       other interests of our friends and partners in the
       Commonwealth.

2.   Freedom as at present to pursue our own foreign
       policy.

3.   Fulfilment of the Government's pledges to our
       associates in the European Free Trade Area.

4.   The right to plan our own economy.

5.   Guarantees to safeguard the position of British
       agriculture' (Labour Party, 1962, p.1.)

This was the line consistently advocated by Gaitskell.
Philip Williams quoted at length from a memorandum sent by
the Labour leader to President Kennedy:

'As for the Opposition, we certainly took the conditions
very seriously and always meant to stand by them. There
were two reasons for this attitude. First, I myself and
my leading colleagues all happened to believe and still
believe that the arguments of principle were fairly
evenly balanced for and against and that the balance
would be tipped in favour of our entry only if our
conditions were fulfilled. Secondly, this policy of
making our final judgement depend on the conditions was
the only one which could have been accepted by the Party
as a whole.' (Williams, 1979, p.729.)

Indeed, in his television broadcast on the 8th of May 1962,
this provided the centre piece of his argument, with notable
emphasis upon the Commonwealth:

'To go in on good terms would, I believe be the best
solution to this difficult problem. And let's hope we
can get them. Not to go in would be a pity, but it would
not be a catastrophe. To go in on bad terms, which
really meant the end of the Commonwealth, would be a step
which I think we would regret all our lives and for which
history would not forgive us.' (quoted in Labour Party,
1962.)

Equally, in his second broadcast he emphasised the
inadequacy of the terms which had been negotiated in respect

of New Zealand, Canada, Australia, India and Pakistan's trade. Secondly, he raised the question of federation, suggesting that if this was what Britain was entering 'we become no more than a 'Texas' or 'California' in the United States of Europe.' (Williams, 1979, p.729.)

Gaitskell's preoccupation with conditions of entry was reflected within Party debate on the matter. For instance, Camps summarised the 1962 Conference saying that Jenkins and about thirty others thought that the Government decision was good if the terms were right, that Foot and the left wing stated their opposition on any terms, and that Jay and about thirty others opposed entry on any terms that seemed likely' (Camps, 1964, p.445.) George Brown recalled that although the 1961 Conference had turned down a motion which rejected the whole European concept it insisted 'that the matter could not be judged until the precise terms of entry were known'. (Brown, 1971, p.216.)

This emphasis upon conditions of entry, whilst assisting the cause of those who opposed British EEC membership, was not confined to this group. Brown himself at the 1961 Conference described the issue as a very complicated one, and asserted that Labour's position hinged upon the terms of entry proposed: he specified the subjects of agriculture, consumer prices, Commonwealth relations and EFTA commitments. Even Roy Jenkins, whose reasons for supporting British entry were based more firmly upon political principle, devoted about half of his speech at the 1962 Conference to objections raised to entry based on loyalty to the Commonwealth in general and Imperial Preference in particular. Similarly Bob Edwards, MP, a long-time advocate of a fuller British role in European integration, devoted over a third of his speech to objections to entry based upon what was, in his view, a false impression of the workings of the EEC. These related to the extent of national autonomy and the extent of economic isolation experienced by the Six.

The emphasis on terms for Commonwealth trade became central to the debate within the Labour Party. Douglas Jay reported that the confirmation of Gaitskell's opposition to entry on the terms available developed as a result of a conference with Socialist Commonwealth leaders and especially after conversations with the Prime Minister of Singapore, Harry Lee. (Jay, 1980, p.282.) Two of the six issues of Talking Points, published by the Labour Party on the EEC, were devoted entirely to the implications of British entry for the Commonwealth; particulary regarding arrangements for the latter's food and raw material exports. An earlier, more general edition of <u>Talking Points</u> suggested that the main factors in any decision were the effects of British entry upon the Commonwealth, upon Britain's own trade and industry, on her agriculture, her ability to control her own economy, and the extent of supranationality involved. A further two editions were devoted to considering the effect of British EEC membership upon economic planning, notably on the problems arising from liberalisation in some sectors of the economy. The paucity of references in Labour Party publications to themes more usually associated with pro marketeers (eg the contribution Britain could make towards a more democratic and socialist Europe, the third force notion, the export access to European markets, the high growth rates within the EEC and the advanced welfare systems) may well have been a consequence of the early interest taken by Denis Healey and Harold Wilson (both sceptics) in the Party's research into this subject, and the fact that Peter Shore, a renowned opponent of EEC membership, was head of the Research Department.

Miriam Camps has argued that criticism of the terms of entry by the Labour Party 'was undoubtedly prompted by a desire to strengthen the Government's bargaining position'. (Camps, 1964, p.447.) She provided no evidence for such an assertion. It does though remain the case that despite the existence of a vocal and well placed minority who favoured British EEC entry, their impact upon the character of the debate within the Party was clearly minimal. The publications of the Party and the debates on the issue at Conference displayed an emphasis on terms of entry at the expenses of themes whigh might have illustrated benefits of entry. The deliberate balance noted in the 1962 Fabian Society meeting (above) and the Fabian Tracts which devoted one issue to the Jay and Jenkins speeches at the meeting and one each to spokesmen for and against entry (Evan Luard and William Pickles respectively), was not (for whatever reasons) matched elsewhere in the Party.

It can be concluded that there were no serious disparities between the Parliamentary anatomy of the issue and that noted within the Labour Party. Of additional significance are the similar levels of equivocation: the high level of neutral statements in the House of Commons debate was reflected in the "wait and see" attitude within the Labour Party, which Gaitskell encouraged at least until October 1962.

The Liberal Party treated the European issue as one of paramount importance in earlier periods, with the possible exception of P3 when some wavering took place largely as a result of the EFTA developments. The Liberals' treatment of the issue in P4 was broadly consistent with their earlier evaluations of it. A Council meeting of June 1961 deplored the vagueness of Ministerial statements on 'the vital question of Britain's relations with the European Common Market'. Thus the Liberal Party continued to designate the European issue as one of critical importance, though in P4 this was a common evaluation.

What of the themes raised by Liberals in the debate on this question? The most significant distinguishing feature of Liberal characterisation of the question was that it gave less emphasis to the right terms for entry, and more to the principle. For example, the 1961 Council

'believing that the essential prerequisite of successful negotiations with the six Common Market countries is British acceptance of the basic principles of the Rome Treaty, calls upon H.M. Government to make an unequivocal declaration of this country's willingness to enter into full membership of the European Economic Community.' (Liberal Party, undated, p.7.)

Whilst most other groups were discussing concessions which the EEC could make to Britain in order to provide acceptable terms, the Liberal Assembly resolution of 1962 gave emphasis to changes Britain should make with membership in mind

'it is essential... to reduce tariffs and adapt the economy to enable it effectively to compete in the Common Market... This Assembly therefore advocates: the preparation of a five year plan for industry integrated with the European target rate of growth... the pooling of British currency reserves with those of the Common Market after British entry therein.' (Liberal Party, undated, p.8.)

The small group of free traders within the Liberal Party, led by Oliver Smedley, who opposed entry into the EEC because of its protectionist implications had little impact on the overall Liberal treatment of the issue.

In contrast to previous periods, the salience of the issue recorded within Parliament matched that within the Liberal

Party: it was no longer just the Liberals who considered this to be a highly important issue. However, one disparity remained. The anatomy of the issue as discussed in Parliament differed markedly from the depiction of the European question by Liberals. The emphasis by the latter upon what Britain could and should do to facilitate entry was in no way matched within the Parliamentary anatomy.

BUSINESS

The Federation of British Industries (FBI) had played a very active role in the discussions surrounding the idea of a free trade area and the formation of the EFTA. Even though the possibility of British membership of the EEC had not previously been countenanced by British business, this representative organisation had at least some experience of negotiations at a European level. However, it should be noted that there had been no concerted campaign either in public or by way of its functional access to the Government to press for this policy option until just prior to the Government's July 1961 announcement. Indeed in a letter from the FBI President (Sir William McFadzean) to the Chancellor of the Exchequer in January 1961 on the future of the economy and the role of manufacturing industry, there was no mention of EEC membership even as a possible solution to the problems identified.

Just prior to the Government's announcement of intent, the FBI did publish a statement for its members on the question of British entry into the EEC (FBI, 1961.) That the FBI did not engage in public campaigning activities on the question during the subsequent months is not necessarily indicative of low importance attached to the issue. Given the compatibility of the FBI and Government aims on the matter, and given the 'insider' status enjoyed by the FBI, such public activities would have been superfluous. Instead, the FBI made full use of its functional access to Whitehall during the negotiations, institutionalised by the creation of a small liaison group with the Board of Trade. In addition, the FBI placed emphasis upon international consultations through the Council of European Industrial Federations. Whilst the FBI played a small role in the formation of Government policy and virtually no role in campaigning or in the conduct of negotiations, it is undoubtedly true that the Government would not advance along the path towards EEC membership had not the FBI backed this policy.

Despite the absence of a public role for the FBI, the organisation did devote considerable resources to informing and consulting its own members, suggesting that considerable importance was attached to it. The Observer's business correspondent in May 1962 noted that:

'If any British businessman has not yet attended a Common Market conference, it can hardly have been because of lack of an invitation. Scarcely a day passes without news of some fresh gathering to discuss the effects of 'going into Europe', whether it is a mass jamboree by the seaside or a select houseparty of two dozen industrialists in a provincial city.' (quoted in Lieber, 1974, p.100.)

The Association of British Chambers of Commerce (ABCC) and most notably its Overseas Policy Committee, like the FBI, had taken a close interest in the possibilities of bridge building, rather than EEC membership per se, prior to the Macmillan announcement. Afterwards, in common with the FBI, the ABCC devoted resources to the provision of information for its members on this issue. A survey conducted in 1961 asked 'Do you consider that the UK should join the Common Market?' Thirty six chambers replied (representing about 36,000 members), thirty were in favour (though usually with some qualifications), two against and four undecided/divided (ABCC, Overseas Policy Committee, 7.6.61.) A further poll was conducted in the following year with 75% of members (as opposed to Chambers) responding in favour of entry. The evidence then as far as the FBI and ABCC are concerned indicates that the issue was held as important, and that there was a broad duplication of views between Government and these business organisations. The President of the ABCC referring to the Prime Minister's announcement of July 1961, 'welcomed it as reflecting the views of the Chambers of Commerce', (ABCC, General Purposes Committee, 2.8.61.) The exception to this broad correspondence of views was that of the Commonwealth Industries Association (CIA) which, whilst considering the issue to be an important one, was firmly opposed to EEC entry. The CIA provided speakers for nearly 300 public and private meetings, as well as directing a campaign specifically aimed at the Conservative Party.

What then of the anatomy of the issue within the mainstream British business circles? Lieber concluded that

'FBI leaders were always sensitive to avoid describing the role of the Federation as one of pressuring anybody: rather they preferred to speak of consultations. Indeed the organisation displayed a striking unwillingness to touch what it considered to be political issues.' (Lieber, 1974, p.104.)

(It should be noted that this description does somewhat camouflage the essentially political nature of functional relations: the mutual reinforcement of certain Whitehall and FBI attitudes.) The FBI statement to its members on the subject in July 1961, confirms Lieber's view, giving strong emphasis to the commercial themes. The statement bore no principled objection to a common external tariff nor to the gradual disappearance of the Commonwealth, though it did specify concern over certain Commonwealth imports, notably cheap Asian manufactured goods, and the prospect of some difficulty over agricultural provisions. The overriding objective stated however was to increase British exports in any market (FBI, 1961.) In his study of FBI, Stephen Blank (1973) laid great stress on industrialists concern at Britain's comparative lack of growth, which led them to take an interest in continental economic planning methods as well as in EEC membership. The commercial emphasis is further highlighted by the Overseas Trade Policy Committee of the FBI which

'gave much attention to the changing pattern of world trade; it called for detailed studies of the EEC institutions and of the harmonisation objectives and their effect on ourselves as potential members. The result was a series of FBI brochures of which one in particular – 'Taxation in Western Europe' – was in tremendous demand.' (Kipping, 1972, p.175.)

The FBI's concern with the likely terms of entry was communicated at a functional level via the liaison group with the Board of Trade (BoT). A report was made to the BoT based upon manufacturing organisations (210 in total with an 85% response rate). It detailed the industries which would expect 'real hardship' with the adoption of the common external tariff, and gave specific reasons. In some cases special provisions which would alleviate hardship were outlined.

In June 1960 the Overseas Committee of the ABCC, whilst recognising that the decision on EEC entry was primarily political:

'It was recognised that some sections of industry and commerce would find themselves in an uncompetitive position whatever the decision and this was unavoidable.

It was important, however, that Commonwealth trade should be developed as much as possible as this would certainly remain very important'. (ABCC, Overseas Policy Committee, 7.6.61.)

This Commonwealth concern prior to the Macmillan announcement, was somewhat overridden as negotiations unfolded, as attention broadened to take account of the implications for British firms. The European Panel of the ABCC set up September 1960 (replacing the Free Trade Area Panel) encouraged firms to contact the BoT directly if they saw damaging prospects of EEC entry. At the end of 1961, the panel noted that 'it was impossible to estimate the position (i.e. as to how the ABCC viewed the talks) before the terms of our entry were known'. (ABCC European Panel, 23.11.61.) During 1962 the panel gave great attention to detail particularly regarding agricultural and Commonwealth products, receiving papers on such subjects as the role of chambers of commerce in the EEC, the powers of EEC institutions and the implications for EFTA.

The London Association of Chambers of Commerce produced a booklet on the subject in 1961, giving an introduction to the history and development of the EEC and discussing implications of British membership. It oulined three main obstacles to British entry: (i) Commonwealth interests (ii) Domestic agriculture and (iii) EFTA interests. In a later chapter however, it assumed that 'reasonable provision' would be made in these three spheres on entry, and that Britain would thereby enjoy the opportunities of equal competition in an expanding market. It dismissed the threat to sovereignty arising from EEC membership. Overall the approach of the booklet was to give a pros and cons discussion, with special attention to commercial themes. Whilst the claims for some special conditions were reported, it was considered that the increase in competition might require adjustments in British industry.' (London Association of Chambers of Commerce, 1961.)

Like the FBI, the ABCC avoided public campaigning on the issue and devoted itself to information gathering and provision for its members, and to making some use of access to Government departments.

The large banks did not appear to play a strongly pro European role, even though it was evident from annual reports that by the end of 1961 some of their number did advocate British entry into the EEC. Westminster Bank (1961) did publish a booklet on the question, giving details on the historical background, and the organisation of the Community, with some reference to the problems regarding the Commonwealth EFTA and British agriculture. It considered that the balance of the advantage will depend on the competitiveness of British industries, and continued by giving a sector by sector approach with emphasis on the removal of internal tariffs, looking also at British agriculture (notably prices and efficiency) and upon the consumer (effect upon the cost of living).

As noted above, there was one business organisation, whose views on British membership of the EEC did not match those already noted, viz general preference for entry qualified by concern for certain commercial implications. The Commonwealth Industries Association (CIA), as its name suggests, had a specific concern with the repercussions of British entry upon Commonwealth trade. This also extended to the political implications of membership from its impact upon the cohesion of the Commonwealth to the consequences for British sovereignty. Lieber quoted from the CIA Monthly Bulletin: 'It is not necessary to approve of socialism to claim that it is the right of the British people to make the decision.' A later issue also spoke of Britain's debt to the Commonwealth, 'written in blood from Flanders to Gallipoli.' (Lieber, 1970, p.102.)

It does seem clear from the foregoing that the salience of the issue noted within the House of Commons was reflected within British business circles. The latter, with the exception of the CIA, did not express this high evaluation of the issue by means of public campaigning activities, but such salience is betrayed by the attention given to the issue within the respective organisations.

Turning to the issue's anatomy, the major organisations, the FBI and the ABCC were primarily absorbed with commercial themes, pertaining not only to EFTA, agriculture and the Commonwealth, but also to the likely effects upon the various branches of British industry. Lieber argued that it was the innate importance of the business sector which led to Government spokesmen giving such attention to commercial issues. It should also be borne in mind though that the Government had a variety of other divergent interests to reconcile in making pronouncements on this issue. Whilst the FBI and ABCC did acknowledge the Commonwealth economic dimension, this was not their central concern. However, it was the main preoccupation of the CIA, and it has been demonstrated above that this sphere dominated the Economic aspect. Thus the depiction of the issue by the main-stream business organisations, whilst represented within the Parliamentary anatomy, certainly did not dominate it. Indeed, the smaller and perhaps more idiosyncratic CIA had reason to be well satisfied with the emphasis within the Parliamentary anatomy both upon economic and political implications of British EEC entry for the Commonwealth.

TRADE UNIONS

Generally speaking, the trade union movement during the 1950s had been in agreement with successive Government policies towards the ECSC, the EEC and EFTA. When the Government's intention to investigate the possibilities of EEC membership became clear in 1961, although a few individual constituent organisations of the TUC held strong views in one direction or another, the Congress itself was reticent to make a final policy commitment. This is not however to say that the issue was of low stature. In 1961 the General Council reported to the 1961 Congress that it had

'continued to devote considerable attention to the development of the European Free Trade Association and the United Kingdom's relations with the European Economic Community.' (TUC, Report of General Council, 1961, p.247.)

It had been informed of early changes in the UK's relationship with the EEC, and had met the President of the Board of Trade to discuss the matter. The General Council prepared a special report on European economic unity which was presented to the 1961 Congress, at which almost 15% of the debating time was taken up with this subject. At the 1962 Congress about 10% of debating time was taken up with the European issue. The General Council then reported that it had

'continued to give detailed attention to the progress of negotiations between the UK and the European Economic Community. They have held regular meetings with the Lord Privy Seal and have also maintained contact with the trade unions in the European Economic Community and the European Free Trade Association.' (TUC, Report of General Council, 1962, p.259.)

In addition it submitted an extensive and detailed memorandum to the Lord Privy Seal on various themes arising from the issue. Thus at both the Congress and Council

levels of the TUC, the European question was certainly one
of high salience. However, no definitive policy was
expressed; judgement was deferred until the final terms
were to be known.

The salience of the issue within individual unions varied
considerably. The National Union of Agricultural Workers
(NUAW) considered it important as the effects of entry upon
its members were probably more prominent than upon workers
in other sectors, given the preoccupation of the EEC with
agriculture. Other unions who took particular interest in
the issue usually did so out of broader economic or
political motives. For instance, the Association of
Supervisory Staffs, Executives and Technicians evidently
attributed the issue some stature, by submitting motions on
the subject to the 1961 and 1962 Labour Party Conferences,
and it was the subject of many leader and other major
articles in the union journal, during 1961 and 1962.

With regard to policy preferences, R. Colin Beever (1963)
pointed out that two factors restrained the TUC from
adopting a strong position on the EEC. The first was the
general disparity between the predominantly favourable views
of the General Council and the more antagonistic attitudes
of the active rank and file. The second factor was the need
to maintain the unity of the General Council: the small
number of opponents of entry were effectively able to
restrain the enthusiasm of the majority who were sympathetic
to EEC entry.

There was considerable variety in the depiction of the
European issue among individual British trade unions. The
NUAW was primarily concerned with the agricultural terms of
entry and the likely consequences of these for its members.
This bore a direct relation to the Parliamentary anatomy of
the issue, as the 1961 Annual Report indicated that the
NUAW sponsored MPs interjected in debates on the Common
Market, by making speeches related to safeguards for British
agriculture. However, these contributions account for only
a very small number of points of detail within this sphere.
Equally the Confederation of Shipbuilding and Engineering
Unions gave attention to implications relevant to its
industries, and the executive decided unanimously to send a
report to the TUC on the advantages of entry for the British
car industry. Other unions, however, adopted a broader
approach. On the economic side the Iron and Steel Trades
Confederation (ISTC) executive adopted a resolution which
argued that British 'industries would be encouraged by the
expansion of economic frontiers which would follow Britain's

entry into the Common Market...' (ISTC. Executive Council, 17.5.62.) The ISTC journal gave extensive coverage to broad economic dimensions of the European question, particularly regarding the tariff system and British industrial competitiveness, in addition to the possibilities of increasing steel exports. In this period the journal included articles from members of the European Labour movement on such subjects as 'Fighting Unemployment in the ECSC', 'Socialists in the Common Market', and 'As a Frenchman Sees It', which dealt with planning and the extension of public ownership within the EEC.

Other unions, particularly those which opposed British membership of the EEC outright, also drew on more political themes in addition to economic ones. The National Union of Mineworkers, for example, adopted the following resolution:

'This conference of the NUM believes that the Common Market is an alliance of the upholders of anti-trade union capitalism, and can do nothing but harm to the masses of the population of this country by: (a) worsening our economic problems (b) deepening the division of Europe and thereby further endangering peace (c) depressing further wage standards and increasing food prices to British families (d) forcing Britain further away from access to the world wide markets which we sorely need, and (e) taking away the right of our people to decide their own affairs.' (NUM, Annual Report, 1962.)

This general portrayal of the EEC took no account of any specific issues for British miners and the coal industry, but simply made broad economic and political assertions. Similarly in a press statement put out by the Transport and General Workers' Union in 1962, most concern was expressed over the failure of the Government to secure broad British and Commonwealth interests, and it asserted that the British people, who it thought opposed entry, should be consulted by the Government. The statement concluded by requesting fuller details on such matters as the price levels of basic commodities, the prospects for full employment, agricultural implications, Commonwealth relations, peace, world trade and progress of 'backward peoples.' (TGWU, General Executive Council, September 1982.)

In contrast to the individual trade unions, the General Council of the TUC had been kept well informed of developments at a governmental level, and had responded by maintaining a dialogue with Heath throughout the negotiations. This took the form of memoranda running in both directions based upon economic implications of membership. Such an emphasis was also evident in the General Council's report to the 1961 Congress, European Economic Unity. This reserved judgement on the question of entry until the conditions were disclosed, although agreement in principle with the Government's decision was expressed. The report discussed the Commonwealth economic dimension, British agriculture and the repercussions of British EEC entry on EFTA. It further argued that a pragmatic, rather than a theoretical view of supranationalism was necessary to evaluate its effects, particularly in the fields of full employment, economic growth and better living standards. Other topics touched upon included the likely impact of entry upon Britain's balance of payments, labour mobility, the harmonisation of social policies and labour representation. In summary then, this report reflected the General Council's main preoccupation with the economic and social nuts and bolts of the question. This was distinct from the emphases of a number of the TUC's constituent organisations, which tended either to dwell upon implications for their own industry or else take a much broader view with particular emphasis upon political considerations.

It appeared that despite the level of regular communication between the TUC General Council and the Government, the unions had little impact upon Government policy. This was not only because the Government's decision to enter would not ultimately be influenced by TUC opposition to it, but also because what became the crucial issues of the negotiation were not those over which unions might have been most closely concerned, viz labour policies, social harmonisation and living standards. While the Government, and particularly Heath who had been Minister of Labour, was glad to be able to reassure the TUC General Council on several counts, there was no evidence of a bargaining relationship over this issue. It would not be accurate to suggest that the TUC's depiction of the issue was necessarily representative of those of its constituent parts. A diversity of portrayals occurred among trade unions, ranging from attention to implications for a union's own industry to broad political and economic argument.

The depiction of the issue by the General Council, which attempted to provide a thorough account of the economic pros and cons of entry was not synonymous with the dominant themes of the Parliamentary anatomy. The latter did bear more direct relation to the substantive issues under negotiation, namely the Commonwealth, agriculture and tariff arrangements.

THE NATIONAL FARMERS' UNION

The National Farmers' Union of England and Wales (NFU) was founded in 1908, and from the outset attempted to embrace all categories of farmers, whether owner-occupiers or tenant farmers. It has assumed the role of the major spokesman for broad farming interests. Despite early links with the Conservative Party, the wartime experience and the success of the NFU's relationship with the post-war Labour administration prompted a modification of its image. The NFU chose to concentrate its energies on access to Whitehall rather than persist with its direct Conservative Party links. The special relationship which it enjoyed with Government dates from the 1947 Agriculture Act. Although this provided little concrete specification

'The theory of the Act was that agriculture should enjoy a permanent degree of "security" in return for measures designed to raise its "efficiency"'.

The Annual Price Review which commenced in 1945, provided a practical bolster to this theory. The subsidies and guaranteed prices for agricultural producers derive from this yearly "agreement" between the Government and the NFU. Not only does the NFU enjoy a monopolistic position in the representation of farmers, but also by virtue of this advantage is the major source of information on agricultural matters for the Government.

The importance of the compatibility of the British agricultural system, based upon the Agriculture Act and the Annual Price Review, with the proposed European Common Agricultural Policy, inevitably drew the NFU into a central position in the Common Market debate. The threats posed by EEC membership to the guaranteed price system for the main agricultural products and to the protective tariff system against imported horticultural products aroused considerable interest on the part of the NFU.

As far as policy preference was concerned, the NFU was generally critical of what it considered to be the most likely agricultural terms of entry. Harold Woolley, the NFU President from 1960-66, in contrast to his predecessor, was consistently critical of the whole membership proposal in speeches during the period. Whilst NFU policy generally

189

reflected the views of Woolley, the larger farmers, in contrast to smaller farmers, dairymen and horticulturists tended to divide over the issue in similar proportions as the rest of the country (Lieber, 1970, p.125.) Nevertheless, the NFU views were those which achieved prominence, and their tone was set early, when, well prior to the Government announcement, Woolley warned of the dangers of joining the Six in a major article in the National Farmer (3.9.60), the NFU journal.

The relevant indicators demonstrate that the issue achieved significant stature within the NFU. National Farmer devoted considerable editorial and news space to the issue throughout P4; this extended to devoting seven pages of one issue to Woolley's appraisal of the prospects for British farmers on EEC entry (7.7.62.) The annual report of the NFU for 1961 clearly indicated that the issue had preoccupied the NFU bureaucracy. In addition to the publication of documents, meetings were held with MPs from the three major political parties, with the chairmen of marketing boards, with the Country Landowners' Association, the National Union of Agricultural Workers and the FBI. Also close contacts were developed with leaders and officials of European farm organisations. The question of British membership of the EEC was the subject of the main motion to be debated at the Annual General Meeting of 1962. Finally, Woolley devoted a high proportion of his speeches during this period to the European question.

Turning to the depiction of the EEC issue by the NFU, their views were established in an eleven page policy statement of July 1961, which won the unanimous approval of its Council (NFU, 1961.) As might be expected, agricultural factors constituted a major part of the discussion. The document outlined, in considerable detail, the main features of the Agricultural Acts, and their contribution to the British farming system. The second section gave an equally detailed account of agriculture within the EEC, which, it concluded was incompatible with the British system of guarantees and protective tariffs. Having devoted the first half of the document to specifically farming matters, the NFU broadened its discussion to take up several related and clearly sensitive themes. In addressing the Commonwealth question, it asserted that

'Unless we are prepared to revoke the traditional system of duty free entry for Commonwealth products it is difficult to see how we would be able to join with the rest of the Community in implementing the target price system.' (NFU, 1961, p.11.)

The report discussed the impact of EEC membership on food costs, and suggested that the adoption of the proposed common agricultural policy would result in higher farm costs and thus higher food prices. It was advocated that an international food trade policy, tackled through the OECD was preferable to a more limited European settlement. The document concluded on the agricultural theme and stated firmly that the negotiations had no prospect of success unless the Six recognised the special needs of British agriculture and horticulture. The sentiments expressed in the motion passed unanimously at the 1962 Annual General Meeting provide a good summary of the main elements of the question which preoccupied the NFU:

'This AGM of the NFU is opposed to the UK's entry into the Common Market under the terms of the present proposals for common agricultural policy provided for in the Treaty of Rome, and considers that the conditions of Britain's entry into an enlarged European Community must include: (a) A continuation of the system of annual reviews of the economic condition and prospects of the agricultural industry. (b) The maintenance of guaranteed prices for agricultural products and effective support for the horticultural industry. (c) That the government support should continue to be given to producer-controlled marketing.' (British Farmer, 10.2.62.)

The subjects of the annual review, guaranteed prices, horticulture and a form of market mechanism proved pre-eminent within discussion of the issue by NFU spokesmen and within the columns of the British Farmer. In addition, debate would periodically settle upon the several commodities which were under negotiation in Brussels at any one time. For instance, one article in British Farmer (13.1.62) expressed unhappiness with the EEC Commission's proposals for grading cauliflowers, apples, pears, tomatoes and peaches. In a lengthy report on the negotiations up until July 1962, Woolley gave specific attention to the particular problems that might ensue for individual sectors of British agriculture on joining the EEC eg milk producers would be competing with farmers in the Six who did not have to comply with stringent hygienic and quality standards. (British Farmer, 7.7.62.) The notion that British agriculture should simply adjust to the EEC pattern as a necessary cost of membership was not countenanced. Rather, a leading article in the British Farmer concluded that

'The Government's attitude in the forthcoming
negotiations must not therefore be one of asking for
concessions for British agriculture, but of insisting
that any changes in our present methods in favour of
common arrangements in an enlarged Community should be
such as to provide firm arrangements whereby the wellbeing of British farmers and growers, and those of
agricultural interests in the Community as a whole can be
assured. As they stand at the present time, the general
arrangements upon which the Six have agreed for their
countries do not provide such an assurance.'
(British Farmer. 3.3.62.)

A theme which did not occur within NFU characterisation of
the European question, was the advantage which certain
British farmers might enjoy in exporting their products to
Europe, by virtue of the more efficient means of production
in the UK, and the relatively higher consumer costs within
the EEC.

In assessing the relevance of the NFU's depiction of the
issue for the anatomy noted in the House of Commons' debate,
several background factors should be borne in mind. First,
the NFU engaged in campaigning activities not normally
associated with an organisation enjoying close functional
links with Whitehall. This is borne out by the evidence
from the 1961 Annual Report cited above: the NFU adopted
the tactics of a promotional organisation, with a large
output of information and press statements (which found
special favour with the Daily Express). The intention was
to influence public opinions, rather than simply civil
service opinions. In addition, the NFU endeavoured to make
personal contact with the MPs of all parties representing
rural constituencies. Thus in contrast to the FBI, the NFU
made a conscious effort to influence public debate, and the
anatomy of the issue recorded for P4 suggests some measure
of success. Over 30% of the European Economic sphere was
occupied with perceptions of agriculture in the EEC, and
just under 30% of the British Economic sphere with
discussion regarding British agriculture - most notably the
support system and the sectors endangered by free entry of
European products.

A further testimony to the success of the NFU's depiction
of the EEC issue is that two themes which could potentially
have run counter to the Union's argument, were not evident
in the Parliamentary anatomy: that of the export benefits
of entry for many British farmers, and of whether Britain

could make some sacrifice in this section in order to join the EEC. Of course, agriculture was inherently important in the continuing negotiations, which may (though not necessarily), have accounted for its stature within the anatomy of the issue. Such an effect was reinforced, however, by the NFU which provided a ready fund of information and causes which MPs of both Conservative and Labour Parties could exploit.

In assessing the relevance of the NFU's depiction of the issue for the anatomy noted in the House of Commons' debate, several background factors should be borne in mind. First, the NFU engaged in campaigning activities not normally associated with an organisation enjoying close functional links with Whitehall. This is borne out by the evidence from the 1961 Annual Report cited above: the NFU adopted the tactics of a promotional organisation, with a large output of information and press statements (which found special favour with the Daily Express). The intention was to influence public opinions, rather than simply civil service opinions. In addition, the NFU endeavoured to make personal contact with the MPs of all parties representing rural constituencies. Thus in contrast to the FBI, the NFU made a conscious effort to influence public debate, and the anatomy of the issue recorded for P4 suggests some measure of success. Over 30% of the European Economic sphere was occupied with perceptions of agriculture in the EEC, and just under 30% of the British Economic sphere with discussion regarding British agriculture – most notably the support system and the sectors endangered by free entry of European products.

A further testimony to the success of the NFU's depiction of the EEC issue is that two themes which could potentially have run counter to the Union's argument, were not evident in the Parliamentary anatomy: that of the export benefits of entry for many British farmers, and of whether Britain could make some sacrifices in this sector in order to join the EEC. Of course, agriculture was inherently important in the continuing negotiations, which may (though not necessarily), have accounted for its stature within the anatomy of the issue. Such an effect was reinforced, however, by the NFU which provided a ready fund of information and causes which MPs of both Conservative and

Labour Parties could exploit.

PROMOTIONAL GROUPS

If the formation of and prominent activity by promotional pressure groups is any indication of a high level of political salience, the indicators in P4 corresponded with evidence of a high level of salience noted in the Hansard content analysis. In 1961 several prominent groups were formed specifically on this issue: The Anti Common Market League, Britain and the Common Market, the Common Market Campaign, the Forward Britain Movement, the Labour Common Market Committee and the United Europe Association. In addition the European Movement took on a more active role during this period having adopted a low profile during P2 and P3 compared with its early flourish of activity between 1948 and 1950. As well as these groups, there were smaller promotional organisations without the prominent personnel of the former organisations: the Campaign for British Freedom, Keep Britain Out Campaign and The True Tories. Also previously existing groups with somewhat broader aims addressed themselves to the European question: Federal Trust for Education and Research, the Federal Union and the European-Atlantic Group.

To combine all these organisations under the one banner of 'promotional groups' is to slightly mislead: their aims and spheres of operation differed significantly. Britain and the Common Market (Anti), the Forward Britain Movement (Anti) and the Labour Common Market Committee (Pro) all operated within the Labour movement, whilst the Anti Common Market League initially devoted its attention to stimulating and consolidating Conservative opposition to the Government's policy (though it later became an all-party organisation). The United Europe Association, an offshoot of the European Movement, was dedicated to stimulating mass education and membership, in contrast to the more discreet mother organisation which primarily performed a coordinating role for its constituent bodies, and provided a focal point of elite pro European opinion. The Common Market Campaign performed a public role, having been launched because of disappointment over the more restrained position of the Federal Union. The latter, in common with Europe House

194

endeavoured to perform an educational role at a mass level. These bodies organised many meetings and published a plethora of tracts and booklets. This level of promotional group activity is consistent with the Parliamentary salience of the issue. In addition, that several of these organisations operated within the major political parties and in many cases were led by MPs, suggests that the Parliamentary stature of the issue and the high level of group activity may well have been mutually reinforcing phenomena.

Clearly these groups espoused a variety of policy objectives which were reflected both in their tactical approaches and their characterisations of the European issue. The Common Market Campaign's main aim was to convince elite opinion of the value of British entry into the EEC. Lord Gladwyn recalled being invited by Roy Jenkins to be chairman of the Campaign. The latter remarked that

'We must mount a campaign to show the Government that important people in every party and in every walk of life are in favour of this.' (Gladwyn, 1972, p.338.)

He also recalled speeches he made in the House of Lords on the matter, which expressed sentiments consistent with prevailing themes in the House of Commons anatomy, though more commonly associated with opponents of entry:

'I said that they (the British public) would not only have to be prepared, on the economic front, to change their way of life to a considerable extent and accept certain short-term disadvantages and upsets, but also that they would recognise that, if we came into the Community, certain decisions affecting our whole future would be taken elsewhere than in Westminster by a body on which we should, of course, be well represented, but on which we should have no absolute veto. It would be pathetic to oppose our entry into the EEC thus to prejudice the defence of the free world against Communism – because it might in a few years conceivably put up the price of a British sausage...' [he was anxious that] 'the political issue should by no means be pushed under the rug.' (Gladwyn, 1972, p.338.)

The emphasis of the Campaign was not on which terms of entry were acceptable, but a desire for a clear statement that Britain was prepared to assume her responsibilities in Europe. Such a view was not reflected in the Parliamentary anatomy of the issue. Perhaps the most important contribution of the Campaign was in publishing a statement advocating British entry, and signed by over one hundred and fifty influential figures from a wide range of backgrounds, prior to Macmillan's announcement, which constituted one of several pre-disposing factors in the latter's decision. The Campaign did not court a mass membership being more concerned to influence elite opinion, although some local cells were established in the regions. Speakers were provided for meetings, and the number of these was estimated at about two hundred engagements between May 1961 and October 1962. The Campaign also produced eight editions of a broadsheet advancing a range of arguments in favour of entry, which in addition to countering prevalent objections, did attempt to give positive political and economic reasons for joining the EEC. The latter did not achieve significance in the Parliamentary anatomy.

For the most part, however, the groups in favour of European entry did not seek to embarrass the Government in any way, by advocating a more outright commitment to the EEC than the Cabinet spokesmen adopted at any one time. Thus these groups made small distinctive contribution to the broad debate. The Common Market Campaign did set up the Labour Common Market Committee with a view to impinging upon debate within the Labour movement, but its main achievement was to provide a source of information for those already committed. The Committee did produce a monthly newsheet entitled **Newsbrief**. This took up questions of special relevance to the Labour movement, especially later in the period when Labour sentiments seemed to be more sceptical of, if not opposed to, EEC membership. Items discussed included social services, nationalization and cooperatives in the EEC, and the strength of trade unions and socialism in Europe, but had negligible impact at the Labour Party Conference or in Parliamentary debate.

The promotional groups operating against British entry into the EEC did have a more discernible effect upon the anatomy of the issue. Two explanatory factors worth identifying are that these groups deliberately sought to undermine the Government's case, in contrast to pro entry groups, and they conducted a more active and popularly oriented operation. The Anti Common Market League (ACML), though initially created as a pressure group within the Conservative Party soon became a broad based organisation boasting 30,000 members by the time of the collapse of the negotiations. It has been estimated that the ACML produced as much literature on the EEC issue as the Conservative Party did (Windlesham, 1966, p.270.) The themes most frequently adopted in their publications were the Commonwealth, sovereignty, agriculture, living standards and employment, which had immediate appeal irrespective of party and achieved considerable status within the Parliamentary anatomy. The League organised a series of about thirty public rallies, the largest being attended by around 2,000 people at Central Hall Westminster. In addition, large advertisements were taken out in popular and quality newspapers for recruitment, and to draw attention to the Commonwealth theme during the 1962 Commonwealth Prime Ministers' Conference. Perhaps the most effective piece of propaganda the ACML produced was a single-sided leaflet, which achieved a circulation figure of about one million. This effectively drew attention to the themes of food prices, the Commonwealth, sovereignty (drawing upon intolerance of European national characteristics), agriculture and employment.

The two smaller anti EEC groups, the Forward Britain Movement, (FBM) and Keep Britain Out (KBO) united with the ACML in organising meetings and rallies and also in the themes which they promoted. Their own special emphases were describing the EEC as a capitalist conspiracy (FBM), and the dangers of free trade posed by the EEC (KBO). The ease with which groups oriented at opposite ends of the political spectrum were able to unite in opposition to EEC entry, was in large part due to their combined emphasis of the Commonwealth and sovereignty themes, and the broad appeal of these.

In summary, whilst the pro EEC groups especially the European Movement and the Common Market Campaign, were of importance prior to Macmillan's announcement, in persuading him of the considerable extent of informed and influential support for British entry into the EEC, as the negotiations proceeded, the ACML in particular succeeded in achieving wide impact, and in emphasising and reinforcing topics which became significant themes in the wider debate and in the Parliamentary anatomy.

THE PRESS

In discussing the relationship of the national press in Britain to the salience and anatomy of the European issue in P4, two periods will be distinguished: that before (ie P4a) and that after (ie P4b and P4c) Macmillan's announcement to the House of Commons in July 1961.

During the earlier period, there had been rumblings among the quality press particularly, that Britain should consider EEC membership. There is no evidence to suggest that this prompted Macmillan's initiative, but it is probable that his resolve was strengthened by such sentiments. Woodrow Wyatt MP believed that the expression of the Daily Mirror's pro EEC sentiments proved

> 'the vital tip-over factor which had decided the Government to stop havering about and really start the negotiations. Because they thought that if they had the Daily Mirror behind them, then all would probably be all right.' (quoted in Windlesham, 1966, p.157.)

The Economist was an early advocate of a change in British policy towards the EEC, due largely to the costs of staying out. In an editorial (28.5.60) these were discussed, and whilst commercial costs of separation from the Six were acknowledged, emphasis was placed upon political considerations. It was suggested that a serious division of Europe may proceed if Britain stayed out and that entry would provide Britain with the opportunity to influence European affairs. It also argued that the Soviet threat meant that Europe needed to be united in order to remain free. The concomitant problems of the implications of entry for British trade with America, the Commonwealth and EFTA were noted. The Daily Telegraph considered that British entry into the EEC would make the country, and specifically British agriculture and the Commonwealth more prosperous.

These themes expressed in The Economist and the Daily Telegraph were somewhat tangential to the main features of the Parliamentary anatomy of the issue, however they were in harmony with the depiction of the EEC question which Macmillan might well have wished to predominate.

Also during this period, the Daily Express pre-empted the Government's initiative by asserting as early as March 1960 that Britain should never join, due to the need to maintain her agriculture, which should not be 'abandoned to foreigners'. The Commonwealth theme was maintained consistently and in an article in the following year, it was stated that

'In many minds the Commonwealth seems to have become an unpleasant word. It is regarded as a hindrance by Little Englanders who think our future lies in becoming a small cog in the European machine, with its policies dictated by Washington.' (Daily Express, 2.4.61.)

This emphasis upon the sacrifice of the Commonwealth for British entry into the EEC, if not contributing to, was at least consistent with some worries expressed by Macmillan on this count, as witnessed by his references to the Commonwealth in his speech of July 1961.

During the early summer of 1961, when the Government's change in attitude towards the EEC was becoming more obvious, the Daily Herald gave prominent coverage to policy developments. In June 1961, a front page headline read "The Rome Treaty: Why Britain should sign and join the Common Market." In common with the Daily Express, the Daily Herald was concerned about Britain's role in world affairs, but presumed that her prosperity and her civilised voice could only be assured by accession to the EEC. It argued that Britain's ties with EFTA and the Commonwealth would not be sufficient if Britain was to remain a major trading nation and have a great influence in the world.

In the period after the Macmillan announcement, and particularly during 1962, the issue of Britain's accession to the EEC became a major item within the British press. This extended to the publication of several pamphlets on the subject by major dailies. Special articles by prestigious guest authors also became commonplace in the efforts of the newspapers to either parade their own views or add further fuel to the debate.

One further notable feature should be pointed out; that of the prevalence of pro EEC sentiments among the national dailies. The only exception to this pattern was of course the Daily Express, which maintained strong, and at times, vehement opposition to the EEC and to the Conservative Government for its European policy. Whilst a considerable proportion of the criticism of Government policy emerged from the ranks of the Labour Party and the trade union movement, their traditional allies among the national dailies – the Daily Herald and the Daily Mirror adopted a consistent pro EEC stance. The Daily Worker, the organ of the Communist Party, was the sole daily left wing critic of the Government's European policy. Among the major weeklies, The Economist, Spectator, Observer and Sunday Times gave gave broad support to the Government, whilst the New Statesman and Tribune were critical. It should also be noted that when negotiations appeared to get bogged down and the terms of entry more complex and unfavourable in autumn 1962, several of these pro EEC papers began to exhibit some misgivings over the likely cost of membership.

In discussing the characterisation of the EEC issue in the British press after Macmillan's announcement, special attention will be given to three papers, the Daily Express, the Daily Herald and the Daily Telegraph. The Daily Express, with a circulation figure at this time of about 4.3 million adopted a crusading style during this period in opposing British EEC entry. (All circulation figures from Williams, 1962). This was achieved by means of editorial comment, front page news reports and regular special features. The Daily Express also maintained a 'Fact a day' series on the front page, designed to cast the EEC in poor light. Given the longstanding identification of the Beaverbrook press with the Commonwealth, it is not surprising that this would be a major theme. This is best illustrated during the 1962 Commonwealth Prime Ministers Conference, when one Daily Express (18.9.62) headline ran 'No, No, No Again'. It also exploited statements made by Europeans to this end. Adenauer (the West German Chancellor) was quoted on a front page as saying that the

Commonwealth could not survive in its present form if Britain went into the Common Market. Great appeal was also made to historical sentiments. An editorial condemning John Hare (Minister of Labour 1960-63) for depicting the behaviour of Commonwealth countries on the EEC issue as childish, asked whether Gallipoli, Vimy Ridge and the Channel invasion were childish. Another emotive issue used was the threat of an influx of foreign labour. In an appeal to the trade unions to oppose the Common Market, a Daily Express editorial (5.2.62) stated that 'If Britain enters the Common Market, foreigners will swarm here.' This somewhat racially motivated attitude was often invoked: another editorial asked 'Do you want your children to belong to some British, French, German, Italian hotch potch?' (Daily Express, 6.1.62.)

Finally, the question of domestic food prices was regularly discussed. One feature described 'the foreign giant looming over breakfast - and every other meal.'(Daily Express, 7.11.62.) It proceeded to outline the threat to British housewives' purses of the agricultural terms of British EEC membership and the accompanying loss of Imperial Preference. Details of the price of sirloin, butter and eggs in the EEC countries were given, and it was also held that the British ate more calories per head than the Europeans. (Daily Express, 13.4.62.)

The fervour with which the Daily Express pursued its campaign did lead to a Press Council ruling that one headline stating that 'Amory lets it out, Common Market will bring painful changes', was misleading. Examination of Amory's speech found that he favoured EEC entry. Whilst the style of the Daily Express's depiction of the issue was perhaps not always typical of Parliamentary debate, the actual subjects and sentiments of discussion, particularly that of the Commonwealth, were consistent with the preoccupations of the House of Commons. Certainly, the Daily Express reproduced the Parliamentary speeches and sentiments of those opposed to entry from both major Parties, though the extent to which it contributed directly to Parliamentary debate is not verifiable, The Daily Express undoubtedly did provide a major platform for the aggregation and articulation of views which were not conducive to the Government's desired outcome.

The Daily Herald, with a circulation figure of about 1.4 million, maintained its broadly pro EEC stance after Macmillan's announcement. In an editorial at an early stage in the campaign, the problems of access for Commonwealth goods and the need for a fair deal for EFTA were acknowledged, though the Daily Herald continued to give emphasis to the political advantages of entry: a strong and united Europe constituting a strong economic unit to compete with the USSR and the USA. Considerable editorial space was devoted to discussing the Commonwealth theme, though this mainly consisted of rebuttals of criticisms of entry on this count. One editorial (1.6.62) asked

'will the Commonwealth ministers have the largeness of vision to judge the plan as a whole and its effects on Britain's relationship with the Commonwealth as a whole?'

The Daily Herald was not so pro EEC that it ignored the complexities and conflicts of interest encountered in the negotiations, and it stated in July 1962 that Britain was being sqeezed very hard, and asked 'is the Market to be a closed community acting in the interests of the French farmer, and without Commonwealth guarantees?' (Daily Herald, 30.7.62.) Equally, it did report when and where progress had been made: eg regarding gains for New Zealand food exports. Thus the Daily Herald recognised the terms of entry as important, but even as late as November 1962, when the magnitude of the problems of negotiation were becoming evident, it expressed its desire for entry squarely within the political theme. It urged the British Labour movement to recognise, like its European counterparts, that national policies were no longer adequate, and that a United States of Europe provided the best hope for social justice. (Daily Herald, 5.11.62.)

Although the Daily Herald dealt with the problems of the entry into the EEC, both for Britain and the Commonwealth, in rather a more discriminating fashion than many other organisations, nevertheless by discussing them it further fuelled the salience of these very problems. The political reasons for membership which the Daily Herald espoused did not however attract a great deal of attention either within Labour Party debate or within the Parliamentary anatomy.

The Daily Telegraph, with a circulation of about 1.25 million in this period, consistently supported the Government's EEC policy. It provided extensive coverage of the debate within the UK and Commonwealth and of the negotiations. Like the Daily Herald, it considered the main reasons for entry to derive from the implications for the prosperity and destiny of Britain, Europe and the world, although it acknowledged that the issue would be discussed in 'bread and butter terms'. Whilst considerable attention was given to the themes of agriculture, the Commonwealth and sovereignty. In addition it did draw on such wider topics as the impact of entry upon the British car manufacturing industry, and social and labour conditions within the EEC. The Daily Telegraph was prepared to defend British and Commonwealth interests in the course of the negotiations, but it was equally prepared to argue that because talks were difficult, there was no reason to jump to gloomy conclusions: it added that the 'aloofness of some Commonwealth Governments, including Canada, is less than helpful'. (Daily Telegraph, 26.3.62.) In contrast to the Daily Express and the Daily Herald, the Daily Telegraph was in broad agreement with its political ally, the Conservative Party. This gave the Daily Telegraph the opportunity to level criticism at the Labour Party for its stand on the EEC. Commenting on the 1961 Labour Party Conference, it said that any idea that the British Labour movement had any ideas of international socialism had long gone overboard, and that the policy of the Labour Party would not encourage the Six. In the following year, the Daily Telegraph suggested that it would be best for the Labour Party to wait until the terms had been negotiated before it attacked them: again the Daily Telegraph urged that the issue be not treated simply as an economic one. The Daily Telegraph developed the major themes evident within the Parliamentary anatomy, viz agriculture, the Commonwealth and sovereignty, but what it saw as political imperatives for entry did not enjoy corresponding salience within the House of Commons.

Assessment of the overall impact of the press regarding any political question is problematical. It has already been established that the salience of the issue within Parliament was clearly duplicated among the national press, whether quality or popular. Evidence in Table 2 suggests that the

Daily Express and Daily Herald readers did not exhibit views clearly reflecting those of the editors. Indeed, if anything there appears to be some deviation from editorial cues when the proportions of readers in favour of entry are compared.

Table 2

Policy Preferences of Daily Herald and Daily Express Readers

Response of Readers	Daily Herald	Daily Express
For	38%	45%
Against	25%	29%
Don't Know	37%	26%

(Cited in Lieber, 1970, p.224.)

What though of the relevance of the press for the anatomy of the issue? The pro EEC press may have succeeded during the formative stages of the issue in P4, in assuring Macmillan of support among editors and journalists. However, despite the weight of numbers of these pro EEC papers, they appeared less successful in contributing to the anatomy of the issue as deduced from Parliamentary debate. The positive reasons for entry as expounded by the Daily Herald and the Daily Telegraph, for example, did not feature significantly in Parliamentary debate. These papers, in common with the other pro EEC papers, were reduced to discussing the very terms of entry which were the campaign weapons of the Daily Express. In summary, it was the latter newspaper which, while occasionally depicting the EEC issue perversely, did most propound the themes of the Commonwealth, EFTA, agriculture and sovereignty. In that these proved to be the undoing of Government (being unable in consequence, to make a positive commitment to the EEC), this paper was more instrumental in the anatomy and outcome of the issue than its competitors.

Kenneth Younger (1964) has commented that foreign affairs are generally too remote for concerted and coherent opinions of the public to be formed. The events of 1982 in the Falkland Islands have at least proved that under certain conditions, foreign affairs can win the concentrated attention of the public and elicit a range of strongly held views upon them. The EEC issue obviously did not constitute a war, but unlike many foreign issues (eg the Palestinian problem or El Salvador), it did include implications close to home (eg the impact of entry upon consumer prices) and close to contemporary British political sensibilities (eg the Commonwealth).

Nevertheless a large, though varying proportion of the British public did remain undecided about the EEC (though this does not in itself imply that they considered it unimportant: no relevant data are available on this). In answer to the Gallup Poll question 'If the British Government were to decide that Britain's interest would best be served by joining European Common Market, would you approve or disapprove?', the percentage of Don't Knows ranged from 20% to 42% over P4, with a mean of 31.2%. Although those who Disapproved never exceeded those who Approved in the Gallup Poll, the mean for the latter was only 45% (cited in Gallup Poll, 1966.) The Daily Express did commission its own opinion surveys, which asked the more direct question, 'Are you for or against Britain joining the Common Market?' Predictably, perhaps, this produced a lower level of approval.

Popular approval of EEC entry tended to shift in direct relationship with the popular standing of the Government. This would suggest that opinion towards the EEC was not firmly held, and despite the direct relevance of the issue, Younger's verdict (above) seems upheld.

The data available on the elements of the European issue considered important by the public is neither systematic nor extensive, and thus only tentative conclusions can be drawn as to popular estimations of the issue's anatomy. It is certainly the case that in the latter half of 1962, some notion of the significance of terms of entry developed.

(All data from Gallup Poll, 1966.) For example, 62% of
respondents thought that the Government would be 'right not
to give way' if the negotiations were to collapse. In
response to a question in October 1962 asking which of a
range of listed effects EEC entry would be likely to cause,
the highest response rate (58%) was for a 'rise in the food
prices'. However, arguments which appeared to be rather
muted in the Parliamentary debates, such as a rise in
British exports and a wider choice of goods available,
achieved higher responses (42% and 54% respectively) than
might have been expected. Further, arguments such as a
reduction of the power of Parliament and the Commonwealth
collapse, were not treated seriously among the respondents.
Thus while the latter themes, along with agricultural
implications of entry, dominated Parliamentary debate, the
wider public were not convinced of their relevance at this
point in time. However, a year earlier, 39% of respondents
had thought that the Commonwealth interests were of such
over-riding importance, that Britain should not join unless
these were satisfactorily accommodated. A 25% proportion
answered similarly for the farming interests. It should be
added that 25% of the respondents thought no difficulties
were so over-riding, and 24% did not know. Another example
of fluidity in public opinion concerns prices. In October
1962, as noted above, the threat of a rise in food prices
was perceived to be the most likely consequence of entry.
However, a year earlier, the most likely consequence was
thought to be the keeping down of the cost of living and the
advent of cheaper goods.

The problem remains of course that the public opinion polls
are measuring and aggregating the views of a variety of
publics, and that the publication of polls in itself
constitutes a tactic in the political process: contrast the
questions and responses of the Daily Express polls and
Gallup Poll. Thus these factors mask different opinions
towards, and different evaluations of the issue held by
different groups in the system. James Spence, on studying
more detailed data, concluded that

'The polls showed that the antis tended to be
concentrated among the poorer working class, women and
older groups, to whom the threat of price increases was
likely to be critical. Middle class groups, men and

younger groups tended to be more in favour.' (Spence, 1976, p.23.)

This corresponds with his earlier assertion that those opposed to entry tended to specify unemployment and high prices as their principal objections. He also found that the reasons people gave for supporting membership tended to be vague and general. This finding does seem to reflect the problems encountered by advocates of EEC entry in advancing the clear merits of entry, rather than simply minimising the objections.

The political party adhered to by the members of the public proved to be an important cue in shaping their attitudes towards the EEC. In April 1962, whilst overall only 38% favoured entry and 33% were opposed to it, Conservative respondents preferred entry by 58% to 22%. When, in October 1962, the Labour Party finally opposed entry on the terms that were likely to be available only 27% of Labour partisans favoured entry and 36% were opposed. (cited in Lieber, 1970, p.232.)

DISCUSSION

What factors account for the anatomy of issue in P4? The comparatively high salience of the issue noted in the Parliamentary content analysis was reflected throughout the British political system in P4. Whilst clearly it was the Government who, after advice from some senior civil servants, took the initiative in pushing the issue to the forefront of political debate, this had a domino effect among numerous political organisations. The Conservative Party Conference and Central Office, all sections of the Labour movement, the Liberal Party, sectional groups, promotional groups and the press, all indicated in their respective fashions that they considered the issue to be one of high salience. This reinforced the ascending salience of the issue within Parliament. Thus the political system proved to be responsive to the Government initiative, in terms of attributing importance to the issue.

It seems clear that the initial Government presentation of the issue gave emphasis to commercial considerations, as

Macmillan was unwilling to risk a principled decision for
entry due to fear of dividing his own party. This was
despite the fact that Macmillan's own memoirs revealed that
he personally valued the political consequences of British
EEC entry very highly. Thus from the beginning of
Macmillan's public campaign on the issue, in his July 1961
announcement to the House of Commons, he included the themes
of the Commonwealth, agriculture and EFTA, presumably
thinking that this would draw the sting from any criticism
from within the Conservative Party. In simple terms of
Parliamentary behaviour, he was successful in this. He also
managed to win the confidence of successive Conservative
Conferences. However, Macmillan's assertion that the terms
of entry should be acceptable in these policy areas, proved
to be crucial. It was these themes in addition to that of
the sovereignty questions, which came to dominate the
Parliamentary anatomy of the issue, to an extent which
Macmillan probably eventually found unwelcome. His decision
to give a Prime Ministerial broadcast on the subject on
September 19th 1962 reflects a desire towards the end of
the period to raise the issue out of the morass of
commercial minutiae which were coming to dominate the issue.
The Government, of course, contributed to this state of
affairs by not taking Monnet's advice of going in and then
sorting out the details (due to adverse anticipated
reactions). Instead, the negotiating procedure was
instigated leading to several White Papers dealing solely
with the terms under discussion: what had been agreed and,
often more importantly, what had not. In addition, the
Government's main source of ideas and advice, the civil
service, was also fully immersed in the conduct of
negotiations and the squabble over terms.

This trend of emphasis on these terms was influenced from
several quarters opposed to EEC entry, or opposed to it on
terms which seemed likely. The Labour Party gave primacy to
the need for acceptable terms of entry, as was manifest in
their 1962 Conference resolution on the subject and in
Gaitskell's television broadcasts. The five safeguards
which were propounded (Commonwealth safeguards, an
independent economic policy, guarantees for EFTA, the right
of independent economic planning, and safeguards for British
agriculture) were regularly drawn upon by Labour MPs at
Conferences and in Parliamentary debate; even by known pro

Europeans such as George Brown and Roy Jenkins. The NFU was a fairly constant critic of the Government's European policy and naturally gave special attention to farming matters, though much was also made by the NFU of the impact on food prices of the loss of Imperial Preference. The NFU's views were easily communicated to the public by way of press interest, notably by the Daily Express (see below), by the connection of the active Conservative EEC opponents with agriculture (notably Viscount Hinchingbrooke whose role in the South Dorset by-election of sponsoring a Conservative anti EEC candidate produced a Labour victory in this Conservative stronghold), and by the interest shown in NFU pronouncements by anti EEC promotional groups. In addition, the functional links of the NFU with the MAFF ensured that the Ministry and the negotiating team were always made aware of the NFU'S views on developments. This scenario is consistent with E. Liggett's view (1971) that the MAFF was obstructionist.

Whilst the views of the British trade union movement were far from cohesive on this subject, certain of the larger and influential unions took up these themes related to the terms of EEC membership though they were often outside their normal functional concerns. The Transport and General Workers' Union, for example, expressed concern over the interests of British agriculture and the Commonwealth.

Turning to promotional groups, whilst it is believed that pro EEC groups might have played some part in convincing Macmillan that there was support, at an elite level at least, for British entry, once the debate began in earnest, it was the anti EEC groups, notably the Anti Common Market League, that had much greater impact. The ACML produced a large amount of literature on the subject, and the themes which it deemed important (the Commonwealth, sovereignty and agriculture) achieved considerable stature within the Parliamentary anatomy.

Equally, whilst certain pro EEC newspapers and journals had contributed to a climate which gave Macmillan the confidence to go ahead with his initiative, it was the Daily Express whose characterisation of the issue was most akin to that of the Parliamentary anatomy. It should be added that towards the end of P4, The Times and the Daily Herald both expressed increased concerns over the themes of the Commonwealth and agriculture.

It appears from analysis that many of the groups and individuals who favoured EEC were unsuccessful in imposing some of the themes most conducive to their case upon the Parliamentary anatomy of the issue. This has been proved to be the case among Conservative MPs, Labour MPs, the Liberal Party and various pro EEC promotional groups. Indeed, advocates of entry spent most of their debating opportunities in combating objections to entry - usually on the subjects of the Commonwealth, sovereignty and agriculture. The combined effects of the emphasis of these themes by opponents or sceptics of British EEC entry, and the concentration upon them by advocates of entry, proved to be undermining to the British Government's negotiating position and gave de Gaulle good cause to question Britain's readiness for membership. Indeed, it is wrong to depict the veto as simply a personal expresssion on de Gaulle's part. Adenauer is reported to have been exasperated with Britain: "You don't seriously think Macmillan is ready for Europe do you? You don't really think Britain can catch that bus?" (Ball, 1982.)

This state of affairs accelerated during P4. The content analysis highlighted a clear increase in the Economic aspect from P4a to P4c and that this was mainly composed of details related to the Commonwealth and agriculture. Events proved that Macmillan's attempt to inject notions of the political needs for Britain's EEC membership into the debate in his television broadcast of September 1962 were too late to be effective. It is possible, though not demonstrable, that such an initiative at the outset may have precipitated an issue with a rather different anatomy, giving emphasis not only to sovereignty and federalism (which were well represented within the P4 anatomy) but also Britain's increasing political isolation, the virtues of a united Europe providing independence from the USA and a bulwark against Communism, and the opportunity for Britain to lead Europe from within.

In conclusion, it is clear that the salience the issue achieved within Parliament, was not only a function of the issue's Prime Ministerial sponsorship, but also the controversy which the issue aroused. This not only directly prompted a desire to contribute to the debate among members of all parties, but also must have, by virtue of anticipated reactions, put pressure upon the Government to report back to the House regularly on the negotiations, thus further contributing to the issue's high salience. Despite the controversy over the issue, it was noted that the level of party scoring was low in contrast to that during P1. Whilst the latter period was one of exceptional inter-party conflict, this finding, in conjunction with that of the high level of substantiation, suggests that the attention to the frequently complex implications of the issue was high, as opposed to attention to superficial slogans associated with the issue or to the exploitation of the issue for party political purposes in P1. In many cases this may have been related to the preoccupation of the terms of membership which prevailed, but which had not achieved such salience when the possibility of ECSC or EEC entry was less likely in earlier periods. It should be noted that the party scoring component increased in status towards the end of P4 coinciding with the Labour Party's strengthened resolve to oppose membership on the terms likely to be available and Macmillan's attempt to further politicise the issue in the autumn of 1962.

The fact that the British Economic sphere and the European Economic sphere of the issue's anatomy were so largely dominated by agricultural considerations is a reflection of the fervent campaigning on this theme by the NFU and regular reference to it by the Labour Party, rural Conservative interests, the **Daily Express** and the ACML. Had the Government adopted the approach of trying to secure entry and then sorted out the details, there would have been no immediate agricultural implications, as the Common Agricultural Policy was not yet agreed by the Six. Little attention was given to potential advantages for the British economy of EEC entry within the British Economic sphere, and this is further testimony to the minimum impact upon the debate of advocates of British entry.

The status of the Commonwealth themes within the Extra European Political and Economic spheres also matches the emphasis put on the debate by opponents or sceptics of entry. They were successful in communicating doubts on

the part of Commonwealth leaders into the British debate.
As with the subject of agriculture, advocates of membership
were obliged - largely by the negotiating procedure adopted
as well as the potency of the antiEuropeans' arguments - to
resort to countering objects to the EEC, rather than putting
forward positive reasons for entry.

In summary, Macmillan can be held partly responsible for
the anatomy which prevailed in that he introduced the issue
in the context of negotiable terms. This was capitalised
upon by opponents of entry who, although vocal and
enthusiastic, would not normally be said to be dominant
forces within Parliament, the press, industry or the trade
union movement. As has been illustrated by the views of de
Gaulle and Adenauer, and the warning of Monnet, this
emphasis on the terms of entry especially regarding
agriculture and the Commonwealth, proved crucial in the 1963
policy outcome.

8 Conclusions

The object of this study has been to demonstrate the
contribution that issue salience and issue anatomy can make
to a fuller understanding of the policy making process.
This has been attempted on the supposition that initial
attention to the nature of political issues and the changes
therein may be more profitable and less value-laden than the
simple adoption of issues to validate a particular view of
the policy making process in general, and more specifically,
of political influence and power. Accordingly, a content
analysis was conducted on the House of Commons debate of the
European question over a period of years during which it was
thought that the issue would be subject to considerable
fluctuation in salience. It was also exected that swings
would occur in broad policy preferences, although no more of
the issue's anatomy could be predicted confidently on the
basis of a simple historical knowledge of the period.

In order to verify expectations of the issue's salience and
to provide a full picture of the issue's anatomy the content
analysis of House of Commons debate was carried out.

What light have the results of the content analysis thrown upon the European question over the specified years? First, the expectations concerning the issue's salience were confirmed. In one period, P4, the issue was characterised by comparatively high status, and in another, P1, it had a short-lived, moderate salience. In P2 and P3 however, the issue achieved only a very low salience, such that the issue in these periods was described as muted. The salience of the issue was so low in the case of P3, that there was insufficient data to enable content analysis of the issue's anatomy.

Turning to the issue's anatomy, the most significant trend between P1 and P4 was a reduction in status of the Political aspect, and the rise in that of the Economic aspect. Whilst in P1, the Political aspect accounted for about 70% of the points of detail, in P4, this aspect achieved on a 43% share. The Economic aspect rose in stature from 24% in P1 to 49% in P4, thus compensating for the decline in the Political aspect. The Social aspect had a low stature throughout, and achieved more than a 10% share of the details only in P2.

There were also discernable shifts in the status of each geographical focus, though there were no clear trends as in the Political and Economic aspects of policy between P1 and P4. The stature of the Extra European focus was particularly erratic. It fell from a 30% share in P1 to 9% in P2, only to rise again in P4 to become the foremost focus in P4, with a 39% share of the details. The European focus acquired the highest status in P1 and P2 (accounting for almost half of the details in the latter period) yet in P4, when entry into the process of European economic integration seemed most likely, the stature of this focus fell to a 34% share of the details.

Examination was also made of the changes within the individual spheres (ie aspect stratified by focus) over the different periods. Generally, the relative size of spheres was in accordance with the statures of the individual aspect and focus which comprised each sphere (eg in P1 and P2, when the Political aspect and the Economic focus were pre-eminent, the European Political sphere accounted for 48% of the points of detail in P1, and 59% of them in P2). However, other findings were less predictable. For example, in P1 whereas overall the British focus accounted for 30% of the points of detail, these occurred disproportionately in the Economic aspect: the British Economic sphere accounted for 53% of the details. In contrast when the Political aspect was stratified by focus, the British Political sphere achieved only an 18% status. A similar pattern of a skew of British details towards the Economic aspect was evident in P2. In this period it was also noted that <u>all</u> of the points of detail arising in the Extra European focus fell within the Political aspect. In P4, the British focus (29% overall) was markedly under-represented (19%) within the Political aspect.

There were other changes in the anatomy of the European question which were highlighted by the content analysis. The most dramatic of these concerned the status of the party scoring component. In P1 this accounted for almost half of all statements made, and about a third of the points of detail (ie when statements were substantiated). In P2 this component's share of the total points of detail fell to 10%, and in P4 to 8%. The component of the state and nature of the negotiations was not subject to such dramatic changes as that of party scoring, though it did almost double in status from P2 (7.9% of detail) to P4 (15%).

Patterns of policy preference were also subject to considerable change over the three periods. P1 was characterised by a high proportion of statements for and against, with the lowest finding for neutral statements throughout. Predictably perhaps, in P2 the proportion of statements for was at its lowest throughout, but the share of those against was also surprisingly low. In P4, despite the obvious contention over the issue, neutral statements not only predominated, but accounted for over 60% of all statements made.

Finally, the levels of substantiation also varied over the three periods, indicating different depths of analysis of the issue. The levels of substantiation were highest in P4 and lowest in P2.

215

Together all this evidence indicates that the European question between 1950 and 1963 was neither static nor monolithic. It was not static, because its salience varied considerably. It was not monolithic because its constituent features (aspect, focus, party scoring, policy preference and substantiation) - collectively labelled the anatomy of the issue - also displayed a marked tendency to change. This conclusion constitutes the first achievement of study. However, it was also suggested at the outset that if it was possible to demonstrate that the salience and anatomy of an issue was subject to such shifts, then it would be desirable to try to explain these. A related objective in so doing was to ascertain the extent to which the Parliamentary findings were representative of broader perceptions of the issue.

P1, SALIENCE AND ANATOMY

In the case of P1, it was concluded that the salience which the issue did achieve was primarily a function of the role of the Conservative Party in Parliament and further, that this was symptomatic of the adversarial political climate of the time. There was no real possibility of the issue being elevated by the Labour Government, Whitehall, British busines organisations, or the British trade union movement, given their general lack of interest in European economic integration. Although the Liberal Party was known to favour British participation in the Schuman Plan, it was only by means of a partnership with the Conservative Party in Parliament that the Liberals succeeded in being associated with, what was in the short term at least, an issue of moderate Parliamentary salience. There is no evidence that any sections of the British press sought to raise the status of the issue prior to Churchill's espousal of it. The Times had given coverage of the developments preceding the Schuman Plan, though it did not mount a campaign for full British participation, and the other major national dailies simply responded to Parliamentary cues on the issue. Thus the stature of the issue within the press was a reflection of its Parliamentary salience.

Turning to the issue's anatomy within Parliament, the main emphasis within the Political aspect was on the European focus. Almost half of the points of detail raised in this sphere were related to the location of sovereignty within the proposed community. Such references (generally raised as objections to a British role in the scheme) outnumbered by almost three times the details concerning the contribution of the Schuman Plan to a strong, united and free Europe (generally raised in favour of British participation). Similarly, within the Extra European Political sphere, details relating to the Commonwealth (usually raised in order to object to British participation in the Schuman Plan) accounted for over a third of the total. The Economic Aspect was dominated by British concerns, almost half of which were related to the effects of British entry into the proposed Community upon the British coal, iron and steel industries. There were usually perceived as detrimental.

In summary, the perceptions of the European question were dominated by debate over what fundamentally were objections to British entry. Matching the depiction of the issue by Government spokesmen, the Conservative front bench spokesmen in Parliament were instrumental in raising the salience of the issue, and in so doing, responsible for the comparatively high level of statements for entry. They were not however successful when it came to affecting the anatomy of the issue. Conservatives spent more time refuting objections to entry than giving positive reasons for Britain going in. The perceptions of the issue which prevailed inside Parliament were essentially those which were unconducive to British entry. Why was this? Given that the Conservative leadership did not agree with, and thus did not promote some of the themes advanced by the Liberal Party, which gave more emphasis to positive benefits of British membership, there was no sufficiently powerful quarter from which the prevailing view of the issue could be challenged.

The stature of the party scoring component in P1 is highly significant. It indicates that the issue was not solely concerned with the inherent questions raised by the Schuman Plan, but that also it was tainted by the adversarial political climate which pervaded the period between the General Elections of February 1950 and October 1951. This goes some way towards confirming the view that the Conservative Party was not really interested in a full

British role in European economic integration.   It further
explains the failure of the Party's spokesmen (having
succeeded in elevating the salience of the issue), to
impinge upon the issue's anatomy in such a way as to
validate the policy preference which they purported to
desire, namely British support for the principles of the
Schuman Plan and participation in the developments leading
to the ECSC.

P2, SALIENCE AND ANATOMY

The Parliamentary salience of the issue in P2 was described
as low, and this seemed representative of the stature of the
issue outside the House of Commons.   The Government made no
effort to pose ECSC membership as a policy alternative,   nor
did the Parliamentary Opposition, business and trade union
representative organisations or any sections of the British
press.   The extent to which the issue was ignored in P2 is
further illustrated by the temporary cessation of the
activities of the European Movement in the UK.

The dominance of the European Political sphere and the
British Economic sphere noted in P1, was extended into P2.
Over two thirds of the details in the former sphere were
taken up by just two themes; first, that of the operation of
supranational authority in the ECSC, and secondly, that of
the acceptability of association with the ECSC.   The
sovereignty theme also dominated the British Political
sphere.   Turning to the British Economic sphere, this was
monopolised by details as to the impact of ECSC membership
upon the British coal, iron and steel industries;   these
normally suggested a detrimental impact.   Thus, it is clear
that the prevailing anatomy of the issue did not include
perceptions of the question which might have encouraged
favourable policy preferences.   This was consistent with
the views of all major groups and organisations within the
political system during P2.   British membership of the ECSC
was virtually a non-existent policy alternative in these
quarters.   Robert Schuman, writing in The Times (30.1.53)
during this period, described the major obstacle to British
participation in the ECSC as one of 'political psychology'.
This is another way of saying that somehow the feeling
prevailed in Britain that she should not join the ECSC: the
reasons given for such a policy were secondary.

Such an interpretation is backed up by other characteristics of the issue's anatomy in P2. The comparatively low level of substantiation which occurred indicates that the issue was not explored as much as in P1 and P4, and suggests that the policy outcome was taken for granted by more contributors to the debate than in other periods. Secondly, there was quite a low level of party scoring, and indeed most of this did not concern the issue at the time, but consisted of justifications and denouncements of policies held during P1. Thus in P2, the combination of the low salience of the issue and its particular anatomy served to ensure that ECSC membership was barely seen as theoretical alternative, let alone a viable one.

P3, SALIENCE AND ANATOMY

So little debate relevant to the issue occurred in P3 that content analysis was not possible to identify the issue's anatomy in this period. However, the low level of salience identified was compatible with wider views on the issue. British membership of the EEC was not considered as a viable policy alternative by the Government, the Labour Party, the trade union movement, British business organisations, the press or any promotional groups. Emphasis instead was given to the efforts made to deter the establishment of the EEC by means of the proposed Free Trade Area, and to the formation of the limited trading alliance, the European Free Trade Association. References which were made outside Parliament to Britain's relations with the EEC either reinforced the supposition that membership was out of the question, or were simply manifestations of Britain's routine relations with the Six (cemented by her Associate Status of the ECSC in 1955), mainly consisting of the exchange of information. This does suggest a relationship between the anatomy of an issue and its salience: it was considered virtually irrelevant and thus acquired no stature within the British political system.

P4, SALIENCE AND ANATOMY

P4 saw a dramatic change in the salience of the issue. Some responsibility for this can be attributed to press

219

articles and elite promotional group activity in promoting the European question and in assuring Macmillan of some support for British EEC membership. However, the most significant factor in the initial elevation of the status of the issue was undoubtedly the decision of Macmillan and the Government to seek EEC membership. The Government announced its intention to the House of Commons, thus raising the Parliamentary salience of the issue. This had knock-on effects throughout the political system whereby the European question achieved high salience in Whitehall, among interest groups, promotional groups, the press and public opinion.

One of the major changes in the anatomy of the issue since P1 and P2 was that the Extra European focus in P4 accounted for the largest number of points of detail within the Political and Economic aspects. This was the result of a single factor: the status of Commonwealth considerations within debate on Britain's part in European economic integration in P4. The Extra European Political sphere related mainly to Britain's leadership role within the Commonwealth and to the need for British loyalty to the Commonwealth. Questions as to the location of political authority within the EEC continued to be significant within the European Political sphere. The British Political sphere was of low stature, as it had been in P1 and P2: sovereignty questions prevailed here also.

The Extra European focus of the Economic aspect was dominated by the Commonwealth to an even greater extent than the Extra European Political sphere. The details raised in this sphere usually dealt with implications of British EEC entry for a specific Commonwealth country or product. Whilst the British Economic sphere was smaller than it had been in P1 and P2 it was still of some significance and was largely occupied by details on a single subject – agriculture. This theme was also of some stature within the European Economic sphere.

What interpretations can be made from this summary of the issue's anatomy? The themes which received most attention, were related to those very topics which embraced the most potent argument against British EEC entry. Macmillan was in a position to elevate the salience of the issue within

Parliament and outside it, but he adopted a more cautious approach than he might otherwise have desired, due to anticipated reactions of others in the Conservative Party. This cautious approach consisted of emphasising at the outset that the terms of membership had to be acceptable and he specified in this respect that they had to be acceptable from the perspectives of the Commonwealth and of the British agricultural community. Opponents of British EEC entry were able to exploit this negotiation approach, by emphasising these themes (in addition to that of sovereignty) to such an extent that advocates of entry were preoccupied with refuting these arguments at the expense of putting forward possible benefits of entry. Thus, the anatomy of the issue inside Parliament and discussion of it outside were characterised by these themes which were unconducive to convincing the country, and particular interests therein, of the advantages of EEC entry. Further, as witnessed by de Gaulle's termination of the talks on the extension of EEC membership, the anatomy of the issue within Britain did nothing to advance the chances of convincing EEC countries of Britain's commitment to European economic integration.

THE EUROPEAN QUESTION - CONCLUSIONS

As the House of Commons provided the primary research material for this study, it is appropriate first to examine the role of Parliament in the policy making process on the European issue. In P1, when the issue enjoyed considerable status in Parliament, although in terms of the numbers of votes cast on the motion to take part in the Schuman Plan, those MPs voting against the Government were only narrowly beaten by those supporting the Cabinet, Parliament had no impact upon the policy pursued by the Government. Alternatively it could of course be argued that the policy of non-participation in the talks illustrated significant Parliamentary influence in that the view of the Parliamentary majority prevailed. It was illustrated however that on the basis of their earlier behaviour, one might have expected a great number of Labour MPs to favour a more positive response to the Plan, had they been unconstrained by Party loyalties at a time when the Government was desparate for every vote it could muster. There was no opportunity for such a group to effect some form of compromise position (eg Britain attending the talks under certain explicit conditions, or putting forward alternative proposals) at for instance a House of Commons Committee and there is no evidence to suggest that they used the Whips office to this end. A zero-sum alternative existed and as the Government won the day, neither the potentially dissident Labour MPs nor Her Majesty's Opposition enjoyed even marginal influence.

It was concluded that a crucial factor in reinforcing this state of affairs was the anatomy of the issue within Parliament. It was noted that despite the significance attached to the issue by the Conservative front bench, the anatomy of the issue was consistent with the Government's perceptions of the issue. One explanation given for this was the mixed motives of the Opposition: did Churchill and Eden really desire British participation in the Schuman Plan? However, there were individuals among all parties who did, and their failure to effect the issue's anatomy must to some degree be a function of the executive domination of the House of Commons. The Government not only enjoyed the backing of a Parliamentary majority, and agenda setting and time-tabling advantages, but also considerable authority in defining the nature of policy alternatives.

In P2 and P3, the position was somewhat different in that there is no evidence that significant groups within Parliament (whether among Government backbenchers or the Opposition Party) advocated a policy on the European question which diverged from that of the Government. Literally only a handful of MPs even appeared to consider British participation in the ECSC, and later the EEC, as a realistic policy alternative. The inability of this group to raise the salience of the issue, let alone change Government policy, can again be interpreted in two ways. First, it can be argued that the view of the majority prevailed (assuming that an absence of policy on an issue constitutes a view ie in favour of no policy change). Alternatively, it might be argued that the organisation of business within the House of Commons denied the minority the ability to expound their views: thus the majority fell in line behind the Government by default, not as a result of an airing of different points of view, ie this was a non decision.

The Parliamentary anatomy of the issue in P2 was seen to be consistent with the Government's evaluation of the issue: no perceptions of the issue which might have undermined the Government's policy achieved prominence. Thus, when the issue existed in almost a political vacuum, the executive's portrayal of the issue was virtually unquestioned.

In P4 a different situation again prevailed. The Prime Minister, Macmillan, and his Government were responsible for introducing the issue and with it the proposal for policy change to the House of Commons. Subsequently however, the House of Commons began to have a significant impact in relation to the issue's anatomy. As was seen there was great emphasis in the Parliamentary debate on themes not conducive to facilitating British entry into the EEC. The emphasis upon the terms of membership, particularly regarding the Commonwealth, British agriculture and the location of sovereignty, seriously undermined the position of the Government, not only within Britain, but also in relation to the negotiations with the EEC countries. The influence of Parliament was never tested by a vote on British EEC entry with a set of known terms. However, the fact that such a bill was never presented to Parliament in P4 is itself illustrative of the ability of the House of Commons to portray the issue in such a way as to detract seriously from the Government's achievement of its policy objective: the Government was never in a position to put a final package before the House.

This study has not been conducted solely in order to provide an assessment of Parliamentary influence and thus no comprehensive conclusions can be drawn in this respect. The analysis has, however, enabled certain insights into the impact of the House of Commons upon the policy making process. The role of the Commons varied from one situation to another. It was clearly extremely difficult for the few motivated MPs to draw attention to the European question in order to achieve policy change during P2 and P3, when there existed no support for their views from either front bench. When the Opposition front bench did sponsor the issue in P1, it might be argued that Parliament had a considerable impact upon the salience of the issue. Despite the very small

223

Government majority the Commons had no impact whatsoever on the Government's policy. In P4, when the Government had taken the initiative by suggesting a policy change and given that the process of negotiation extended the life of the issue, Parliamentary opinion did contribute to the failure of the Government to achieve policy change. During P2 and P3, when there existed no support for their views from either front bench. When the Opposition front bench did sponsor the issue in P1, it might be argued that Parliament had a considerable impact upon the salience of the issue. Despite the very small Government majority the Commons had no impact whatsoever on the Government's policy. In P4, when the Government had taken the initiative by suggesting a policy change and given that the process of negotiation extended the life of the issue, Parliamentary opinion did contribute to the failure of the Government to achieve its policy goal, even though de Gaulle was personally responsible for terminating the talks.

The influence of Parliament by means of its impact upon an issue's salience and anatomy and upon the related policy outcome has been seen to be conditional. When the Government enjoys a working Parliamentary majority, the Opposition front bench can significantly raise the salience of an issue, though this by no means guarantees a policy change. Individual MPs are generally impotent even to affect an issue's salience (though there are of course celebrated exceptions to this proposition). If a Government desires a policy change it has no problem in raising the salience of that issue. However, as was illustrated in the case of P4, the ability of the Government to secure a favourable anatomy of that issue within Parliament, should not be taken for granted. In this case, Parliamentary influence was effective. It may be significant that Parliamentary influence was greatest, not in achieving a policy change (P1), but in preventing one (P4). The departure from previous policy advocated by the Macmillan Government was considered too radical. The notion of EEC membership and all it entailed had not sufficiently permeated the political consciousness of MPs who spent the previous decade in accord (if for the most part, silent accord) with the perception held by successive governments that such a policy change was inappropriate for Britain. These findings correspond with other studies of the role of Parliament in policy-making during the nineteen fifties and sixties: executive domination prevailed except in special circumstances.

The study of debate in the House of Commons was conducted primarily in order to enable a contribution to the understanding of the policy making process by the adoption of the concepts of issue salience and anatomy. Thus some assessment should be made of the usefulness of the employment of the Parliamentary debate to this end: how representative were the content analysis findings for the issue's salience and anatomy of wider evaluations and perceptions of the issue? It was pointed out that the salience of the issue in P1 did slightly exaggerate the prominence of the issue, when contrasted with the attention accorded to it by Whitehall, the main political parties and the major interest groups. It was more representative of press attention to the issue, if only for a two month period. The Parliamentary salience of the issue in the other periods did match more closely its standing within the political system.

Turning to the issue's anatomy, the Parliamentary findings generally accorded with the balance of viewpoints which prevailed elsewhere. In P1, the small fraction of the anatomy devoted to positive benefits of British participation in the Schuman Plan was consistent with the comparative political impotence of those who expressed such a view. It should be emphasised that although the Conservative Party leadership did advocate participation it did not do so on the conviction that the Schuman Plan was good for Britain, but merely that there might be something to be gained from participation, and that the objections raised by the Government were not insuperable. The high profile of party scoring within the anatomy was consistent with the party political press coverage of the issue and with the text of the Labour Party document, European Unity.

The anatomy of the European question in P2 reflected the absence of Conservative and Labour conflict over the issue: the party scoring element had considerably declined since P1. In common with P1, there were few statements drawing attention to positive benefits of ECSC membership; this matched discussion on the issue (such as there was) in

225

Whitehall, political parties, pressure groups and the press. The more even balance of the Political and Economic aspects, also resembled the pattern noted outside Parliament. Similarly, the disappearance of the Commonwealth theme in the Parliamentary debate paralleled its demise in wider perceptions of the issue.

In P4 also, the Parliamentary anatomy of the issue was broadly representative of the wider debate. The emphasis on terms of EEC membership and the sovereignty, Commonwealth and agriculture themes in particular, not only reflected the perceptions of those expressly opposed to membership, but also of the waiverers and many of the supporters of British EEC membership. It also matched press coverage of the issue. The high proportion of neutral statements found in the Parliamentary anatomy was thought to be related to uncertainty over terms. This also mirrored uncertainty in many spheres of the Labour Party (until October 1962), the quality press and popular opinion.

In conclusion there was good reason to be confident about the representativeness of the Parliamentary salience and anatomy of the European question in the years covered. The applicability of this method for the measurement of salience and anatomy of other issues will be discussed in the final section of this chapter.

The main aim of the study has been to evaluate the usefulness of the concepts of issue salience and anatomy for a fuller understanding of the policy-making process: what has been achieved in this respect?

This study has confirmed what might have been expected; that the ability of different groups and individuals to effect the salience of an issue is variable. It has been shown that in P1 the Leader of the Opposition and in P4, the Prime Minister, were primarily responsible for elevating the issue's salience: their iniative was followed in P1 by a flurry of press attention and in P4 by a more sustained level of attention throughout the political system. This contrasts vividly with the ineffectual efforts of the European Movement prior to the Schuman Plan, and of the Liberal Party and the handful of motivated backbench MPs during P2 and P3, to draw attention to the European

226

question.

The study has also illustrated that an increased level of issue salience is no guarantee to securing a policy change. The Conservative leadership's success during P1, in elevating the salience of the issue was not matched by any influence on the outcome. It was concluded from the analysis of this period, that the issue's anatomy was of crucial importance in this respect. A view of the European question prevailed within the Government Whitehall, business and trade union organisations, the political parties and the press, which discouraged recognition of the possibility of benefit of British participation in the Schuman Plan. The issue was consistent with a pluralist model in that there appeared to be an open conflict on the question (press discussion, and Parliamentary debate) and in that groups with a variety of support and powers bases took part in the debate. It is however difficult to attribute the anatomy of the issue to one group or even to several. With the exception of that by the Daily Express, little active campaigning took place. Indeed, the anatomy of the issue in P1 seems more a function of the 'collective and systemic forces' to which Lukes referred in this third view of power. A state of mind existed which coloured views of Britain and her role in Europe, the Commonwealth and the world. These in turn significantly impinged upon reactions to the Schuman Plan.

A similar explanation was posed for the British policy towards the ECSC in P2 and the EEC in P3. A group model seems particularly inappropriate as the issue had such a muted status inside and outside Whitehall. The prevailing view of Britain's relations with European economic integration went virtually unchallenged. This is not just to say that it was rarely suggested that Britain should join the Six, but more importantly, that the perceptions of what was entailed in this policy alternative were not conducive to achieving a policy change.

Circumstances changed in P4. After Macmillan had initiated a significant rise in the salience of the issue by his proposal of a policy change, the issue entered the group arena and became the subject of considerable promotional and sectional group activity. This was both within the public forum and within the sectional group - Whitehall channels. It was indicated that, notwithstanding the Government's commitment to EEC entry and support for this by most Whitehall departments, the FBI, several trade unions, prominent Labour Party spokesmen and the majority of the British press; the anatomy of the issue did not suit this policy objective. Indeed the issue's anatomy was more akin to the policy goal of those opposed to entry on the terms likely to be available, notably some of the trade unions, important sections of the Labour Party, the NFU, the Anti Common Market League and the Daily Express. This, it has been argued, was crucial to the policy outcome. A group explanation is more appropriate in this case, though the view of the issue presented by opponents and sceptics of EEC entry drew upon the very themes which in P1-P3 seemed, so firmly embedded in the British political consciousness at every level. It can be concluded from this that even issues which are debated and decided upon in an open debate are susceptible to the very 'invisible' forces which operated in the case of the muted issue. The past is never erased before the decision making process once an issue is set into motion: well-established perceptions linger and these may bear fundamentally upon the outcome. It could be observed, however, that given the eventual accession of Britain to the EEC, in 1973, confirmed by the 1975 Referendum, an important achievement of those favouring entry in the early nineteen sixties was to begin to change perceptions of Britain and her position in Europe and the world, at all levels of the political system.

The conclusions outlined above can be made with much more confidence than had they been offered simply on the basis of an historical acquaintance with the period. The precise quantification of the changes in the issue's salience and anatomy have been made possible by the content analysis. The findings for salience and anatomy have permitted insights into overall changes of the issue. Thus, the perceptions and aims of individual groups and organisations have been assessed in the context of the wider standing and nature of the issue. Reference to the salience and anatomy of the European question as intervening variables between various competing policy objectives on one hand and policy outcomes on the other, has provided an additional dimension to an understanding of the evolution of the issue and of the policy-making process in operation.

WIDER CONCLUSIONS

It now remains to outline the implications of the findings of this study for previous work in the field and to assess the practical use that could be made of the related concepts of issue salience and anatomy in future research. The previous section illustrated how the application of these concepts could refine analysis of an issue at different stages of its evolution. Reference will now be made to other studies of issues which it is believed could be improved by the application of the salience and anatomy concepts.

Christoper Hewitt's study (1975) of the exercise of power in British politics in defence of the pluralist perspective considered the European question in P4. He suggested that the antimarketeers were successful because they imposed conditions on the Government such as to oblige the latter to adopt a negotiating position which was likely to contribute to the breakdown of the talks. In fact no inviolable conditions were placed upon the Government, rather the latter deemed it domestically expedient to defend certain interests (notably agricultural and Commonwealth) and positions (notably a degree of national autonomy). Hewitt is unable to account for this because he omitted the notion of issue anatomy – the vital intervening variable between groups opposed to EEC entry and the Government approach. Although Hewitt acknowledged Macmillan's success in achieving a policy change, he did not look at the European question prior to P4 to ask why such a policy change had not occurred earlier. Had he done so he would have encountered the muted issue; the explanation of which requires reference to the anatomy of the issue in these earlier years.

Attention to issue anatomy may provide a more sophisticated account of the issues which Morriss (1975) raised as objections to Hewitt's approach to the study of political influence. Analysis of their anatomy might provide further insights into the very examples of issues which Morriss suggested were not susceptible to pluralist analysis: the plight of Catholics in pre 1969 Northern Ireland, dangerous

229

working conditions and the issues which are deemed 'routines'. Like Hewitt, Morriss did not pay sufficient attention to the changes which characterise issues: the former (like many pluralists) was pre-occupied with 'big' issues and the latter (like many elite theorists) with 'small' issues. Neither Hewitt nor Morriss gave sufficient attention to changes in issue salience, nor did they give sufficient consideration to changes in issue anatomy which might account for the transformation of an issue's position on the spectrum of salience.

In summary, the analyses of Hewitt and Morriss have been unnecessarily crude, each assuming issues to be static and monolithic and neither confronting the crucial question of issue change. The salience and anatomy variables not only provide means of identifying issue change, but also illustrate that issues are much more complex than either pluralist or elite theorists have assumed. This study of the European question has indicated that factors associated with a pluralist explanation have co-existed with factors normally found in an elite perspective. In P1, the salience of the issue was attributed to group factors, but its anatomy seemed more a function of the prevailing ideology about Britain and her place in the world. The salience and anatomy of the issue in P2, appeared to be compatible with an elite analysis in that the policy to remain outside the ECSC was the consequence of a non decision. However, it would be untrue to say that the European question was a non issue in this period: it existed at a muted level within Parliamentary circles. The success of the anti EEC groups in P4 is not simply attributable to a pluralist explanation. Whilst the groups concerned would not normally be described as elites, they drew upon the very factor which contributed to the non decisions noted in P2 and P3 ie established perceptions of Britain's world role. Equally, the reason Macmillan himself gave for his particular manner of presentation of the issue was that of anticipated reactions: this too is normally associated with the elite perspective.

Robert Lieber's study (1970), of Britain's relations with EFTA and later the EEC between 1961 and 1967, was clearly concerned with changes in the conditions under which issues are debated and decided, in terms of the role of groups, and using various indicators of politicization. Unfortunately there existed an ambiguity in that these indicators (the level of attention by political parties, the involvement of a wider public, and the identity of the government department responsible for the issue) are not only presented as a means of identifying politicization, but also as the means by which this politicization comes about. Attention to the issue's anatomy and salience, independent of these factors would therefore provide an important refinement to this form of analysis. Indicators of different types of politicization are thus possible (eg its salience, the level of party scoring, the proportionate size of the Political aspect) independent of the range of possible causal factors.

William Solesbury (1976) recognised the changing salience of issues, and the relevance of their definition (ie presentation) to the policy outcome. The notion of an issue's anatomy as employed in this analysis was related to Solesbury's contribution to the study of issues. However, Solesbury lacked precision in discussing the changes in issue salience. Secondly, he was unable to verify his assertion of issues benefiting from having some compatibility with dominant values of the political system. Had he adopted a similar method of analysis used in the present study, Solesbury might have been able to contrast the anatomy of an environmental issue when it did not enjoy high salience nor attention of policy-makers, with its anatomy at a point of high salience. This could then be related to the extent of policy change. Such an approach would permit assessment of whether the manner in which the issue was defined had been a significant factor in the changed status of the issue and the policy outcome.

This point also applies to the Stringer and Richardson thesis (1980); that problem definition is a crucial factor in the policy-making process. Their study would also have benefited from accurate depiction of issue salience and anatomy. This would be particularly apposite in cases where issues initially deemed technical and of low status, were transformed into issues of high salience within the political system. Thus, the sort of analysis employed in this study would have permitted Stringer and Richardson to trace the changing salience of the issues with more precision and to illustrate more conclusively the relevance

231

of the issue definition to policy outcomes regarding for instance the problem of drug abuse and air pollution.

One problem which would be encountered in these possible improvements to the above studies, and in any future work along the lines advocated herein, is that of finding a suitable data base. The Hansard record was considered appropriate for the study of the European question 1950-1963. It would be obviously impossible for issues which do not receive Parliamentary coverage, but are settled within the Whitehall based issue communities, to be analysed in this way. Equally, it may be thought that Parliamentary debate might over-represent attention to an issue in the wider political system. Alternatives are available (eg analysis of press coverage, or the literature and statements emerging from the interested parties). However these must pass the tests of representativeness and some independence from the major casual factors. It is impossible to attain complete detachment from the latter as any source of views on an issue is itself part and parcel of the policy making process. More specifically, Parliamentary debate, for instance, may not be simply a reflection of something going on outside, but also the means by which the salience and anatomy of an issue are changed. Account should be taken of such a factor in the analysis as it was in the case of P1, when it was considered that Parliament was a major vehicle in raising the issue's salience.

The approach adopted in this study was born out of a feeling of a need for precision in discussing political issues, and especially in talking about changes therein. The goal of precision has brought with it the task of content analysis, the sheer size of which might deter students of politics from following up and building upon this work. There are now, however, computer facilities capable of conducting such content analysis (as opposed to their use in the present study for the aggregation and handling of data collected). This would require a key-word type analysis, providing advantages of speed which would still be offset by a level of analysis inferior to the thematic approach adopted in this study. The latter provides insights into the meaning of spoken and written material, rather than the frequency of certain words. For instance, in P2 the phrase "in association with the ECSC"

232

was generally interpreted as meaning something different from membership of it, and more akin to the terms of the Treaty of Association passed by Parliament in 1955. However, in the case of a few speakers, the context of their speeches clearly indicated that in using this phrase, they were referring to full participation in the ECSC. Such fine points of analysis would be lost in all but the most sophisticated key-word analyses.

It may well be that, because of constraints of time and finance, any future studies, will adopt some form of word count system. This is regretable in that the precision achieved in this thesis may not be repeated, but is preferable to solely impressionistic assessments of issue anatomy. Other authors have advanced the study of policy making, firstly by reference to differences in and changes of issue salience, and secondly by the identification of the significance of the definition of issues. However, progress can be best made in this field by sharpening up means of verification. This would be particularly rewarding in that it would enable students of politics to speak with more confidence about the 'definition' or 'presentation' of the issue in question.

What then has this analysis contributed to the study of politics? It has suggested the notion of a spectrum of salience, as an alternative to previous two dimensional approaches, (issues/non issues, on/off the agenda), and employed a method of assigning issues to a position on this spectrum relative to each other. Further, the concept of issue anatomy has been posed, and operationalised by means of the content analysis. The findings suggest that in combination the concepts of salience and anatomy are of use in the study of issues particularly in identifying issue changes. The adoption of this approach may have benefits for several areas of research. It provides an additional dimension to interest group studies: the relative abilities of different groups to influence issue salience and anatomy can be explored. For certain issues it might be appropriate to contrast their salience and anatomy outside, with their standing and character within Whitehall-based issue communities. The relative impact of political parties (or factions within parties) upon the anatomy of an issue may aid the work of students of party politics.

Studies which endeavour to account for policy persistence and change may benefit from the application of these concepts. Also, studies of the press and media could benefit from contrasting individual portrayals of an issue with some aggregate measure of its anatomy. In all these examples there will be methodological diffulties to be overcome, but the adoption of the concepts of issue salience and anatomy offer the prospect of clarifying and deepening our understanding of different areas of the study of politics. Although the salience and antomy of an issue at a particular point in time should be traceable to other factors in the political system (eg group activity, ideological permeation), it should be recognised that an issue also takes on something of a life of its own (definable in terms of salience and anatomy), and that this itself becomes a factor in the policy process. An issue is thus not simply a dependent phenomenon, but in some ways also an independent one. Thus the study of issue change should not be solely considered as an indicator of the relative balance of political forces, but also as an intervening variable in the process of policy change.

Appendix I: Identity of components and points of detail

Component 1:   Sovereignty

    Detail 1   Implications for Parliamentary Sovereignty
    Detail 2   Implications for Independent Foreign Policy
    Detail 3   Implications for Economic Planning
    Detail 4   Implications for Public Ownership
    Detail 5   Desirability of Supranational Authority
    Detail 6   Acceptance of Loss of Sovereignty in Other
                    European Spheres
    Detail 7   Preference for Functional Organisations
    Detail 8   Ability   to   Democratically   Control   a
                    Supranational   Authority   (ie   through   a
                    European Parliament or Court)
    Detail 9   Safeguard of Veto/Council of Ministers

Component 2:   Political Perceptions

    Detail 1   Federal Implications
    Detail 2   Towards Strong and United Europe
    Detail 3   Towards Break Up of Europe
    Detail 4   Isolation of Britain
    Detail 5   American Desire to See Europe United and
                    Britain Involved
    Detail 6   Slow Process Towards Future Unity
    Detail 7   Britain's Role as Leader of Europe
    Detail 8   Britain's Wider Political Role (ie 3 Circles)
    Detail 9   Franco German Unity
    Detail 0   France's Willingness to Admit Britain

Component 3:   Political Perceptions (ii)

    Detail 1   Socialist Strength in EEC

Component 4:   Defence

    Detail 1   Against Communism/USSR
    Detail 2   Against Germany
    Detail 3   Independence from/Alliance with USA

Detail 4	Inadequacy of Other Organisations
Detail 5	British Military Isolation and Inadequacy
Detail 6	Alternative EFTA/Commonwealth Bloc
Detail 7	World Polarisation and World War
Detail 8	Economic Means for Defence
Detail 9	Neutral Role for Britain

Component 5: Britain's Historical Traditions

Detail 1	"Splendid Isolation"
Detail 2	World Role
Detail 3	Participation in Functional Organisations
Detail 4	Maintenance of the European Balance of Power
Detail 5	Britain's Destiny in Europe
Detail 6	Language Problem
Detail 7	Distrust of Foreigners
Detail 8	Europe's Perceptions of Britain's Intransigence

Component 6: General Utility of Unity

Detail 1	Desirability of Nations Federating
Detail 2	Preference for Cooperation Rather Than Federation
Detail 3	Progress Made By Community
Detail 4	Desirability of the 'Free' Countries Uniting
Detail 5	Practical Step Toward Peace
Detail 6	Economic Morality
Detail 7	Furthering Democracy
Detail 8	Should Disregard Varying Political Opinions of Partners
Detail 9	Desire to be Associated with Project though not Totally Involved

Component 7: Commonwealth

Detail 1	Loyalty to Commonwealth
Detail 2	Britain's Leadership of Commonwealth
Detail 3	Trade Obligations and Sterling Area
Detail 4	Wider Markets Available to Commonwealth if Britain in Europe
Detail 5	Commonwealth Views on a United Europe
Detail 6	Britain's Commonwealth Role not Threatened if in Europe

236

Detail 7	Britain's Trade Disadvantages/Advantages with Commonwealth
Detail 8	Commonwealth Benefit/Loss from an Independent Britain
Detail 9	Consultation with Commonwealth
Detail 0	Associate Status for Commonwealth Countries

Component 8: Commonwealth (ii)

Detail 1	Australia
Detail 2	New Zealand
Detail 3	Producers of Sugar and Other Tropical Products
Detail 4	Canada
Detail 5	West Africa
Detail 6	India, Pakistan, Hong Kong
Detail 7	Raw Materials
Detail 8	Manufactured Goods
Detail 9	Transitional Period
Detail 0	Other Commonwealth Areas

Component 9: Third World

Detail 1	Economic Expansionism
Detail 2	Political Imperialism
Detail 3	Opportunity for Aid
Detail 4	Opportunity for Trade Extension
Detail 5	Threat of Political Division of Third World
Detail 6	Ability to Make Better Production Plans for Associated Countries

Component 10: Britain's Wider Trade Commitments

Detail 1	EFTA
Detail 2	Commonwealth
Detail 3	World Free Trade
Detail 4	GATT
Detail 5	Trade and Aid on Extra European Scale
Detail 6	Trade with Eastern Europe

Component 11: Economic Implications of Entry

Detail 1	Balance of Payments
Detail 2	Growth

237

Detail 3	Britain's Trade Trends
Detail 4	Access to European Markets
Detail 5	Britain's Ability to go it Alone
Detail 6	Britain's Access to World Markets
Detail 7	Inevitability of Economic Association
Detail 8	Threat of Economic Isolation
Detail 9	Benefits of Competition

Component 12: Perceptions of European Economy

Detail 1	Advantages of Free Trade
Detail 2	Advantages of Planning and Protectionism
Detail 3	Advantages of Pooling
Detail 4	Broad Benefits of Economic Unity/Economies of Scale/ Rationality
Detail 5	Economic Terms of Entry are Negotiable
Detail 6	Particular Economic Advantages Enjoyed by Participants
Detail 7	"Capitalist Plot"
Detail 8	Britain's Economic Freedom Inside EEC
Detail 9	Cartels in Europe

Component 13: Commercial and Industrial Suitability

Detail 1	Technological Advantages
Detail 2	High Consumer Prices
Detail 3	Iron/Steel
Detail 4	Coal
Detail 5	Sugar Beet
Detail 6	Car Manufacture
Detail 7	Consumer Responsiveness
Detail 8	Industrial Investment
Detail 9	Transport
Detail 0	Companies Developing European Links

Component 14: Commercial and Industrial Suitability (ii)

Detail 1	Chemical Engineering
Detail 2	Small Manufacturers and Producers
Detail 3	Jute and Textiles

Component 15: Economic Alternatives to EEC

Detail 1	Free Trade Area of OEEC Countries

Detail 2	Association Better Than Exclusion
Detail 3	No Alternative to EEC
Detail 4	Expanding Commonwealth Group
Detail 5	World Tariff Solution

Component 16: Agriculture

Detail 1	CAP and Budget Contribution
Detail 2	Inefficient European Farmers Compared to British
Detail 3	Agreement Possible on Agricultural Terms
Detail 4	British Agriculture's Need of Common Market
Detail 5	British Agriculture's Support System
Detail 6	Areas in Need of Protection, eg Horticulture
Detail 7	Effects on Food Farm Prices
Detail 8	Farmers'/Horticulturists' Views
Detail 9	Transitional Period
Detail 0	Farmers' and Labourers' Living Standards

Component 17: Regulations

Detail 1	VAT and Indirect Taxation
Detail 2	Imperial Measures
Detail 3	Effect of Regulations on Particular Products
Detail 4	Currency Unity
Detail 5	Abolition of Passports
Detail 6	Common External Tariff and Prices in Europe
Detail 7	Pricing Policies
Detail 8	Bureaucracy

Component 18: Welfare Implications

Detail 1	Britain's Relative Wage
Detail 2	Social Implications for Workforce
Detail 3	Health/Safety at Work
Detail 4	Achievments in Europe (Wages, Holidays, etc.)
Detail 5	Influx of Migrant Labour (Social Security Costs)
Detail 6	Cost of Living
Detail 7	Product Quality
Detail 8	Social Services

Component 19: Trade Union Affairs

Detail 1   Effect on Industrial Relations for Trade
            Unions
Detail 2   Uniform Treatment of Trade Unions
Detail 3   Representation and Consultation for Trade
            Unions
Detail 4   Loss of Work
Detail 5   Industrial Unrest

Component 20: Employment

Detail 1   Threat of Migrant Labour (on British Jobs)
Detail 2   Effect of Inflow of Investment re Jobs
Detail 3   Effect of Outflow of Investment re Jobs
Detail 4   Effect of Cheap European Imports
Detail 5   Effect of Increased British Export Markets
Detail 6   Effect of Coordinated European Employment
            Policy
Detail 7   Preference for National Control in Employment
Detail 8   Entry as Irrelevant to Employment

Component 21: Popular Opinion

Detail 1   British Belief in Rule of Parliament
Detail 2   Grassroots Opposition to European Alternative
Detail 3   Attitudes of those in Iron/Steel Industries
Detail 4   Ignorance of ECSC/EEC
Detail 5   Need for Election or Referendum on Issue

240

Appendix II: Policy aspect

	Component	Points of Detail

Political

1	Sovereignty	1-0
2	Political Perceptions	1-0
3	Political Percentions (ii)	1,0
4	Defence	1-0
5	Britain's Historical Traditions	1-0
6	General Utility of Unity	1-0
7	Commonwealth	1,2,5,6,9,0
9	Third World	2,5,0

Economic

7	Commonwealth	3,4,7,8
8	Commonwealth (ii)	1-0
9	Third World	1,3,4,6,0
10	Wider Trade Commitments	1-6,0
11	Economic Security and Suitability	1-0
12	Broad Economic Perceptions	1-0
13	Commercial and Industrial Stability	1,3-0
14	Commercial and Industrial Stability (ii)	1-3,0
15	Economic Alternatives	1-5,0
16	Agriculture and Horticulture	1-6,8,9

Social

13	Commercial and Industrial Stability	2
14	Agriculture and Horticulture	7,0
17	Regulations	1-0
18	Welfare	1-0

19	Trade Union	1-0
20	Employment	1-0
21	Popular Opinion	1-0

Appendix III: Geographical focus

Britain

Component	Points of Detail
1	1-4,0
4	5,8,9
5	1,7,0
7	7
11	1-3,5,8-0
12	8
13	1-9
14	1-3,0
16	4-8,0
17	1-5.0
18	1-3,5-0
19	1,3-0
20	1-5,7-0
21	1-0

Europe

Component	Points of Detail
1	5-9
2	1-4,6,7,9,0
3	1-0
4	2
5	4,5,6,8
6	3,5,6-9,0
10	1
11	5,7
12	1-7,9,0
13	0
15	1,2
16	1-3,9
17	6-9
18	4
19	2
20	6

Extra Europe

2	5,8
4	1,3,4,6,7,0
5	2,3
6	1,2,4
7	1-0
8	1-0
9	1,3,4,6,0
10	2-6,0
15	3-5,0

Appendix IV: Spheres

SPHERES

	Britain		Europe		Extra Europe	
	Comp.	Detail	Comp.	Detail	Comp.	Detail
Political						
	1	1-4,0	1	5-9	2	5,8
	4	5,8,9	2	1-4,6,7,9,0	4	1,3,4,6,7,0
	5	1,7,0	3	1,0	5	2,3
			4	2	6	1,2,4
			5	4,5,6,8	7	1,2,5,6,8,0
			6	3,5,6-9,0	9	2,5,0
Economic						
	7	7	10	1	7	3,4,8
	11	1-3,5,8-0	11	4,7	8	1-0
	12	8	12	1-7,9,0	9	1,3,4,6,0
	13	1,3-9	13	0	10	2-6,0
	14	1-3,0	15	1,2	15	3-5,0
	16	4-6,8	16	1-3,9		
Social						
	13	2	17	6-9		
	16	7,0	18	4		
	17	1-5,0	19	2		
	18	1-3,5-0	20	6		
	19	1,3-0				
	20	1-5,7-0				
	21	1-0				

Appendix V: Illustration of the method of content analysis

This appendix demonstrates how records of the Parliamentary debate were broken down into quantifiable units of analysis. A speech by Dingle Foot (Labour) has been selected, and this is reproduced below with key numbers appearing therein. These refer to divisions which have been made within the speech, which are explained in the table following the text of the speech.

Mr. Dingle Foot (Ipswich): (1) I listened with somewhat mixed feelings to the hon. and gallant Member for Lewes (Sir T. Beamish), but I entirely agree with his concluding sentence. It would be a tragedy for this country, for Europe and the world if, at the end of these negotiations, we did not, for whatever reason, become a member of the Community. I do not think that there is any hon. Member who is prepared to join on any terms, but I feel that our ultimate decision – and it is a decision which, at the end of the day, will have to be taken by every individual member of the House – cannot turn simply on a nice assessment of economic profit and loss but must be determined by wider political considerations.

(2) This is our fourth or fifth debate on the Common Market. The division has run right across the House. It has always seemed to me that the real division is between those who are looking for ways to enter the Community and those who are hunting for excuses to keep out. Throughout these debates we have been faced with an unholy alliance between the isolationists of the Right and the isolationists of the Left; people whom I might describe, to use a title of the late Mr. Galsworthy as 'The Island Pharisees' – those who are always beating their breasts and thanking God we are not as other nations are.

I can understand that coming from hon. Member opposite, because they have a very long isolationist tradition going back as far as Bolingbroke. I find it a little less comprehensible in some of my hon. Friends who pride themselves on being internationalists. Indeed when I hear some of them, I cannot help recalling the lines of G. K.

Chesterton:

'Oh, how I love the human race
With love to pure and pringlish,
And how I hate the horrid French
Who never will be English.'

(3) In turning to the arguments addressed to the House about
the position of the Commonwealth, I should first say that
the Commonwealth ties mean as much to me personally as I
think they do to any other hon. Member. During the last
fourteen years or so I have been very great priviliged. In
the exercise of my profession I have had the opportunity of
visiting most of the Asian and African Commonwealth
countries. I have been to many of them several times over,
and I can say without any exaggeration that I have
friendships that I greatly value in all those countries, not
least in Nigeria.

But do not let us pretend - and I think that this is the
danger - that the Commonwealth today is something which
quite clearly it is not. And do not let us deceive
ourselves about our own position in relation to the
Commonwealth. A rather favourite phrase nowadays,
particularly among the opponents of Common Market entry, is
that we are the centre of the Commonwealth. That is the
sort of question-begging phrase which covers up realities.

There are a great many people today both inside this House
and outside it who speak of the Commonwealth as though it
were simply the old British Empire in a new suit of clothes.
It is nothing of the kind. The British Empire was the
product of British seapower, and was held together chiefly
by the British Fleet. Through a very long period of time,
the British Empire was a great power bloc. In the last war
we had fighting on our side 2 million Indian soldiers and
0.5 million soldiers from Africa. Nobody supposes that
those troops would be available today if we were involved in
war. Above all, until the end of the last war, the other
members of the Commonwealth - even those which were
completely self-governing because they had attained Dominion
status - were content to follow our British lead in matters
of foreign policy. That again, has passed away, and it is
a state of affairs which is unlikely ever to recur.

Still less are the Commonwealth countries inclined to follow our lead – or, indeed, to consult our interests – in matters of commercial policy. At the Prime Ministers' Conference the various Prime Ministers, quite rightly from their own point of view, expressed apprehension about the effect on their economies of British entry into the European Community, but, as far as I could follow – and it was not difficult to follow most of what happened at this Conference – there was no single Commonwealth Prime Minister who, on behalf of his Government, offered to alter the commercial policy of his own country in order to help meet the needs and possible difficulties of the United Kingdom.

It is only a few weeks since we had a series of letter in The Times from exporters who complained bitterly of the obstacles – not only tariffs and licences, but in some cases embargoes – which they had to confront when they exported to Commonwealth countries. I do not say this in criticism of the countries concerned. Those countries are perfectly entitled to consider their own economic interests. Those countries, and the African countries particularly, wish to build up their secondary industries even if it be at the expense of our exporters, but surely we, on our side, are also entitled to consider the economic wellbeing of our own people and especially in this House, the economic wellbeing of those whom we represent.

(4) What remains? Of course, a good deal. There is the habit of consultation between Commonwealth countries and I do not think that anyone should underrate it. There is the use of the English language, not indeed a universal language throughout the Commonwealth but certainly it is the lingua franca both in Africa and in Asia. There are similar conceptions of law and similar systems of legal administration, and, of course, there is a very great fund of goodwill, particularly among those who have been trained and educated in this country. Perhaps I may say that, going as I have often done to Africa, and in particular to West Africa, I found African members of the legal profession continuing to take the very greatest pride in the fact that they had been called to the bar by one of the Inns of Court in London. I do not underrate any of that, but none of these things make the Commonwealth into a unit, and none of

these things can possibly make the Commonwealth into an alternative to the European Economic Community.

(5) I come to another matter which troubles a good many hon. Members and which clearly troubled my hon. Friend the Member for Nuneaton (Mr. Bowles) a few minutes ago. That is the question of the loss of sovereignty, particularly in the realm of foreign policy. Whenever this country has been about to enter into any fresh commitment, whether in the military sphere or the commercial sphere, precisely the same fears have been expressed on one side or another in this House. I quote one speech which was made not in connection with the Common Market but a little earlier and which expressed, I think, a good deal of what has been said by the opponents of entry, in these debates:

> "It is a really necessary principle of British foreign policy, whatever the complexion of the particular government, that while we have our definite commitments, and while we have principles on which we should all agree, it is essential that we should not enter into extensive, indefinite commitments with the result that the control of our own action, and to a large extent the control of our own foreign policy, will depend not on this country, on this Parliament, on these electors, but upon a whole lot of foreign countries." - (OFFICIAL REPORT, 15 March, 1939: Vol. 345, c. 554).

That is the sort of plea we have heard throughout the debates. As I have said, it was not in these debates; it was said by Sir John Simon speaking from the Dispatch Box on 15 March, 1939, just after the German troops had marched into Prague, and when Sir John Simon was still resisting any movement towards collective security on the Continent of Europe.

No doubt we have to safeguard ourselves against any loss of freedom to determine our own foreign policy if we go in, but it does not seem to me that that is the most vital question. The real question is how much freedom shall we have in determining our foreign policy if we stay out, because an effective foreign policy does not consist of simply wringing one's hands over events one does not like, or in making gestures of one kind or another. An effective foreign

249

policy consists in influencing events outside one's own shores, and if this country was left in a position of isolation how much effective foreign policy would then be left to us?

(6) We have heard the use of the terms "neutralism" and "neutrality". They always ring a bell in my mind because for five years during the war I had the honour to serve as a junior Minister in the Coalition Government which was formed by the right hon. Member for Woodford (Sir W. Churchill) in the summer of 1940. My principal task during those years was to conduct negotiations with the neutrals to get them to put down, so far as possible, their trade with the enemy.

There were quite a lot of neutrals in 1939 and 1940. Each one had, relatively speaking, an independent foreign policy. It happened to Belgium, Holland, Denmark, Norway, Yugoslavia, Greece and Finland. Each pursued its independent foreign policy, with the result which we all know. But there were six that were left – Eire, Portugal, Spain, Sweden, Switxerland and Turkey. Those six, it is perfectly true, remained outside the area of actual hostilities. They were not invaded and they did not have to engage their troops in the war. But that was not through their own choice; they had no choice. They only remained immune because it did not suit either of the belligerents to bring them into the war. Throughout the five and a half years they were subject to constant pressure from both sides. On the one side, there was the threat of German invasion, and, on the other, the economic pressure constantly exercised by the allies, particularly by Britain and the United States, and as the balance of the was gradually tilted, so they had to alter their policy. But at no stage were they masters of their own destiny. They were completely at the mercy of decisions taken by other powers.

I do not say that that is an exact analogy, but it illustrates the impossible position of a neutral country that is not itself overwhelmingly powerful. If we were outside the European Community, and if there were to grow up in Europe a closely integrated European super State, we should be in a position not very different from the smaller neutrals at the beginning of the last war, and it might well happen that decisions of the utmost consequence would be taken at Washington and Brussels, decisions over which we ourselves in this country would have little or no influence.

(7) I believe that the paradox is true that we can only exercise an effective foreign policy if we are members of a larger combination, and we shall have far more influence over our own foreign policy if we are members of the European community than if we remain outside. It is for those mainly political reasons that I hope it will be possible for us to enter the European community.

(8) I return for one moment to the Commonwealth Prime Ministers' Conference. It is perfectly true that particularly all the Prime Ministers opposed our entry into the Community, but they did so not only for economic reasons but to some extent for political reasons. I remember - I was in India at the time - reading an interview that Mr. Nehru gave to the Indian Press before he left for the Commonwealth Prime Ministers' Conference. He said that one of the reasons why he was against Britain's entry into the Community was that it would strengthen N.A.T.O. That may have been a perfectly good reason to Mr. Nehru - and I speak of him with great respect - for our staying out, but it is a very compelling reason for us to go in.

(9) 1Therefore, my right hon. Friend the Leader of the Opposition may well be right when he says that the economic advantages and disadvantages are very nearly balanced. But it seems to me that the political considerations are overwhelmingly on the side of British entry. I believe that we must have reasonable terms, that we cannot accept anything that is offered, but it will be a very great tragedy if at the end of the day Britain does not join the Community.

Hansard Reference	Whether Substantiated Component		Points of Detail	Policy Preference	Columns Occupied
1	Character and state of negotiations (22)	Yes	6	For	0.3
2	Party scoring	Yes (23)	9	For	0.4
3	Commonwealth (7)	Yes	2,3,7	For	1.5
4	Alternatives to Europe (EEC, ECSC) (15)	Yes	4	For	0.4
5	Sovereignty (1)	Yes	2	For	1.0
6	Defence (4)	Yes	9,5	For	1.1
7	Sovereignty (1)	Yes	2	For	0.2
8	Commonwealth (7)	Yes	5	Neutral	0.3
9	Political Perceptions (2)	No	–	For	0.2
	Other		None		0.0
				Total	5.5

In the first section, Foot discussed the basis on which the negotiations should proceed: whether on an economic bargaining or political commitment basis. Secondly, he made criticism of political opponents within his own Party, though mainly of those to the right of the Conservative Party. In the third section he discussed the Commonwealth at some length, touching upon Britain's leadership role within, her trade obligations to, and trade advantages with the Commonwealth. He then continued in the fourth section of his speech to outline alternatives to British EEC membership, specifically of a more cohesive Commonwealth

unit.   In the fifth section, Foot turned to the question of
sovereignty and notably the impact of EEC membership upon an
independent British foreign policy.   He then discussed
defence questions before returning to the question of
British independence in foreign policy-making.   In the
eighth section he discussed the views of the Commonwealth
upon the prospect of British entry and concluded with an
unsubstantiated remark as to the political value of British
EEC entry.

Bibliography

PRIMARY SOURCES

GOVERNMENT PAPERS

Cabinet Papers and Minutes 1947-1950

Including:

Minutes of European Economic Cooperation Committee of Ministers, 1947-48.

Minutes of Cabinet, May-June, 1950 (on Schuman Plan).

Integration of French and German Coal and Steel Industries, Report of Committee of Officials, 1950.

Integration of Western European Coal and Steel Industries, Report of Committee of Ministers, 1950.

Parliamentary Debates (Hansard), House of Commons Official Report

All debates on European question 1950-1963 subjected to content analysis.

Also debates 1945-1963 on matters related to the European question.

Government Publications

Cmd 7388, European Economic Cooperation, Convention for, together with the Resolutions Transmitted to the Council by the Committee of European Economic Cooperation (with covering memorandum by the Foreign Office), Paris, 16 April 1948.

Cmd 7970, Schuman Plan, Anglo-French Discussion regarding French Proposals for the Western European Coal, Iron and Steel Industries, May-June 1950.

Cmd 9304, Paris Conference, Documents agreed on by the Conference of Ministers held in Paris, 20 October 1954.

Cmd 9346, European Coal and Steel Community, Agreement concerning the Relations between the United Kingdom of Great Britain and Northern Ireland and the European Coal and Steel Community (and connected documents), London, 21 December, 1955.

Cmd 9525, Western Europe, Correspondence arising out of the Meeting of the Foreign Ministers of the Governments of Belgium, France, the Federal Republic ot Germany, Italy, Luxembourg and the Netherlands held at Messinsa on 1-2 June, 1955.

Cmnd 72, European Free Trade Area, United Kingdom Memorandum to the OEEC, February 1957.

Cmnd 641. Negotiations for a European Free Trade Area, Documents relating to the Negotiations from July 1956 - December 1958.

Cmnd 823, Stockholm Draft Plan for a European Free Trade Association, July 1959.

Cmnd. 906, European Free Trade Association, Text ot Convention and other Documents approved at Stockholm, on 20 November, 1959.

Cmnd 906-I, European Free Trade Association, Text of Schedules to Annex B to Convention approved at Stockholm on 20 November, 1959. Lists of Qualifying Processes and of Basic Materials; Forms ot Documentary Evidence of Origins.

Cmnd 1026. European Free Trade Association, Treaty Series No. 30, 1960, Convention Establishing the European Free Trade Association, Stockholm, 4 January 1960.

Cmnd 1449, Commonwealth Consultations on Britain's Relations with European Economic Community, Statements on Talks between Ministers and other Commonwealth Governments, 1961.

Cmnd 1565, European Economic Community, Miscellaneous, No. 14, 1961, United Kingdom and European Economic Community. Text of the Statement made by the Lord Privy Seal, the Rt. Hon. Edward Heath, M.B.E., M.P., to the Ministerial Council of the Western European Union, London, 10 April 1962.

255

Cmnd 1790 , <u>European Coal and Steel Community</u>, Miscellaneous, No. 2, 1962. The United Kingdom and the European Coal and Steel Community. Text of the Statement made by the Lord Privy Seal at the meeting with Ministers of Member States of the European Coal and Steel Community at Luxembourg, 17 July 1962.

Cmnd 1805, <u>European Economic Community</u>, Miscellaneous, No. 25, 1962, The United Kingdom and the European Economic Community, Report by the Lord Privy Seal on the Meeting with Ministers of Member States of the European Economic Community at Brussels from 1-5 August, 1962.

Cmnd 1838, <u>European Communities</u>, Miscellaneous, No. 33, 1962, The United Kingdom and the European Communities, Report by the Lord Privy Seal on the Meetings with Ministers of Member States of the European Coal and Steel Community at Luxembourg on 4 October 1962 and with Ministers of Member States of the European Economic Community at Brussels on 8 October 1962.

Cmnd 1847, <u>European Economic Community</u>, Miscellaneous, No. 36, 1962, The United Kingdom and the European Economic Community, Report by the Lord Privy Seal on the Meeting with Ministers of Member States of the European Economic Community at Brussels from 25-27 October, 1962.

Cmnd 1882, <u>European Communities</u>, Miscellaneous, No. 37, 1962, The United Kingdom and the European Communities, Report by the Lord Privy Seal on the Meetings with Ministers of Member States of the European Atomic Energy Community on 14 November 1962 and with Ministers of Member States of the European Economic Community from 15-17 November 1962 and with Ministers of Member States of the European Coal and Steel Community on 19 November 1962.

Cmnd 1910, <u>European Economic Community</u>, The United Kingdom and the European Economic Community, Report of the Lord Privy Seal on the Meeting with Ministers of Member States of the European Economic Community at Brussels on 19 and 20 December 1962.

POLITICAL PARTIES

Conservative Party

Annual Conference Reports, 1947–1962.

Britain and European Unity, Ursula Branston, 1953.

Towards a Free Trade Area, 1959

European Unity: The Political Issues (Notes on Current Politics, No. 16), 1960).

Britain and the Common Market (Notes on Current Politics, No. 16), 1961.

Britain and Europe (Weekend Talking Points, 349), 1961.

Commonwealth and Common Market, Sir Alec Douglas Home, 1961.

Britain and the Commonwealth and Europe, Harold Macmillan, 1961.

Britain and the Common Market (Weekend Talking Points, 385), 1962.

Common Market Negotiations (Weekend Talking Points, 392), 1962.

Lead from Llandudno (Weekend Talking Points, 396), 1962.

The Economic Case (Common Market, Common Sense 1), 1962.

The Political Case (Common Market, Common Sense 2), 1962.

The Commonwealth (Common Market, Common Sense 3), 1962.

The Cost of Living (Common Market, Common Sense 4), 1962.

Employment Prospects (Common Market, Common Sense 5), 1962.

The Farmers (Common Market, Common Sense 6), 1962.

Would Britain Get Pushed Around? (Common Market, Common

Sense 7), 1962.

European Stability (Common Market, Common Sense 8), 1962.

Religious Freedom (Common Market, Common Sense 9), 1962.

The Law (Common Market, Common Sense 10), 1962.

The Monarchy (Common Market, Common Sense 11), 1962

Tell us the Facts (Common Market, Common Sense 12), 1962.

Why the Rush/Delay? (Common Market, Common Sense 13), 1962.

Farewell to Welfare? (Common Market, Common Sense 14), 1962.

Commonwealth Trade (Common Market, Common Sense 15), 1962.

Food Prices (Common Market, Common Sense 16), 1962.

Commonwealth and Common Market, Harold Macmillan, 1962.

Britain, the Commonwealth and Europe, Harold Macmillan, 1962.

Leaders of Industry and the Common Market, 1962.

European Political Unity 1962.

European Political Unity 1962.

The Commonwealth and the Common Market, 1962.

British Agriculture and Horticulture and the Common Market, 1962.

National Sovereignty in the European Community, 1962.

Social Security in the Common Market, 1962.

Common Market Progress Report, Sir Alec Douglas-Home, 1962.

Common Market Topics, No. 1, 1962.

258

Common Market Topics, No. 2, 1962.

Common Market Topics, No. 3, 1962.

Common Market Topics, No. 4, 1962.

Common Market Topics, No. 5, 1962.

Common Market Topics, No. 6, 1962.

Common Market Topics, No. 7, 1963.

Labour Party

Annual Conference Reports, 1947-1962.

European Unity, A Statement by the National Executive Committee, 1950.

Labour and the Common Market, A Statement by the National Executive Committee, 1962.

European Trade (Talking Points, No. 13), 1959.

The Common Market, No. 1 (Talking Points, No. 10), 1961.

The Common Market, No. 2 (Talking Points, No. 11), 1961.

Common Sense on the Common Market: Planning (Pt. 1) (Talking Points, No. 10,) 1962.

Common Sense on the Common Market: Planning (Pt. 2) (Talking Points, No. 11,) 1962.

Commonwealth and Common Market (1) (Talking Points, No. 14), 1962.

Commonwealth and Common Market (2) (Talking Points, No. 15), 1962.

Internal Documents (The Labour Party record keeping system does not appear to be comprehensive):

The European Commitment, A Paper to the Home Policy

259

Committee, 1961.

Selected Minutes of Sub-Committees of NEC.

Selected Memorandums from Labour Research Department.

Liberal Party

Extracts from Assembly and Council Resolutions, 1945 onwards, 1973(?).

Moore, Richard and Morgan, Christine, The Liberals in Europe (undated).

The Commonwealth and the Common Market, 1962.

Europe after Britain Joins, 1962.

The National Farmers' Union

British Farmer (Weekly Journal of N.F.U.), 1961-62. Journal contains copies of Annual Reports, General Purpose Committee Reports, N.F.U. Policy Statements and Speeches by the N.F.U. President.

British Agriculture and the Common Market, An N.F.U. Policy Statement, 1962.

SECTIONAL GROUPS

Business Organisations

Chamber of Commerce

Overseas Committee Minutes, Association of British Chambers of Commerce, 1948-1962.

European Panel Minutes, A.B.C.C., 1960-62.

General Purposes Committee, A.B.C.C., 1948-68.

Annual Report, Federation of Chambers of Commerce of the British Empire, 1946-62.

The European Common Market: What Will it Mean to You?,
Westminster Chamber of Commerce, 1957.

Approach to Europe, London Chambers of Commerce, 1961.

Federation of British Industry

(F.B.I. records are not comprehensive).

Executive Committee Minutes, 1945-53.

Overseas Policy Committee Minutes, 1947-50.

European Recovery Programme Committee Minutes, 1948.

Economic Policy Committee Minutes, 1949-58.

A Statement by F.B.I. to Members on British Industry and Europe,
1961.

Trade Unions

Annual Reports, Trades Union Congress, 1947-1962.

Economic Association with Europe: T.U.C. Statement of Policy
 and Backg round Report, 1956.

General Executive Council Minutes,   Transport   and   General
Workers' Union, 1945-1962.

Finance and General Purposes Committee Minutes,   Transport
and General Workers' Union, 1945-62.

Report of National Executive Committee, National Union of
Mineworkers,   1947-62.   Report   includes   proceedings   of
Conference proceedings.

Quarterly Reports, Iron and Steel Trades Confederation,
1949-62.

THE PRESS

Daily Express, 1947-62.

Daily Herald, 1947-62.

Daily Telegraph, 1947-62.

The Times, 1947-62.

Selected copies of:

Daily Mirror.

Manchester Guardian

New Statesman

The Economist

PROMOTIONAL AND EDUCATIONAL GROUPS

Anti-Common Market League

British Industry and the Common Market, 1961(?)

British Sovereignty and the Common Market, 1961(?)

Britain's Future Lies with the Commonwealth, 1961

British Agriculture under a European Common Policy, 1961

The European Common Market Is Britain Already Committed?
1961.

Corbett, R. Hugh (ed.), Britain, Not Europe: Commonwealth
Before Common Market, 1962.

Britain in Europe

Minutes of Britain in Europe Ltd. Committee, 1960-1963.

Assorted copies of Britain in Europe Newsletter, 1959-63.

Common Market Campaign

Minutes of Common Market Campaign Directing Committee, 1961-1963,
Statement on Europe: call by more than 100 leading citizens for British Membership of the Common Market; list of signatories, 1961.

European Movement (U.K. Council)

Minutes of European Movement (U.K. Council) Executive Committee, 1948-1963.

Minutes of European Movement (U.K. Council) Management Committee, 1961-1963.

A Free Trade Area in Europe, 1957 (?)

Agriculture and the Free Trade Area, 1957(?)

Britain's Food and the Common Market, 1961.

The U.K. Economy and the Common Market: Report of a Bankers' Conference, London, 1961.

Fabian Society

The Common Market and its Forerunners, Shirley Williams, Fabian International Bureau, Research Series 201, 1958.

Britain's Role in a changing World, Kenneth Younger, Fabian Tract 327, 1960.

Britain and Europe, Evan Luard, Fabian Tract 330, 1961.

Commonwealth and Common Market: The Economic Implications, Fabian Commonwealth Bureau, Research Section 230, 1962.

The Common Market Debate, Douglas Jay and Roy Jenkins, Fabian Tract 341, 1962.

Federal Trust for Education and Research

Assorted Annual Reports, 1950-1962.

<u>Inside the Common Market</u>, 1961(?)

<u>Transport and the Common Market</u>, 1962(?)

<u>Sovereignty and the Common Market</u>, 1962(?)

<u>Industry and the Common Market</u>, 1962.

Forward Britain Movement

Assorted numbers of <u>Forward Britain Movement Newsletter</u>, 1961-1964.

Leighton, Ron, <u>The Case Against Britain's Entry into the Common Market</u>, 1962(?)

Labour Common Market Committee

Assorted copies of <u>Newsbrief</u> (monthly newsletter), 1961-1963.

SECONDARY SOURCES

Abrams, Mark, 'British Elite Attitudes and the European Common Market',. Public Opinion Quarterly, Vol. 29, no. 2, pp. 236-246.

Amery, Julian, 'The Conservative View of the Commonwealth', Political Quarterly, Vol. XXIV, no. 2, April-June 1953.

Attlee, C.R. As it Happened, London, Heinemann, 1954.

Aughey, Arthur, Conservative Party Attitudes Towards The Common Market, Hull Papers in Politics, no. 2, 1978.

Avon, Lord (Sir Anthony Eden). Memoirs of Sir Anthony Eden: Full circle, London, Cassell, 1960.

Bachrach, Peter, The Theory of Democratic Elitism: A Critique, Boston, Little, Brown and Company, 1967.

Bachrach, P. and Baratz, M.S., 'Two Faces of Power', American Political Science Review, Vol. 56, pp. 947-52, 1962.

Ball, George, 'America's Bid to push Britain into Europe', The Guardian, 3/7/82.

Barclay, Roderick, Ernest Bevin and the Foreign Office, 1932-69, Latimer Bucks, Roderick Barclay, 1975.

Barker, Anthony and Rush, Michael, The Member of Parliament and His Information, London, George Allen and Unwin, 1970.

Barnett, Joel, Inside the Treasury, London, Andre Deutsch, 1982.

Bauer, Raymond, A., Pool, Ithiel de Sola and Dexter, Lewis A., American Business and Public Policy: The Politics of Foreign Trade, New York, Atherton Press, 1963.

Beer, Samuel, Modern British Politics, London, Faber and Faber, 1965.

Beever, R. Colin, European Unity and the Trade Union

Movements, Leyden, A.W. Suthoff,. 1960.

Beever, R. Colin, 'Trade Union Re-Thinking', Journal of Common Market Studies, Vol. 2, No. 2, 1963.

Beloff, Max, New Dimensions in Foreign Policy: A Study in British Administrative Experience, 1947-59, London, Allen and Unwin, 1961.

Beloff, Max, 'Labour and Europe: Unreal Romanticism', Time and Tide, 3/5/62.

Beloff, Nora, The General Says No, London, Penguin, 1963.

Beloff, Nora, Transit of Britain, London, Collins, 1973.

Berelson, Bernard and Janowitz, Morriss eds., Public Opinion and Communication, Toronto, The Free Press, 2nd. ed., 1966.

Birch, A.H. Representative and Responsible Government, London, George Allen and Unwin, 1964.

Blank, Stephen, Industry and Government in Britain: The Federation of British Industries in Politics, 1945-65, Farnborough, Hants, Saxon House, 1973.

Boardman, Robert, 'British Public Opinion and the Common Market Issue', Dalhousie Review, Vol. 52, No. 1, pp. 34-46, 1972.

Bogdanor, Vernon, 'The Labour Party in Opposition' in Vernon Bogdanor and Robert Skidelsky eds.

Bogdanor, Vernon and Skidelsky, Robert, eds., The Age of Affluence 1951-64, London, Macmillan, 1970.

Boothby, Robert, 'The Economic Policy of the Conservative Party', Political Quarterly, Vol. XXIV, no. 2, April-June, 1953.

Boothby, Lord (Robert Boothby), Recollections of a Rebel, London, Hutchison, 1978.

Braybrooke, David, Traffic Congestion goes through the Issue Machine, London, Routledge and Kegan Paul, 1974.

Brookes, S.K., Jordan, A.G., Kimber, R.H. and Richardson J.J. 'The Growth of the Environment as a Political Issue in Britain', British Journal of Political Science, Vol. 6, pt. 2, 1976.

Brown, George, In My Way, London, Gollancz, 1971.

Bruce-Gardyne, Jock, and Lawson, Nigel, The Power Game, London, Macmillan, 1976.

Butler, D.E. The British General Election of 1951, London, Macmillan, 1952.

Butler, D.E., The British General Election of 1955, London, Macmillan, 1955.

Butler, D.E. and King, Anthony, The British General Election of 1964, London, Macmillan, 1965.

Butler D.E. and Kitzinger, U., The 1975 Referendum, London, Macmillan, 1976.

Butler, D.E., and Rose, R., The British General Election of 1959, London, Macmillan, 1960.

Butler, R.A., The Art of the Possible, London, Hamilton, 1971.

Butt, R., 'The Common Market and Conservative Party Politics, 1961-62', Government and Opposition, Vol. 12, no. 3, April-July, 1967.

Butterwick, M. and Rolfe, E.N., Food, Farming and The Common Market, London, OUP, 1968.

Camps, Miriam, The Free Trade Area Negotiations, London, Political Economic Planning Occasional Paper, no. 2, 1959.

Camps, Miriam, Division in Europe, London, Political and Economic Planning Occasional Paper, no. 8, 1960.

267

Camps, Miriam, Four Approaches to the European Problem, London, Political and Economic Planning Occasional Paper, No. 12, 1961.

Camps, Miriam, Britain and the European Community 1955-1963, Princeton, Princeton University Press, 1964.

Camps, Miriam, European Unification in the 1960s, London, OUP, 1967.

Charlton, Michael, Price of Victory, B.B.C. Radio Three, Broadcast between 19/2/81 and 30/3/81.

Clark, Colin, British Trade in the Common Market, London, Stevens and Sons, 1962.

Cobb, Roger W. and Elder, Charles D., Participation in American Politics: The Dynamics of Agenda Building, Baltimore, John Hopkins University Press, 1975.

Cook, Chris and Ramsden, John, eds., Trends in British Politics, London, Macmillan, 1978.

Crenson, Matthew, Unpolitics of Air Pollution, Baltimore, John Hopkins Press, 1971.

Crossman, R.H.S., 'Britain and the Outside World', Political Quarterly, Vol. XXIV, no. 1, January-March, 1953.

Dahl, Robert A. A Preface to Democratic Theory, Chicago, University of Chicago Press, 1957.

Dahl, Robert A., Who Governs?, Newhaven, Yale University Press, 1961.

Daily Express, You and the Common Market, London, 1961.

Daily Mirror, Britain and Europe, London, 1961.

Daily Telegraph, Britain and the Common Market, London, 1961.

Dalton, Hugh, High Tide and After, London, Muller, 1962.

Davies, Ernest, 'Labour Party Foreign Policy',

Political Quarterly, Vol. XXIII, no.2, April-June, 1952.

Diebold, W. Jr., The Schuman Plan, A Study in Economic Cooperation 1950-59, New York, Frederick A. Praeger, 1959.

Donoughue, Bernard and Jones, G.W., Herbert Morrison: Portrait of a Politician, London, Weidenfeld and Nicolson, 1973.

Douglas, Roy, History of the Liberal Party 1895-1970, London, Sidgwick and Jackson, 1971.

Downs, A., 'Up and down with Ecology - the issue attention cycle', Public Interest, Vol. 28, Summer, 1972.

Downs, A., 'The Political Economy of Improving our Environment', in Joe E. Bain (ed.) Environmental Decay: Economic Causes and Remedies, Boston, Little Brown, 1973.

Drucker, H.M., 'Two Party Politics in the United Kingdom', Parliamentary Affairs, Vol. XXII, no. 4, 1979.

Dunleavy, Patrick, The Politics of Mass Housing in Britain, 1945-1975 Oxford, Clarendon Press, 1981.

Eatwell, Roger, The 1945-1951 Labour Governments, London, Batsford Academic, 1979.

Economist Intelligence Unit, Britain and Europe, London, 1957.

Economist Intelligence Unit, Britain, the Commonwealth and European Free Trade, London, 1958.

Economist Intelligence Unit, If Britain Joins, London, 1961.

European Movement - Meeting of the Committee of Ministers in Rome, 1950, London, 1950.

European Movement, The Economic Potential of Europe, London, 1952.

European Movement, <u>A free trade area in Europe</u>, London, 1957.

Evans, Sir Harold, <u>Downing Street Diary: The Macmillan Years, 957-63,</u>, London, Hodder and Stoughton, 1980.

Gaitskell, Hugh, 'The Economic Aims of the Labour Party', <u>Political Quarterly</u>, vol. XXIV, no. 1, January–March, 1953.

Gallup Poll, 'British Attitudes to the EEC, 1960-63', <u>Journal of Common Market Studies</u>, Vol. V, no. 1, September 1966.

Gerbner, G., Holsti, O., Krippendorff, K. and Stone, P., <u>The Analysis of Communication Content</u>, New York, John Wiley and Sons, 1969.

Giddens, Anthony, 'Preface' to P. Stanworth and A. Giddens (eds.) <u>Elites and Power in British Society</u>, Cambridge, Cambridge University Press, 1974.

Gladwyn, Lord, <u>The Memoirs of Lord Gladwin</u>, London, Weidenfeld and Nicolson, 1972.

Goodrich, P.S., <u>British attitudes towards membership of the European Community</u>, Ph.D. Thesis, Manchester, July 1975.

Grant, Wyn, <u>Insider Groups, Outsider Groups and Interest Group Strategies in Britain</u>, University of Warwick, Department of Politics, Working Paper, no. 19, May 1978.

Grant, Wyn. 'The National Farmers Union: The Classic Case of Incorporation', in D. Marsh (ed.) <u>Pressure Politics</u>, London, Junction Books, 1983.

Grant, Wyn and Marsh, David, <u>The CBI</u>, London, Hodder and Stoughton, 1977.

Gwyn, W.B., 'British Politics and European Unity', <u>Political Studies</u>, Vol. XX, no. 1, 1972.

Harris, J., <u>Unemployment and Politics : A Study in English Social Policy 1886-1914,</u> Oxford, Oxford University Press, 1972.

Hene, Derek, Decision on Europe, London, Jordan and Sons, 1970.

Hennessy, James, Britain and Europe Since 1945, a Bibliographical Guide, Brighton, The Harvester Press, 1973.

Hewitt, Christopher, 'Policy-Making in Postwar Britain : a Nation-level Test of Elitist and Pluralist Hypotheses', British Journal of Political Science, Vol. 4, pt. 2, 1975.

Hewitt, Christopher, 'Pluralism in British Policy-making, A Reply to Morriss', British Journal of Political Science, Vol. 6, pt. 3, 1976.

Holsti, Ole R., Content Analysis for the Social Sciences and Humanities, Reading, Massachusetts, Addison-Wesley, 1969.

Inglehart, Ronald, The Silent Revolution, Princeton, Princeton University Press, 1977.

Ionescu, Ghita, ed., The New Politics of European Integration, London, Macmillan, 1972.

Jay, Douglas, Change and Fortune, London, Hutchinson, 1980.

Joll, James, Gramsci, Glasgow, Fontana, 1977.

Jowell, Roger and Hoinville, Gerald, eds., Britain Into Europe: Public Opinion and the EEC 1961-75, London, Croom Helm 1976.

Judge, David, Backbench Specialisation in the House of Commons, London Heinemann, 1981.

Kaplan, Abraham, The Conduct of Inquiry: Methodology for Behavioural Science, San Francisco, Chandler, 1964.

Kimber, Richard, Richardson, J.J., Brookes, S.K., and Jordan, A.G., 'Parliamentary Questions and the Allocation of Departmental Responsibilities', Parliamentary Affairs, Vol. XXVII, No. 3. 1974.

Kimber, Richard and Richardson, J.J., eds. Pressure Groups in Britain, London, Dent, 1974.

Kipping, Sir Norman, Summing Up, London, Hutchinson, 1972.

Kitzinger, Uwe, The Challenge of the Common Market, Oxford, Basil Blackwell, 1962.

Kitzinger, Uwe, ed. The European Common Market and Community, London, Routledge, 1967.

Kitzinger, Uwe, The Second Try, Oxford, Pergamon, 1968.

Kitzinger, Uwe, Diplomacy and Persuasion, London, Thames and Hudson, 1973.

Lasswell, Harold D., 'Why be Quantitative?' in Berelson and Janowitz (eds.)

Leemans, Arne, 'Causes of Policy Succession: The Delta/Oosterschelde Case', Paper to Policy Succession Workshop of ECPR, Freiburg, 1983.

Lidderdale, Sir David, Erskine May's Treatise on the Law, Privileges, Proceedings and Usage of Parliament, 19th ed., London, Butterworths, 1976.

Lieber, Robert J., British Politics and European Unity, Berkeley and Los Angeles, University of California Press, 1970.

Liggett, E., Organisation for Negotiation: Britain's first attempt to join EEC, 1961-1963, M.Litt Thesis, Glasgow University, 1971.

Lowi, Theodore, J., 'American Business, Public Policy, Case-Studies and Political Theory', World Politics, Vol. XVI, no. 4, 1963.

Lukes, Steven, Power: A Radical View, London, Macmillan, 1974.

McCarthy, M., 'Child Poverty Action Group : Poor and Powerless?, D. Marsh (ed.) Pressure Politics, London,

Junction Books, 1983.

McEachern, Doug, A Class Against Itself: Power in the Nationalisation of the British Steel Industry, Cambridge, Cambridge University Press, 1980.

McKay, D. and A. Cox, 'Confusion and Reality in Public Policy: the case of the British Urban Aid Programme in C. Pollitt et.al. Public Policy in Theory and Practice, Sevenoaks, Hodder and Stoughton, 1978.

MacKay, R.W.G., Britain in Wonderland, London, Gollancz, 1948.

MacKay, R.W.G., Towards a United States of Europe, London, Hutchison, 1961.

Macmillan, Harold, Tides of Fortune 1945-1955, London, Macmillan 1969.

Macmillan, Harold, Riding the Storm, 1956-1959, London, Macmillan, 1972.

Macmillan, Harold, Pointing the Way 1959-1961, London, Macmillan, 1972.

Macmillan, Harold, At the End of the Day, 1961-1963, London, Macmillan, 1973.

Mayne, Richard, The Community of Europe, London, Gollancz, 1962.

Mayne, Richard, The Recovery of Europe: From Devastation to Unity, London, Weidenfeld and Nicolson, 1970.

Mills, C. Wright, The Power Elite, New York, Oxford University Press, 1956.

Minkin, Lewis, The Labour Party Conference, Manchester, Manchester University Press, 1980.

Morgan, Roger, West European Politics since 1945: The Shaping of the European Community, London, B.T. Batsford, 1972.

273

Morriss, Peter, 'Power in New Haven: a Reassessment of "Who Governs?"', British Journal of Political Science, Vol. 2, pt. 4, 1972.

Morriss, Peter, 'The Pluralist Case not proven: Hewitt on Britain', British Journal of Political Science, Vol. 5, pt. 3, 1975.

Mowatt, R.C., Creating the European Community, New York, Barnes and Noble, 1973.

Nettl, Peter and Shapiro, David, 'Institutions Versus Realities - A British Approach', Journal of Common Market Studies, Vol. 2 no. 1., 1963.

Norton, Philip, The Commons in Perspective, Oxford, Martin Robertson, 1981.

Nutting, A., Europe will not wait, London, Hollis and Carter, 1960.

Orwell, George, 'Towards European Unity', Partisan Review, July and August 1947.

Pelling, Henry, History of British Trade Unionism, London, Penguin, 1965.

Pinder, John, Britain and the Common Market, London, Crenset Press, 1961.

Pliatzky, Sir Leo, Getting and Spending, Oxford, Basil Blackwell, 1982.

Polsby, Nelson, W., Community Power and Political Theory, New Haven, Yale University Press, 1963.

Potter, A., Organised Pressure Groups in British National Politics, London, Faber and Faber, 1961.

Pryce, R., The Political Future of the European Community, Tonbridge, Marshbank, Federal Trust, 1962.

Rasmussen, Jorgen, The Liberal Party, London, Constable,

1965.

Richardson, J.J., and Jordan, Grant, Governing Under Pressure : the Policy Process in a Post Parliamentary Democracy, Oxford, Martin Robertson, 1979.

Robins, L.J., Labour Party and the EEC. 961-1971, Ph.D. Thesis, University of Southampton, 1974.

Robins, L.J., The Reluctant Party : Labour and the EEC 1961-75, G.W. Ormskirk, and A. Hesketh, 1979.

Rose, Richard, 'Parties, Factions and Tendencies in Britain', Political Studies, Vol. 12, no. 1, 1964.

Rose, Richard, ed., Policy making in Britain, London, Macmillan 1969.

Rose, Richard, Politics in England: An Interpretation for the 1980s, London, Faber, 3rd. ed. 1980.

Ryan, M., 'The Penal Lobby : Influencing Ideology?', in D, Marsh (ed.) Pressure Politics, London Junction Books, 1983.

Ryle, Michael, 'The Commons in the Seventies - a General Survey' in Walkland and Ryle (eds.)

Sahm, Ulrich, 'Britain and Europe 1950', International Affairs, Vol. 43, January, 1967.

Schattschneider, E.E. The Semi-Sovereign People, Hinsdale, Illinois, The Dryden Press, 1960.

Self, Peter and Strong, Herbert, 'The Farmers and the State', Political Quarterly, Vol. 29, no. 1, January-March, 1958.

Siedentop, L.A, 'Mr. Macmillan and the Edwardian Style', in V. Bogdanor and Robert Skidelsky, eds.

Sissons, Michael, ed. The Age of Austerity, London, Hodder and Stoughton, 1963.

Sked, Alan and Cook, Chris, Post-War Britain : A Political History,

London, Penguin, 1979.

Social Surveys Ltd., British Attitudes Towards The Common Market 1957-1971, London, Gallup, Ltd.

Solesbury, William 'The Environmental Agenda', Public Administration, Vol. 64, Winter, 1976.

Stanworth, P. and Giddens, A., Elites and Power in British Society, London, Cambridge University Press, 1974.

Stringer, Joan K. and Richardson, J.J. 'Managing the Political Agenda: Problem Definition and Policy-making in Britain', Parliamentary Affairs, Vol. XXXIII, no. 1, 1980.

Sweet and Maxwell, European Community Treaties, London, Sweet and Maxwell, 1972.

Uri, P. ed., From Commonwealth to Common Market, London, Penguin, 1968.

Ward, Hugh, 'The Anti-Nuclear Lobby : An Unequal Struggle?' in D. Marsh (ed.) Pressure Politics, London, Junction Books, 1983.

Walker, J.L., "Setting the Agenda in the U.S. Senate : A theory of problem selection", British Journal of Political Science, Vol. 7, pt. 4, 1977.

Walkland, S.A. and Ryle, Michael, eds., The Commons in the Seventies, London, Martin Robertson, 1977.

Williams, Philip M., Hugh Gaitskell, London, Jonathan Cape, 1979.

Williams, Raymond, Britain in the Sixties : Communications, Baltimore, Penguin, 1962.

Windlesham, Lord, Communication and Political Power, London, Jonathan Cape, 1966.

Young, G.K., Masters of Indecision, London, Methuen, 1962.

Younger, K., 'Public Opinion and British Foreign Policy',

International Affairs, Vol. 40, no. 1, 1964.

Zurcher, A.J., *The Struggle to Unite Europe 1940-58*, New York, New York University Press, 1958.

Index

281